The Untold Story of Shields Green

THE UNTOLD STORY OF

SHIELDS GREEN

THE LIFE AND DEATH OF A
HARPER'S FERRY RAIDER

Louis A. DeCaro, Jr.

NEW YORK UNIVERSITY PRESS

New York

NEW YORK UNIVERSITY PRESS
New York
www.nyupress.org

First published in paperback in 2022

References to Internet websites (URLs) were accurate at the time of writing. Neither the author nor New York University Press is responsible for URLs that may have expired or changed since the manuscript was prepared.

Library of Congress Cataloging-in-Publication Data
Names: DeCaro, Louis A., 1957–   author.
Title: The untold story of Shields Green : the life and death of a Harper's Ferry raider / Louis A. DeCaro, Jr.
Description: New York : New York University Press, [2020] | bibliographical references and index.
Identifiers: LCCN 2020016525 (print) | LCCN 2020016526 (ebook) | ISBN 9781479802753 (cloth) | ISBN 9781479816705 (paperback) | ISBN 9781479802807 (ebook) | ISBN 9781479802791 (ebook)
Subjects: LCSH: Green, Shields, 1836?–1859. | Harpers Ferry (W. Va.)—History—John Brown's Raid, 1859. | African American abolitionists—Biography. | Free African Americans—Biography. | Fugitive slaves—United States—Biography. | African Americans—South Carolina—Charleston—Biography. | Charleston (S.C.)—Biography.
Classification: LCC E451 .D445 2020po (print) | LCC E451 (ebook) | DDC 326/.8092 [B]—dc23
LC record available at https://lccn.loc.gov/2020016525
LC ebook record available at https://lccn.loc.gov/2020016526

New York University Press books are printed on acid-free paper, and their binding materials are chosen for strength and durability. We strive to use environmentally responsible suppliers and materials to the greatest extent possible in publishing our books.

Book designed and typeset by Charles B. Hames

Manufactured in the United States of America

10 9 8 7 6 5 4 3 2 1

Also available as an ebook

For my beloved wife, Michele,

in the year of our twentieth wedding anniversary

There has been a systematic attempt to underrate the bravery of the colored men who fought with Brown at Harper's Ferry. . . . Northern men, always easily impressed when a statement reflects upon black men, saw only old John Brown and seventeen white men.

Weekly Anglo-African, 1860

Contents

Illustrations

Preface

A young man named Shields Green, who
went down with [Frederick Douglass],
staid and joined in the attack.

Rochester Democrat and Chronicle, 1875[1]

ACCORDING to the conventional narrative, Shields Green was a young black man who broke the chains of slavery and fled northward in the late 1850s. A widower, he left a young son behind in South Carolina and was smuggled on a ship traveling northward along the Atlantic coast. Upon reaching the North, Green, who liked to call himself Emperor, made his way to Rochester, New York, where he met Frederick Douglass, the abolitionist orator. Through involvement with Douglass, Green eventually came into contact with John Brown, who sought to enlist him for his imminent liberation effort in Virginia. Despite Douglass's opposition, Green decided to join Brown's small "army" of little more than twenty men in seizing the town and federal armory at Harper's Ferry, Virginia, on Sunday night, October 16, 1859.

Although the raid initially went well, Brown's tactical misjudgments, especially his long delay in town, proved his undoing. By late morning the next day, the tide of advantage turned against him, and his men were now being shot down in the streets—in some cases, captured and murdered outright by angry townsmen. As things fell apart, Brown retreated into the armory's fire engine house with several of his raiders, including his sons Watson and Oliver, as well as some enslaved men and a group of hostage slaveholders.

The narrative continues that Shields Green was yet outside when Brown had taken refuge in the engine house. Admonished to flee by another raider, instead Green chose to go down into Harper's Ferry to join the "Old Man." The raider who had urged him to escape, Osborne Anderson, made it safely back to Canada by means of the underground railroad, and likely Green would have done the same. But the path he chose led him back down into Harper's Ferry, to John Brown, and the gallows.

The raiders withstood a major siege on Monday afternoon and continued to exchange fire from the engine house until night fell. By all accounts, Green was courageous throughout the ordeal, although it was evident that Brown and his men were at an impasse. At first, the Old Man attempted to negotiate terms that would even out the odds of escape, but authorities had no intention of negotiating with one they considered a meddling abolitionist and insurrectionist. To Virginia, along with the rest of the South, the presence of armed abolitionists from the North was as outrageous as it was unprecedented, and Governor Henry Wise was determined to crush these insurgents with the support of President James Buchanan in Washington. The next morning, Tuesday, October 18, a contingent of marines arrived from the capital under the command of Colonel Robert E. Lee. When Brown refused Lee's demand for unconditional surrender, the marines stormed the engine house, taking heavy fire, and finally broke through.

Along with their leader, four captured raiders including Emperor were given hasty trials and sentenced to death. Brown was the first to be executed, being hanged on Friday, December 2. On December 16, four of his men, John Cook, John Copeland, Edwin Coppic, and Shields Green, followed him to the gallows.[2] Although the deaths of these four young men made news throughout the country, most of the nation's attention was focused upon Brown's martyrdom and its aftermath. Rescue plans had been discussed here and there by allies and sympathizers, but the abolitionist leader disdained any such notion, holding that his death would prove best for the antislavery cause. Shortly, the growing number of militia men stationed in Charlestown made any thought of rescue utterly impossible. While Governor Wise of Virginia rejected any notion of commuting Brown's death sentence, some Northerners hoped that perhaps a measure of clemency would be shown to his young followers. After all, Virginia had slain the old lion. Surely, a people purportedly steeped in the Christian faith might have spared his whelps. But those who thought this way could not have understood the implacable spirit that possessed the South.

One man knew better, not only having experienced the depths of slavery's depravity, but also the impact that "Old Brown" and his men had made upon the entirety of the South. "The efforts of John Brown and his brave associates," wrote Frederick Douglass in 1860, "have done more to upset the logic and shake the security of slavery, than all other efforts in that direction for twenty years." Furthermore, as Douglass recognized, throughout Brown's occupation of Harper's Ferry, he had not once acted with malice toward his opponents, but rather had shown uncommon concern for the feelings of the townsmen and had made every effort to shield his hostages. Yet this meant nothing to the Virginians, he concluded. "Slaveholders are as insensible to magnanimity as to justice, and the measure they mete out must be meted to them again."[3]

While he suffered no wounds in the hour of defeat, perhaps Green was the most despised of Brown's captured men, not only because he had proven bold in action and clever in defeat but also because he was the darkest man and thus the least sympathetic to whites. It was typical of reports and observations at the time to not only list whites and blacks separately, but also to distinguish light-skinned and "mulatto" from dark-skinned blacks. During the trials of Brown's men, there was a slight amount of sympathy in the court for John Copeland, a light-skinned raider, but none for Emperor, who was typically described in terms of his dark skin color. Indeed, while Brown and his men were all rushed through the formalities of a slaveholders' court and sentenced to death, the least covered and most easily overlooked by the press was Shields Green—"quite a black negro," as one newspaper report described him. After the executions, some forlorn efforts were made to save the bodies of the black raiders, but more so in the case of Copeland, who had heartfelt support from family and friends in Oberlin, Ohio. Ultimately, neither of the black raiders' remains were honorably interred. However, John Copeland's surviving daguerreotype, correspondence, and legacy in Oberlin have at least sustained his memory in a manner unlike that of Emperor, whose identity and body have nearly been lost to history. What remains is only a skeleton-thin account, almost a legend of a black man who fled the South, was befriended by the abolitionist orator Frederick Douglass, and then was enlisted by the militant John Brown.

* * *

Over the past few years, interest in the Harper's Ferry raiders has been on the upswing among writers, although in this case, artistic interest preceded scholarly effort by two decades. In 1996 *Shields Green and the Gospel of John Brown*, a screenplay by Kevin Willmott, was purchased by filmmaker Chris Columbus, but the project failed in pre-production.[4] Besides this disappointed effort, a number of other artistic ventures have been written for the stage and screen over the years about the black men who followed John Brown to Harper's Ferry. More recently, the sculptor Woodrow Nash has been preparing busts of Brown and his five black raiders to be installed in the John Brown House in Akron, Ohio; and the visual artist Peter Cizmadia's *Invisibles* exhibit at the Harpers Ferry National Historical Park featured twenty-four commemorative portraits of the men and women who supported John Brown, including his five black raiders.[5] Leading up to and following the sesquicentennial of the Harper's Ferry raid in 2009, a number of notable works about John Brown were published, but it was legal historian Steven Lubet who single-handedly produced two definitive biographies of Brown's men—*John Brown's Spy* (2012), the story of raider John Cook, and *The "Colored Hero" of Harper's Ferry* (2015), the story of raider John Anthony Copeland. In 2018 Eugene L. Meyer's *Five for Freedom* was published, a work exclusively focused upon the lives of Brown's black raiders. In the same year it was announced that Mark Amin's Sobini Films had once more taken up the story of Shields Green for the big screen in the film *Emperor*, based upon a screenplay co-written by Amin and Pat Charles and starring Dayo Okeniyi in the role of Green and James Cromwell as Brown. Shields Green also figures among Brown's men in the SHOWTIME adaptation of James McBride's historical fiction, *The Good Lord Bird*, featuring Ethan Hawke as John Brown and Quentin Plair as Emperor.[6]

After I heard news of Amin's film project in late 2018, it occurred to me to search through my own files, simply to see what I might find about Emperor. Having studied John Brown the abolitionist for twenty years, I thought that perhaps I might even be able to write one of those "real story behind the movie" pieces. However, when I began to cull my sources, I started to find little bits and pieces that I had never noticed before, prompting me to revisit the short but conventional narrative of Shields Green that has been passed down by older authors. As I did, questions arose that prompted me to look for more evidence until I found myself doing research with the intention of writing something more than an article about this fascinating but somewhat mysterious figure.

Unfortunately, even after my own scratching and digging, it seems that what can be confidently stated about Emperor remains limited. Indeed, it seems that Emperor has all but slipped away from us, historically speaking, and even with research it seems that key questions may never be answered without some fortuitous discovery. When I made initial inquiries into Emperor's background in South Carolina, a helpful researcher provided what she could unearth, concluding that it is a complicated thing, "trying to track down someone who likely didn't want to be tracked down." Perhaps this is the case with Shields Green, for it seems likely that he did not want to be found after he fled from the South. After all, he had escaped oppression and was all too aware that authorities in his day had the ability to reach to the very border of Canada and snatch him back into bondage and degradation. When he did go south with John Brown in 1859, Emperor was quite aware that he had placed himself, as he put it, back into "the eagle's claw."

On the other hand, I remain hopeful that some small trail into the past may yet be discerned, and that this work, despite its real limitations, may encourage someone else in the effort to further research the life of this Harper's Ferry raider, so well-remembered yet so little-known. To be sure, preparing this work has been obstinate and challenging for me in a manner that I have not known in previous biographical projects. In the most obvious sense, there simply is not enough material to write a substantive biography of Shields Green, while yet the available fragments suggest that it may be possible to get beyond the mere record as it stands.

For this reason, this work is presented as a kind of narrative inquiry in which the solid lines of the story are drawn out as much as possible, followed by the dotted lines reflecting the biographer's effort to distinguish what merits further consideration from what should be dismissed. Most biographers encounter moments in the narratives of their subjects when questions are left unanswered and insufficient evidence leads to some degree of guesswork—the dotted lines that we draw when we can no longer draw solid lines. The problem with writing about Emperor is that there are fewer solid

lines than in most biographical studies, and therefore a greater need
to draw out the dotted lines of the story. Understandably, then, some
may not be pleased with this work, reasonably questioning whether
such an undertaking is worth the effort. My first response is that
readers should be assured that there is neither presumption nor insistence on my part that this book is definitive. Indeed, as history
goes, this work is provisional in that it is intended as a kind of narrative restart, and therefore both criticism and further research are
invited—particularly because my goal is not to present a conclusive
narrative as much as it is to push through the fragments of the past
and rediscover the man known in antebellum newspapers as "Shields
Green, *alias* Emperor." Nevertheless, one might simply ask whether
what we already know about him is enough. Are there not many
other figures in African American history who merit our attention?
Furthermore, John Brown had a small army of followers, and some of
them have yet to receive biographical treatment even though it may
be easier to locate them in the historical record. Why labor further in
such a sparsely sown field? In response, I would argue that there are
yet compelling reasons to look more closely at Shields Green.

First, he is deeply embedded in the narrative of the Harper's Ferry
raid because he is uniquely connected to and dependent upon both
Frederick Douglass and John Brown. Often, when Douglass spoke
of Brown, he also spoke of Shields Green. Second, Emperor was the
only one of the Harper's Ferry raiders who understood flight from
the South. The other raiders were either white men or free black men
living in the North, even if they had been in some way carried or
transported from the South in youth. Green had fled from the South
and made a life for himself in the free states and in Canada. His
alliance with John Brown in some sense closed the loop of his own
story by means of a perilous trek back into the South in 1859. Finally,
Emperor is something of a paradox in the story of the Harper's Ferry
raid: he has only the slightest biographical profile and yet occupies

some of the most dramatic moments of the story; his sketched visage is familiar to students of the raid although he is the only one of John Brown's raiders not to have left a daguerreotype image of himself; and within the conventional record he is both the son of an unidentified father and the father of an unidentified son. Strangely, digging deeper into the record has added slight insight to both Green's parentage and his son, and yet their identities still remain unknown. However, if there is a final reason—even a personal mandate—for my taking on this project, it has been in some sense to restore the life of Shields Green the man who lived, to represent an embodiment of the man whose actual body was stolen by the same racist society that tried to steal his labor, his freedom, and his humanity, and which ultimately stole his life and remains. I think Emperor is owed this much, and whether I have succeeded or failed, in so doing I have tried to follow Old Brown's advice: "Everything worthy of being done *at all* is worthy of being done in *good earnest*, & in the best possible manner."[7]

In the first chapter, before proceeding with his story, then, I thought it best to address some traditional assumptions about Shields Green, raising questions and suggesting possibilities where evidence permits. Readers who are familiar with the story may be surprised, for instance, to discover that Emperor may not have been a "runaway slave" in the conventional sense. In chapter 2, Green's enlistment in John Brown's cause is examined and a closer look is taken at the story that is singly preserved in Frederick Douglass's familiar account, where Emperor famously told the abolitionist orator that he would "go wid de ole man." At some points, however, there is little actual material about Emperor, and in such cases I have made an effort to provide a framework for the setting and context of which he was a part. This is especially the case in chapter 3, which discusses the circumstances in which Emperor and the other raiders lived together under John Brown's roof in Maryland prior to the raid, and again in chapter 4, which includes consideration of a narrative of the Harper's Ferry raid by Green's black colleague, Osborne Perry Anderson. Chapter 5 recalls Emperor's last days, from the Harper's Ferry engine house to the gallows at Charlestown, and chapter 6 closes out this narrative inquiry by reflecting upon the surviving images of Emperor, particularly my effort to discern which of them best represents the man who lived. The epilogue thus reflects upon the absent body of Shields Green and the way in which he somehow pushed back into the realities of the post-Reconstruction era, and the legend of Emperor so bequeathed to us all. Finally, by way of style, the reader should note that in keeping with his own preferred self-designation, I refer to the subject throughout either as Shields Green or as Emperor.

In 1886, looking back at this antebellum drama, an aged Frederick Douglass declared that John Brown of Harper's Ferry was "like all men born before their time, whose bleeding footsteps show us the cost of all reforms."[8] But Brown did not walk alone to Harper's Ferry, nor were the gallows solely his penalty. Those who followed him shared in his suffering, some falling first at Harper's Ferry and others being tried and hanged at Charlestown. Afterward, some who had escaped went on to risk their lives once more in opposing slavery during the Civil War—two of them even dying in the conflict.

It is my contention that the Harper's Ferry raiders were among the best men that this nation could offer in the antebellum era. Indeed, they still represent something that should be admirable for every generation—particularly in their concern for overturning injustice and liberating the oppressed. A just and progressive reading of our nation's history will not permit the Harper's Ferry raid to be trivialized as a prequel to modern terrorism, nor restrict Brown and his young freedom fighters to the margins of our national narrative. John Brown's raiders must be remembered, including Emperor, whose footsteps in history may be the hardest to trace among his brethren. Still, the path of freedom that he followed is certain and his sacrifice is without question. His soul, too, goes marching on.

Emperor Mysterious

To Find the Man Who Lived

Materials from which to furnish a sketch of this
courageous Martyr for Freedom
are meagre indeed.

Pine and Palm, 1861

HE quest to learn about Shields Green is frustrating, especially because the pursuit of evidence seems to raise new questions beyond those that originally were asked by historians. For instance, there is no doubt that his early life and upbringing took place in Charleston, South Carolina. "He had been brought up in the city," recalled Owen Brown, his traveling companion.[1] This means that Green does not conform to the stereotype of the agrarian slave that is most familiar in popular thinking. In a real sense, Green was far more an urban figure than even Frederick Douglass, who knew both the agrarian and urban experience in slavery. But neither was Green unusual in this regard, since, as will be shown below, he was among a significant number of African Americans in the Lower South, half of whom lived in urban centers in the mid-nineteenth century.[2] Yet the particulars of his early life in Charleston remain out of reach.

There is no reason to doubt the tradition that Shields Green had been a married man with a young son prior to his flight from the South. In this tradition we rely upon the testimony of Anne Brown

Adams, the daughter of John Brown, who stayed for a time with her father and the raiders prior to the Harper's Ferry raid.[3] Based upon what Green told her, Anne wrote that he had escaped from Charleston in a "sailing vessel loaded with cotton" bound for New York City, where he was "stowed away by one of the hands" and "aided by friends upon arrival." She said that Green told her that he had left a young son behind when he fled, and that his wife had died prior to his escape.[4] These few details are priceless, but they also raise questions. Benjamin Quarles suggested that the death of Green's wife had "spurred on" his escape.[5] This is dramatic, but nothing in the record suggests that her death had anything to do with his decision to flee from South Carolina.

As to his family life in the South, we do not know, for instance, whether Green's wife was enslaved or free. Free and enslaved blacks "commonly joined together as man and wife."[6] However, without sufficient information, Green's unfortunate spouse remains anonymous to history. To compound the problem, although Anne Brown Adams claimed that Green's wife had died prior to his flight from the South, we do not know the year of his departure. If, for example, his escape from Charleston took place between 1854 and 1855, then his wife might be one of three black women listed as having died just before this period. Of the three, one was enslaved and two were free.[7] Without any certainty as to the identity of Green's wife or the date of her death, it seems impossible to date his flight from the South. Evidence of his presence in the North may put us closer to an estimate of his departure from South Carolina, although even here it remains inconclusive.

According to the *Rochester Democrat* in 1859, Green made his first appearance in Rochester, New York, about three years prior to the Harper's Ferry raid, after which he went to Canada, and then returned to the city in the spring or summer of 1858.[8] This would set Green's first appearance in Rochester at about 1856, although this is not adequate to determine the date of his escape, since he may have wandered elsewhere through the Northern states prior to his first arrival in Rochester.

* * *

Frederick Douglass wrote that Shields Green "called himself by different names," including "Emperor."[9] However, since the 1970s, frequently it has been reported by historians that his real name was Esau Brown. The contemporary source of this claim is the invaluable study *Allies for Freedom: Blacks and John Brown* (1974) by the eminent African American scholar Benjamin Quarles. However, the claim has not been sufficiently examined over the past half century, particularly given the fact that the citation actually was omitted from the book, through an oversight by either Quarles or his editor.

In preparing *Allies for Freedom*, Quarles clearly uses Anne Brown Adams as a source, along with an article in the *Rochester Democrat*, dated October 21, 1859, and its republication in the *New York Daily Tribune* on the following day.[10] While these sources are vital, neither makes reference to Green's real name having been Esau Brown. Most recently, journalist Eugene Meyer has extended this assumption in his narrative, *Five for Freedom: The African American Soldiers in John Brown's Army* (2018). Relying on the assumption as conveyed by scholars since the time of Quarles, Meyer goes so far as to venture that Green's former master may have been a Charleston slaveholder named Alexander H. Brown.[11] While this is a reasonable conjecture, the question remains whether there is sufficient evidence that Esau Brown was Green's actual name.

As it turns out, the original source for the claim—and likely the one that Quarles omitted from his manuscript—was an article in the *Pine and Palm* published in 1861. The *Pine and Palm* was the undertaking of the zealous abolitionist James Redpath, who knew John Brown and had published his official biography the year before. John

McKivigan, Redpath's biographer, says the Scotsman purchased the
Weekly Anglo-African early in 1861, renamed it the *Pine and Palm*, and
placed it under the charge of a nominal black editor named George
Lawrence in New York City. As a measure of control, Redpath "dispatched his old friend Richard J. Hinton to work with Lawrence."
Primarily, the *Pine and Palm* functioned as a means for Redpath, who
was based in Boston, to advocate for immediate emancipation and
black emigration to Haiti, and he maintained a strong control of the
paper in advancing his agenda.[12]

The Esau Brown claim is found in an unsigned article entitled
"Shields Green," which provides both trustworthy and questionable
information.[13] The article was based upon information provided to
Redpath by the abolitionist William C. Nell, who admitted that he
did not know the raiders but had gathered the information from
"friends with some materials." Nell's "friends" with "materials" are unknown, and the article itself is probably edited heavily or actually written by Redpath based upon his notes.[14] The *Pine and Palm* piece states
that in Charleston, South Carolina, Green "was there known as Esau
Brown, but on reaching the North he assumed the name of Shield
Emperor." It also claims that Green had fled from South Carolina
early in the year 1859—this error afterward having been picked up
by Frederick Douglass, who told a Massachusetts audience in 1873
that Green was "only a year from slavery in South Carolina" when he
had joined John Brown. Fortunately, Douglass did not continue to
repeat this error in later speeches or in his autobiography.[15] In 1859
the *Rochester Democrat* stated that Green had been in the vicinity of
Rochester (including Canada) for a few years. The *Pine and Palm* article itself provides a full transcription of Green's Rochester business
card with a date well over a year before the Harper's Ferry raid:

Clothes Cleaning

The undersigned would respectfully announce that he is prepared to do clothes cleaning in a manner to suit the most fastidious, and on cheaper terms than any one else.

Orders left at my establishment, No. 2 Spring Street, first door west of Exchange Street, will be promptly attended to.

I make no promises that I am unable to perform.

All kinds of Cloths, Silks, Satins, &c., can be cleaned at this establishment. **SHIELD EMPEROR.**

ROCHESTER, JULY 22D, 1858.[16]

The *Pine and Palm* article certainly raises important questions pertaining to Green's story, such as the claim that he had made friends in Philadelphia, and whether he had first heard of John Brown through Douglass in Rochester or while he was in Canada. Primarily, however, one must ask, if Green's actual name was Esau Brown, why does every contemporary source refer to him as either Shields Green or Emperor? Whatever Redpath's basis was for the Esau Brown notion, it seems dubious, perhaps little more than hearsay. Although Redpath served history well by preserving Green's business card in the *Pine and Palm*, his article otherwise is more a homage than a well-substantiated record.

To no surprise, the only other place where Green is referred to as Esau Brown is in a piece that probably was based upon the one in the *Pine and Palm*. In a 1907 article in the *Washington Bee*, the alleged real name of Shields Green is mentioned in the context of a dinner meeting of the Pen and Pencil Club in Washington, a private social organization of journalists. The article describes a gathering dedicated to the ninetieth anniversary of the birth of Frederick Douglass, who had died twelve years before. Among the toasts to be given at the affair was one by the abolitionist's own son, sixty-six-year-old

Lewis Douglass. His toast reportedly was entitled, "Esau Brown, martyr, one of John Brown's men." Unfortunately, Lewis was sick that evening and could not present his toast in person, and so it was submitted in writing and apparently read by someone else before the meeting. The reporter who covered the event for the *Bee* stated only that all the speeches were well received but provided no further description of the Douglass toast.[17] In retrospect, however, the younger Douglass was merely echoing Redpath's speculation, even appropriating his martyr title from the 1861 *Pine and Palm* article.

In his last memoir, Frederick Douglass described Green as "a colored man who called himself by different names."[18] However, "Shield Emperor," the name he used on his business card in Rochester, seems only a variation of his real name, Shields Green. Douglass himself makes no mention of Esau Brown, instead referring to him—in all of his speeches over many years and in his autobiography—as Shields Green. Indeed, in all of the reportage from the time of the raid, Green never was identified as Esau Brown and never was quoted as referring to himself by this name. Furthermore, none of his recorded Harper's Ferry associates, including Anne Brown Adams, ever referred to Shields Green as Esau Brown. Finally, none of the most detailed researchers of John Brown ever seem to have found evidence for the Esau Brown notion. Katherine Mayo, whose expansive research made it possible for Oswald Garrison Villard to publish his magisterial biography of Brown in 1910, never mentions Esau Brown in her field notes and interviews. Neither, apparently, did Boyd Stutler, the "godfather" of John Brown researchers in the later twentieth century. Considering the absence of any other reference besides the *Pine and Palm* article and its probable reiteration in 1907, it is doubtful that Esau Brown was Green's real name. Perhaps this was one of his traveling names, although its apparent absence from the record makes even this possibility uncertain.

* * *

Although the popular narrative does not provide a detailed physical description of Shields Green, it correctly describes him as a strapping black man. Green evidenced no "mixed" family heritage, unlike some of the other black raiders who were considered "mulatto." He was described by one white Virginian as being "dark copper-colored," and by a white Baltimore journalist as "quite a black Negro."[19] The notion put forth by Quarles, that Green called himself Emperor because he believed himself to be the descendant of an African prince, is thoughtful speculation.[20]

Of all people, a physician named Alban Payne (whose pen name was Nicholas Spicer) who espoused "scientific" knowledge of alleged black inferiority, provided another physical description of Shields Green. Payne described him as "a negro with a thick, broad neck" and as "uncommonly strong and active." After visiting him in jail, Payne concluded that Emperor had "the appearance of being as tough as a 'pine knot.'"[21] In fact, Payne's description is more reliable than a more familiar one provided by the antislavery journalist Richard Hinton, written long after the Harper's Ferry raid. Hinton, who was an antislavery racist like many others in his time, seems never to have seen Green in person, but presumptively described him in bigoted caricature as "the negro man with Congo face . . . and huge feet."[22]

* * *

Although Shields Green's origin in slavery is a reasonable conclusion of historians, this point too is open to question. Certainly, Green knew the pangs of oppression in the South, but his experience probably is more nuanced in historical terms. While incarcerated in Virginia, Green and the other raiders were interviewed by a man whose description of the prisoners appeared in a New York publication, *Spirit of the Times*, in early December 1859. After describing the black Ohioan John Copeland, the writer summarily reported: "Shields Green, the other black, born, *he says*, in South Carolina of free parents."[23] This heretofore unknown statement in which Green himself claims free parentage requires us to reconsider his background in South Carolina, as well as the circumstances that brought about his flight to the North.

Certainly, there is no reason to doubt the truthfulness of the report. Neither the writer (known to us only as "J.T.") nor Shields Green himself had any reason to lie about having had free parents in the South. In fact, Green probably had revealed his free parentage to his lawyer, who may have chosen to keep the point hidden during the trial.[24] By doing so, Green's lawyer could undermine the count of treason against him because the court found that slaves were not citizens and therefore could not commit treason. After his trial, Green may have found some satisfaction in announcing his freeborn status to Southern visitors.

Green's claim of free parentage may be accepted, although none of the available records from this period thus far examined either verify or contradict it.[25] Assuming his words to be true, however, his flight from the South more likely was a reaction to a changed condition in his status, perhaps one that reflected the racist realities of antebellum South Carolina. In other words, what if Shields Green had lived in South Carolina as a free man, but somehow had found himself threatened with imprisonment or even enslavement? Might not such tragic circumstances have prompted him to flee the South?

As Ira Berlin observed in his seminal work, *Slaves without Masters*, "Southern free Negroes balanced precariously between abject slavery, which they rejected, and full freedom which was denied them."[26] Berlin's study, which highlights the differences between slavery in the Upper and Lower South, is useful in understanding Green's original context. In South Carolina, like the rest of the Lower South, freemen lived in a tenuous position between whites and their enslaved black brethren, a position that "allowed them just enough room to create their own life under the hateful glare of whites and within the slave society." Unless self-employed, free blacks often were obligated to hire themselves out to whites who exploited their labor and deducted expenses from their salaries, often ensnaring them in "perennial indebtedness." If a free black man like Green had found himself either deeply in debt or involved in some other legal problem involving fines, taxes, or jail fees, he would have been imprisoned and possibly sold into virtual slavery without hope of relief or deliverance.[27] Likewise, in his vital study *Black Charlestonians*, Bernard Powers Jr. affirms that, apart from the experience of the most elite free blacks, free persons of color in Charleston led an "imperiled" existence. Not only could they be legally sold into slavery due to the aforementioned financial and legal burdens that were imposed upon them, but sometimes they were also kidnapped and sold into slavery.[28]

According to an abolitionist who knew him after he had fled to the North, Green told her, "I have suffered cruel blows from men *who said they owned me*."[29] These words might just as likely have come from a freeman who had fallen prey to slavery's grip than from one born into slavery. In the late antebellum era, free people of color in the South found themselves increasingly under assault as both previously unenforced laws and new laws were imposed upon them, restricting every aspect of black life.[30] Free blacks convicted of crimes were punished more harshly; for failure to pay city taxes, for example, they were subject to extended periods of forced labor, whereas whites were issued fines. Charleston's free black men between the ages of twenty-one and sixty had to pay a tax of ten dollars if they practiced any kind of trade or art in the city. Likewise, free black males between eighteen and fifty years of age were subjected to a poll tax of two dollars. If a free black man failed to pay this tax, he could be handed over to the sheriff, who was then authorized "to sell him for a period of service not more than five years, sufficient to pay the costs."[31] While enslaved people were routinely beaten, in the 1850s free blacks increasingly were also whipped for violations that whites were only fined for committing. As Leonard P. Curry concluded, free blacks now "lived between two worlds with an unsteady foot in each."[32]

Perhaps Shields Green, born free in Charleston, had somehow found himself in a situation where he was jailed, whipped, and vulnerable to some sort of indentured enslavement. Whether or not he was permanently reduced to the status of slavery or subjected to an extended time of servitude is not clear, although Emperor found the injustice of this treatment intolerable and decided to flee. At this point, too, his manner of flight—as a stowaway on a ship loaded with cotton and bound for New York City—bears consideration, for it may reflect the means by which he had fallen victim to slavery as a freeman.

Recall that Frederick Douglass was able to secure his freedom in 1838 by borrowing a free black sailor's papers, and jumping aboard a northbound train from Baltimore, then going by steamboat to Philadelphia, and thence to New York City. Douglass noted that sailors enjoyed popular favor at the time in Maryland, and that the conductor so readily trusted "the sailor's protection" in lieu of free papers, that he was able to make the risky sojourn to freedom.[33] Green apparently also drew upon the assistance of black seamen, but under very different circumstances.

By the later years of the antebellum era, many states in the Lower South were highly suspicious of free black mariners, particularly South Carolina, which remembered their association with the Denmark Vesey conspiracy of 1822 in Charleston. Beginning with South Carolina, many slave states had passed Seaman Acts, based upon the popularly held belief that the influence of free black sailors upon enslaved people was tantamount to a "moral contagion." The Seaman Acts functioned as "quarantines," whereby free black sailors were immediately detained when coming ashore in port cities like Charleston. Despite this white fixation on keeping "vulnerable" slaves from being exposed to free black sailors, the detainment facilities for free black sailors were also used to imprison delinquent local slaves and free people of color. The contradictions of this racist practice are evident, not only in that both free and enslaved blacks were exposed to the "morally contagious" black seamen while in detention, but also that enslaved black sailors were not detained.[34] In Charleston, had Shields Green actually been arrested and jailed due to unfortunate circumstances, he would have been incarcerated in the looming, cheerless, and rat-infested city jail, exposed not only to criminals of all stripes, but also to free black sailors and white Charleston's other black victims.[35] Certainly, in order for him to have gained access to a sailing ship bound for New York City, most likely he had made connections with blacks on board, either free or enslaved. Did he come into contact with a "morally contagious" free black sailor under detention, and was it through this contact that he arranged to be smuggled aboard?

As to Emperor's former life as a freeman in the Lower South, consideration of other details may provide insight, such as his apparent education. Benjamin Quarles not only assumed that Green was born in slavery, but attributed illiteracy to him—once more reflecting an uncritical dependency upon the 1861 *Pine and Palm* article, which stated that he was illiterate.[36] But since Green had been reared as a freeman, it is more likely that at least he had some basic schooling, certainly beyond what would have been allowed of an enslaved man. The interviewer J.T. described Green as showing "a good countenance, and a sharp, intelligent look," concluding that he was "not much inferior to Fred. Douglass in mind *or education*."[37] The comparison with Frederick Douglass probably was intentional, given that by the time of the interview, it is likely that Green's association with the famous abolitionist had become known. In contrast, another interviewer was determined to belittle Green, as if to spite that same association. The physician Alban Payne was eager to pronounce Green as showing "no evidence of either education or intelligence." But the racist forgot himself, afterward mentioning that Green was "said to be finely educated."[38]

Of course, even if some Virginians thought that Shields Green was "finely educated," they were speaking in the context of racist realities, not the norms of white society. More likely, Green's schooling was incomplete, commensurate with the tenuous existence he had known in Charleston. Just as his economic and political condition reflected the restrictions forced upon free blacks in the Lower South, so perhaps the limitations imposed upon his schooling also reflect his precarious existence in a racist, slavery-based society. One snobbish Virginia clergyman, who had ministered to him in his final days, thus adjudged Green "an uneducated Negro." Likewise, after his death, a journalist from the *Richmond Daily Dispatch* repeated another report that called Green illiterate.[39] But the notion of Green's illiteracy may have been based on prejudice, given that he was a dark-skinned man who was not well spoken, and who was presumed to have been a slave.

In her later years, Anne Brown Adams seems to have lacked the kind of empathy for black people demonstrated by her father and mother, and sometimes even conveyed the impression that they owed her a measure of fealty and support.[40] Reading over her several reminiscences of the Harper's Ferry raiders, one can also see that she tended to favor the white men, of whom she could write about passionately and extensively when asked. In fairness to Anne, however, three of the raiders were her brothers, and two of the black raiders (John Copeland and Lewis Leary) did not even join Brown and his men until after she had left her father and returned home in September 1859. In the 1890s, when she was asked to provide reminiscences of the Harper's Ferry raiders, Anne felt constrained to make her own search for information about Brown's black raiders by soliciting sources in Ohio.[41]

Yet even if Anne's reminiscences of Brown's black men were as benign as they were brief, her remarks about Shields Green are the least flattering. Indeed, in every reference to him, Anne tended to present Green as having been something of a nuisance while at Brown's Maryland farmhouse prior to the raid. Based upon her reminiscences, it seems that Emperor was either always in her way or tediously rambling on, to her annoyance. Belittling even his efforts at conversation, she wrote to Franklin Sanborn that Shields Green was "a perfect rattlebrain *in talk*."[42] In another remembrance from the 1890s, she relayed an incident that took place prior to her departure from Maryland, when Green attempted to make something of a farewell speech. "It was the greatest conglomeration of all the big words in the dictionary, and out, that was ever piled up," she recalled. According to Anne, even fellow raider Osborne Anderson had jested that "God Almighty could not understand" Green's speech.[43] But if Green was aspiring to use words in the dictionary, maybe he could read one too. In his own reminiscence of the Harper's Ferry raid, Osborne Anderson made no such jest about Shields Green. Nor did Frederick Douglass, who described him rather as dignified, yet as "a man of few words" whose "speech was singularly broken."[44] Taken together, these descriptions suggest that despite his desire to learn, it is more likely that Shields Green had labored under the deficiencies of an uneven schooling, or may have struggled with a speech impediment or even a learning disability. That he has been portrayed as illiterate in history seems to be a notion partially rooted in the unreliable *Pine and Palm* article—the same source that gave us the doubtable tale of Esau Brown the runaway slave.

Another hint at Green's former status may be found in the kinds of livelihoods he sustained after he had fled the South. During an extended stay in Canada, he worked as a waiter. In Rochester, New York, he assumed proprietorship of a clothes cleaning business.[45] (Certainly it is quite possible that Green himself wrote the draft for the printer who published his business card.) After his arrest at Harper's Ferry, one journalist who interviewed Green identified him as a barber by trade, and following his death, another reporter noted that he had been a "journeyman barber."[46] Restaurant service, clothes cleaning, and barbering were among a number of livelihoods typically carried on by free blacks in the North and the South in that era. Berlin notes that in the South there was a variety of "drudgery jobs" that working-class whites either avoided or conceded to free blacks in order to elevate their status. These jobs, derogatorily referred to as "nigger work," ranged from serving as coachmen and stable hands to food service, tailoring, barbering, and other roles that whites preferred not to undertake for themselves.[47] Green seems to have had a varied skill set, which may further suggest his original status as a freeman in Charleston.

Another detail that bears reconsideration is Green's age at the time of the Harper's Ferry raid in 1859. Traditionally, it has been presumed that he was a young man in his twenties at the time, especially by Benjamin Quarles, who referred to Green as being twenty-five years old—once more based upon the unreliable reportage in the *Pine and Palm*.[48] Certainly, a few newspaper reports at the time did describe him as a young man in his twenties, although no definitive age was ever established by reporters.[49] As a man of dark complexion, Emperor more likely had a youthful appearance. Still, at least one interviewer concluded, "Green is a dark negro about 30 years of age."[50] In this light, estimation of Emperor's age at the time of the raid cannot rely alone upon random newspaper descriptions.

Another source that has been taken as evidence for Green's youth is a letter written by John Brown Jr. on August 11, 1859, still fresh from a meeting with Frederick Douglass in Rochester. Writing to John Henrie Kagi, Brown's trusted agent in Chambersburg, Pennsylvania, John updated him on the upcoming meeting between the Old Man and Douglass later that month. "The friend at Rochester will set out to make you a *visit* in a few days," he wrote. "He will be accompanied by that 'other young man,'" referring to Shields Green.[51] However, the phrase "other young man" is only a veiled reference to Green as a recruit. As age goes, there is no literal intent in John's words since, if Green was the "other young man," then the first "young man" was forty-one-year-old Frederick Douglass. Richard Hinton seems to have missed this in taking these words literally, although John clearly placed them within quotation marks.[52] There are yet other reasons for suggesting that Shields Green was older than what has been presumed by historians, including the conclusion of an elusive genealogical researcher.[53] Certainly, as observed in chapter 6, the best sketches of Emperor made from life suggest that he was not a twenty-something youth at the time of his death. While it is not yet possible to determine Green's actual age, it is far more reasonable to assume that he was in his mid-thirties at the time of the Harper's Ferry raid.

* * *

A survey of contemporary newspaper accounts shows that much of the reporting about Brown and his men after the raid mainly was picked up from major New York papers like the *Herald* and *Tribune*, or from newspapers in Baltimore and Washington, D.C., from which reporters were also dispatched to Harper's Ferry and Charlestown. In some cases, however, newspapers featured other details, a few of which had substance, while others were based upon transcription errors. To no surprise, details of all kinds traveled across the country, North and South, based upon reprinted newspaper reports. For instance, an antislavery editor in Lisbon, Ohio, published a flawed reiteration of a report originally in the *Baltimore Sun*. In so doing, he mistakenly transformed raider Edwin Coppic's racial identification ("white") into an additional raider named "White." The same report erroneously stated that both Coppic and Green were from Iowa. This line seems to have been picked up by smaller newspapers across the North, suggesting that it was an error first made in a

Northern newspaper.[54] In another report, Shields Green was associated with the city of Pittsburgh, Pennsylvania. In this case, however, the error seems to have traveled south. While it is difficult to be certain as to the origin of this mistake, an early report stating that Green was from Pittsburgh is found in the *Evening Star*, published in Washington, D.C., on October 19, 1859.[55] Within a week of this report, this error seems to have spread among lesser journals in North Carolina and South Carolina, and likely elsewhere in the South.[56]

However, the Pittsburgh reference is worth considering because apparently it had been confused in reports for Harrisburg, the capital of Pennsylvania, which was linked with initial reports about Shields Green after the raid. Most notably, a journalist from the *Baltimore Sun* was among the earliest reporters on the scene at Harper's Ferry, and described Green in two different reports (dated October 19) as "colored, of Harrisburg," and also as a "free negro from Harrisburg."[57] Likewise, another report in the *Baltimore Daily Exchange* initially connected Green with Harrisburg. In his first report, however, either the journalist (or the typesetter) misidentified Green as "Gains"—although the raiders' names sometimes were confused, particularly in those reports made when the smoke was still clearing in Harper's Ferry. The article thus states that "Gains" had been "induced" by Brown "to come over to Maryland and work for him," after which he was further "induced to go into the insurrection."[58] The following day, however, the *Daily Exchange* filed another report, identifying Green by his correct name, and describing him as "a large man" who also went by the sobriquet "Emperor." The updated description says that Green was "raised in South Carolina" but was from Rochester, New York, and the Harrisburg connection is not repeated.[59]

Was there any real connection between Shields Green and Harrisburg? One may very well assume that Green's claim to have been a free man from Harrisburg was a ploy of some kind. It is a matter of record that Green was clever enough to try to elude capture by means of a ruse following Brown's defeat.[60] But when it was clear that he could not pass himself off as a "captured" slave, Green may have changed tactics, telling the marines that he was a free black man from Pennsylvania. However, if the Harrisburg claim was a ploy on Green's part, it is not clear what he hoped to gain by it as a black man captured as an ostensible insurrectionist in a slave state. Certainly, the Virginians would not have been willing to surrender him to Pennsylvania authorities. Perhaps by associating himself with Harrisburg, Green hoped to avoid connecting Frederick Douglass to the raid; or maybe he merely hoped to avoid any word reaching South Carolina that he had been apprehended in Virginia.

But what if Green was telling the truth and his reference to Harrisburg has biographical significance? In the *Pine and Palm* article it is stated that Emperor had made friends in Philadelphia. While it is possible that the reference to Philadelphia is an error, Green may very well have gone there after landing in New York City. Indeed, his possible connection to Harrisburg is interesting, not only given the unusual profile of that city in the antebellum era, but also because there is a well-documented underground railroad connection between Philadelphia and Harrisburg.[61]

Harrisburg was not a typical Northern city in the 1850s. Although it benefitted from trading on the Susquehanna River, Harrisburg was far more political than commercial in outlook. At the same time, it had become appealing to settlers, both white and black, because of its accessibility by canal and railway. While the majority of its citizens were white, African Americans in Emperor's time numbered significantly in Harrisburg, being the city with the leading black population in the state. Considering the importance of Harrisburg to blacks in the antebellum era, it may be that Green had some real connection there, just as he claimed to have had free parents in South Carolina.

As the preferred residence for many blacks in Pennsylvania, Harrisburg saw its African American population reach nearly thirteen thousand prior to the Civil War. Although Pennsylvania had other smaller black settlements, most of them were isolated communities of color in rural areas largely comprised of freedmen and refugees from the South. In contrast, Harrisburg was the home of a sizable free population and a sanctuary for fugitives. Black and white abolitionists provided safe havens to fugitives, so if he had found his way to Harrisburg from Philadelphia in the 1850s, Green was among a population of escapees from slavery that numbered well over one hundred—no small number for a moderate-sized antebellum town. Unlike other cities in the North, Harrisburg even had its own black cultural area, which developed along Tanner's Alley (near today's Capitol Park and Walnut and Fourth Streets), a thoroughfare where free blacks and fugitives from slavery lived and mingled.[62]

What makes the Harrisburg connection even more interesting is a single contemporary source, a report that was filed by a Baltimore journalist on October 18, the day after Brown's capture, appearing the following day in the *New York Herald*. According to the *Herald* report, a "Negro named Green, who was conspicuous in the fugitive slave riot at Harrisburg some years ago, was among the insurgents" at Harper's Ferry.[63] This reported claim, that Green had participated in a "fugitive slave riot" in Harrisburg, appears only once in the annals of the Harper's Ferry raid and therefore it is not quite clear how to evaluate it. Should it be dismissed as yet another error, or should it be considered possibly as granting a new insight into Shields Green's mysterious story? If it was simply an error, it is peculiarly so because the anonymous reporter who filed it would have had no obvious reason to make such a connection. It seems more likely that this Baltimore reporter probably was among the first journalists on the scene following the raid, and that his reference to Green's participation in a "fugitive slave riot" actually was based upon an interview with him.

To be sure, the Harrisburg connection, if altogether dismissed, would have no immediate bearing upon the record of Shields Green and the Harper's Ferry raid. On the other hand, if it is retained as a possibility, then the conventional chronology would have to be significantly adjusted in favor of a much earlier escape from South Carolina, because the only recorded "fugitive slave riot" in Harrisburg took place in 1850. This again raises the issue of Green's age, for if he was a young man in his twenties at the time of the Harper's Ferry raid as typically assumed, then he would have been far too young to have participated in the Harrisburg episode nine years before. But if Shields Green was born in the mid-1820s, then he would have had sufficient time to marry, sire a child, and escape in his later twenties, and would have been in his early thirties by the time of the raid in 1859.

The episode at Harrisburg often has been overlooked in narratives of the antebellum era, perhaps because it occurred just prior to the passing of the Fugitive Slave Act in the fall of 1850. As such, it cannot be numbered among the more memorable "rescues" and "riots" that occurred in the wake of the Fugitive Slave Law of 1850, from the Christiana (Pennsylvania) "riot" and "Jerry Rescue" (Syracuse, New York) in 1851 to the Oberlin-Wellington (Ohio) incident of 1858. To be sure, the legal outworking of the Harrisburg incident unfolded after the law was passed. But the incident itself—in which Shields Green may have participated as a young man—actually shows the kind of antislavery resistance that slaveholders wanted to prevent in the first place by a reinvigorated fugitive slave law.[64]

In the summer of 1850, eight men fled from Clarke County, Virginia, passing through Harrisburg on their way north. Undoubtedly, the underground railroad brought these desperate men to Harrisburg, and likely also to the attention of William A. Jones, the leading black citizen. Jones owned property and ran a popular boardinghouse in the city that doubled as an underground railroad stop. Although five of the fugitives left town, three men remained, only to be apprehended by a party of slave hunters and placed in custody. Less than a week afterward, a committee of black citizens led by Jones was able to bring the three fugitives before a judge on a writ of *habeas corpus*, and then paid two abolitionist lawyers to represent them.

The judge was apparently sympathetic to the fugitives, permitting the slaveholders only to reclaim the horses that the fugitives had taken. Undaunted, the slaveholders entered the jail after the trial with the clear intention of seizing the runaways. This immediately prompted a response from black Harrisburg. When one of the fugitives was seized, the crowd exploded in anger and pushed forward to the jail. During the struggle, a single man was able to get past an iron fence and liberate one of the three fugitives. While sustaining terrible wounds, the hero delivered him to the sympathetic crowd, which promptly armed him and sent him on his way north.

Unable either to escape or to be rescued by the black community, the other two fugitives remained in the Harrisburg jail under armed guard. Unfortunately, they were incarcerated long enough for President Millard Fillmore to sign the Fugitive Slave Act into law that September—essentially dooming them to be returned to bondage in Virginia. The bitter process was overseen by a notoriously racist state commissioner, the scion of some Northern slaveholding family who considered the black population in Pennsylvania as "a tax and a pest" upon white society. Under his auspices, from October 1850 to December 1851, there were nine incidents involving seventeen blacks, ranging from minor disturbances to exasperating episodes for black Harrisburg. Was Emperor involved in some of these incidents as well? While the African American community responded to this incident by forming an ad hoc committee to aid fugitives under the new law, the tragic "fugitive slave riot" of August 1850 was a harbinger of the last and most desperate decade of the antebellum era.[65]

Shortly after Emperor's death in 1859, a journalist inserted a description of the raider in the *Richmond Daily Dispatch*, suggesting that it was based upon another source. The description is clearly derogatory, but also provocative. According to his source, Emperor "was an ambitious, vindictive, but very illiterate negro of the African species" who had "died a victim to his own brutish impetuosity." It is easy enough to dismiss these charges, yet for all of its malicious twaddle, the report also states that Green had been "the head and front of all the negro rescues at Harrisburg, for several years past." Once again, the reference to Emperor's activities in Harrisburg tends to reinforce the notion that he had revealed this background himself, and that possibly he had some connection to antislavery activities there, although there is no certainty as to what is meant by "negro rescues."

In 1885 a longtime Oberlinian named Lewis Clark told a reporter from the *Chicago Inter-Ocean* that Shields Green had also been a resident of Oberlin, Ohio. If this were true, it certainly would have put him in the company of John Brown's other black raiders, John A. Copeland and Lewis S. Leary. A similar claim, that Green had been "a student and citizen of Oberlin," was made by another author in the early twentieth century.[66] However, Green's alleged connection to the famous Ohio town has no basis in fact. In 1860 James Mason Fitch wrote in the *Weekly Anglo-African* that Green "was but little known" in Oberlin except by news of his capture and execution in Virginia. Elias Jones, a longtime resident and activist in Oberlin, likewise denied that Green was ever a part of the community. During the antebellum era, Jones had served as secretary of an antislavery society in Oberlin and insisted that Green could never have been part of the community without him knowing it.[67]

How old was Shields Green when he fled from South Carolina, and what year did he make his escape? What roads had he traveled by the time he knocked on the door of the Douglass residence in Rochester? The conventional narrative portrays Emperor as one who had run away from slavery and then stumbled his way into the historical spotlight by his association with Frederick Douglass. But it may very well be that he was a militant freedom fighter seeking an opportunity to attack slavery—what Manisha Sinha calls a "fugitive slave abolitionist." Sinha has observed how, in the final decades prior to the Civil War, a new generation of black abolitionists had come to dominate the movement. While Frederick Douglass was the most renowned of this new leadership, Sinha concludes that there were many other self-emancipated slaves who also emerged as leaders.[68] Even assuming that Green was not born into slavery, perhaps he had fallen prey to it. His first act of resistance was flight, but like his abolitionist peers, for him freedom entailed more than attaining personal liberty. In this light, Shields Green may be remembered as among the most radical vanguard of the black antislavery movement, rather than simply as an actor in the Harper's Ferry episode. Despite these interesting possibilities, however, our knowledge of Emperor remains frustratingly uneven—at a few points bright and clear, but at many other points obscure and uncertain, still hidden in the shadows of the past.

2

Emperor Enlisted

Yes, I shall probably lose my life, but if my death
will help to free my race, I am willing to die.

Shields Green

As we have seen, based upon what we know about Shields
Green—and more so, what we do not know about him—
any attempt to reconstruct his backstory must be done
provisionally. From the few and scattered bits of information accessible to us, we have observed that he was born of free parents in
Charleston, South Carolina, about the year 1825. We may further
suppose that his early life was beset by the racist realities that constantly imposed themselves upon free black people in the Lower
South. Consequently, both in opportunity and experience, he suffered
the challenges and traumas shared by a population beset by white
supremacy at every turn. Additionally, as a dark-skinned man, Green
was caught between the enslaved community and the mostly light-
skinned free black population in Charleston. According to Bernard
Powers Jr., in Green's time, 75 percent of free blacks in Charleston
County were "mulattoes," and Charleston itself had a disproportion-
ate number of light-skinned free people. While light-skinned free
people in the Lower South were typically referred to as "free persons
of color," dark-skinned free people like Shields Green were excluded
by this reference.[1] As such, he shared the experience of a minority
within a minority—that small society of disdained dark-skinned free
people. In this, Shields Green knew the experience of his ill-fated

forerunner, Denmark Vesey, the South Carolinian liberator who, "as a man of Africa in a light-skinned free community . . . was condemned to remain a stranger in a strange land."[2]

Although we have not yet found specific record of Green's origins in Charleston, it would seem that he was a partaker of the features of life typical of the free black community in work and society. Whatever livelihood he had pursued in Charleston, he had acquired some basic level of schooling, perhaps through the black church. If not, maybe he was fortunate to have received some instruction in one of the independent black schools supported by the wealthier and more successful members of the free black community.[3] Likewise, we know that he was married, although we do not know the name or status of his wife. We also know that he was widowed, but we do not know the year of his wife's death. Their brief union produced a son, whose name also is unknown in the record. It has been supposed by some that Green's wife was enslaved, and perhaps died at the hands of a cruel slaveholder. However, it seems more likely that her death came about by some unfortunate health crisis and a lack of adequate medical care. Given that most free blacks in Charleston "lacked nourishing food, good water, proper clothing, and adequate sanitation," they were not strangers to disease or plague.[4]

It may be more dramatic to imagine that Shields Green had struck down his oppressor and fled, but there is no basis for such a scenario in the record. However, there are other possible scenarios for his flight from Charleston. Perhaps due to debt or some other legal ensnarement, Green had found himself physically abused and threatened with servitude at the hands of a loathsome white man. This seems to align more with what we know of him. Still, as Harlan Greene has observed, "it would have been an event for a free person of color to lose his freedom," so it is possible that Emperor's flight preempted this diabolical process. Another possibility is somewhat less dramatic: What if Shields Green, despite racist abuses, actually fled Charleston with the intention of returning later? As Greene also observes, free persons could not leave South Carolina and return by the 1850s. Did Emperor steal away undercover so as to leave the way open to return to Charleston at a later date, perhaps to claim his son?[5] Whatever the case, it is likely that as a free man, Shields Green was forced into a hard choice: either face continued physical abuse and bondage in Charleston in order to be near his motherless son or leave the child in the hands of relatives and flee northward to freedom.

Sometime between about 1850 and 1856, then, we have surmised, Shields Green worked out a plan and made good his escape from the South, evidently with the support of some trusted black seaman. As a stowaway on a Southern vessel, perhaps bearing cotton to the port of New York, he reached the North undetected. New York City, before and after the Fugitive Slave Law of 1850, was no haven for black people. Frederick Douglass had landed there in 1838, recalling that he found that "New York was not quite so free, or so safe a refuge" as he had expected.[6] This probably was the case for Shields Green as well. Circumstances had not changed for the better in New York City by the last antebellum decade, and the black population, whether free or enslaved, still "lived with the constant threat of abduction and subsequent sale in slave states." Free blacks were subjected to hardcore segregation in public facilities and education, were restricted to menial and unskilled jobs, were vulnerable to violent assaults by white competitors on the job, and typically were confined to the poorest and most crime-ridden wards of the city.[7] One can only imagine what Shields Green, freshly arrived from South Carolina, made of New York City, when he discovered that the whims of white racists often were just as brazen and influential as they were in the South.

One illustration of conditions in New York City for black people should suffice. On a spring morning in Manhattan in May 1855, one of the most prominent black clergymen in New York City, James

W. C. Pennington, boarded a Sixth Avenue train running downtown. Upon taking his seat, Pennington was informed by the conductor that he could not ride in that car. Refusing to give up his seat, he was "forcibly ejected by the Conductor and driver and being roughly handled lost his hat and cane." Undefeated, Pennington "held fast to the car, behind which he ran to the lower depot," at which point he summoned a policeman, demanding that his assailants be arrested. To no surprise, the policeman instead advised Pennington to "drop the matter." Unrelenting in his quest for justice, the minister shortly found himself under arrest and thrown in jail. After this incident was reported in Horace Greeley's sympathetic *New York Daily Tribune*, the secretary of the Sixth Avenue Railroad Company responded with a letter to Greeley, stating that separate cars for whites and blacks were necessary because "respectable gentlemen" objected to sitting in the same cars with "colored persons."[8] If such indignities could befall a prominent black minister, it is not hard to imagine the daily insults and assaults that defined black life in general, and why Emperor would not have remained there long. Even John Brown disliked New York City, probably both for its congestion and for its explicit racism. When his eldest son decided to leave after a period of employment there, the abolitionist wrote in a tone of relief: "I am . . . exceedingly gratified to learn that you have concluded to quit that city."[9]

Assuming there is substance to Green's later statements that he had been in Harrisburg, Pennsylvania, perhaps he had ventured there after having heard that conditions in that place were more favorable than in cities like New York and Philadelphia. Beyond this, however, there is no way of knowing when he arrived in Harrisburg, why he chose to leave, or how long he had been there before venturing farther north.[10] Despite the fact that there was a flourishing black community in Harrisburg, perhaps Green's decision not to remain there pertained to the passing of the Fugitive Slave Law and the fact that it was still too close to the Mason-Dixon Line.

Besides his own reference to Harrisburg, Green's life in the North is not verifiable apart from his residence in Rochester, New York. That he chose Rochester may have been due to its proximity to Canada, but also because that city had attained the reputation of being one of the more racially tolerant communities in the North—in no small part due to the presence of Frederick Douglass, who had relocated there with his family in 1848.[11] In his memoir, Douglass attributed Rochester's benign attitude as largely due to his own presence in the community, especially as a lecturer. "If in these lectures I did not make abolitionists," he wrote, "I did succeed in making tolerant the moral atmosphere in Rochester." Furthermore, with the publication of his paper, the *North Star* (which became *Frederick Douglass' Paper*), he wrote that "colored travelers told me that they felt the influence of my labors when they came within fifty miles."[12] If Douglass's antislavery labors attracted fugitives from a distance, perhaps so did his reputation for hospitality. His chief biographer thus observes that fugitives passing through western New York "frequently ended up on Douglass's doorstep."[13]

Apparently, Shields Green was one of the fugitives who ended up finding shelter in the Douglass household. Yet his host seems not to have shown any interest in keeping Green in Rochester, for we know from the *Rochester Democrat* that after his initial stay, he "was sent" to Canada—perhaps by admonition of Douglass himself. According to the same source, these things took place about 1856, several years before the Harper's Ferry raid.[14] It seems likely, then, that Emperor made his way out of the United States from western New York, passing from Rochester to Buffalo, and then up to the Canadian border. At this point he crossed into Ontario, and then perhaps made his way up to St. Catharines on the Niagara Peninsula, an area corresponding with western New York State. Wherever Green finally settled in Canada West (today, Ontario), he seems to have remained there no less than two years, working as a table waiter or domestic servant until perhaps the spring or early summer of 1858, when he decided to return to Rochester.

Certainly, his decision to relocate to Canada was not uncommon for blacks in the era of the Fugitive Slave Law, given that they were no longer safe from slavery's grasp in any Northern city in the United States. Between fifteen thousand and twenty thousand African Americans fled to safety in Canada from 1850 to 1860, settling in towns and cities just across the border in Canada West that stretched from St. Catharines near the Niagara River to Windsor, opposite Detroit, Michigan.[15] Hundreds of African American expatriates would later return to the United States with the outbreak of the Civil War, and perhaps thousands more with war's end and Reconstruction.[16] However, the fact that Emperor chose to return to the United States at the height of slavery's power over the North raises a question as to his motivation. Certainly, one would assume that a black man who had made his way to Canada would not have been eager to return to Rochester without some compelling reason. Absent alternative evidence, then, perhaps the best surmise pertains to John Brown. While it is quite improbable that Brown had met Shields Green prior to his return to Rochester in 1858, it may be that news about the Old Man's intentions had reached him in Canada, leading him to pack his bags and reenter the United States.

This is not mere speculation, given that Brown actually had made an excursion through Canada West from April 6 to April 24, 1858, in an effort to enlist black recruits for his Virginia campaign. Traveling on the Great Western Railway, Brown traversed the province from St. Catharines to Ingersoll, and then to Chatham before crossing back into the United States at Detroit. While at St. Catharines, he met Harriet Tubman and was greatly encouraged by her enthusiasm and promise of support.[17] Shortly afterward he wrote to John Brown Jr., stating that he had enjoyed "tolerable success" while traveling around St. Catharines and neighboring townships.[18] He made further stops in Hamilton, Brantford, Woodstock, and Ingersoll in seeking out black enlistees.[19] At Ingersoll, a community with about five hundred black expatriate residents, he hoped to meet up again with Harriet Tubman. Unfortunately, she had gone by train to Toronto first and did not arrive at Ingersoll until after Brown's departure, which may have blunted his efforts at recruitment.[20] On April 15, he gave a public address at the Wesleyan Methodist church in Ingersoll, but finally departed on April 19 without any apparent success in enlistment.[21] Brown's last and most important stop was Chatham, located in the southwestern section of Canada West. In Chatham, which had a flourishing community of African American expatriates, he sought out black leaders. The Old Man told them that he had access to money. It was men that he needed.[22]

On April 24, 1858, Brown made a quick trip back into the United States, traveling from Detroit to Springdale, Iowa, where he gathered his own men and then brought them back to Chatham by the end of the month. The purpose for his return to Canada was to convene "a most quiet convention" of his men with interested abolitionist supporters from the black community. The agenda of the meeting was to introduce his plans, gather enlistees for his Virginia campaign, and introduce a document that would serve as the solemn political foundation of his liberation movement, the "Provisional Constitution and Ordinances for the People of the United States." While Brown's most notable abolitionist allies in the United States, both white and black, did not attend the convention, forty-six delegates were in attendance for the Chatham meeting on May 8 and 10, 1858. Of this number, thirty-four of the participants were black, including Osborne Anderson, the only one of Brown's five black men to survive the raid, and the only Harper's Ferry raider to provide a detailed description of the raid as it pertained to enslaved people.[23]

By this time, Brown had modified his long-standing plan to move into the South and draw away enslaved people, liberating and arming them in order to further disrupt and undermine the operations of slavery. To this strategy he added the seizure of the federal armory (not just the arsenal) in Harper's Ferry, as a demonstration to initiate his Southern campaign. As will be seen in chapter 4, he had no intention of raiding its stores despite the claims of the Virginians afterward. In fact, besides rallying a small force of local slaves, Brown's seizure of the armory was intended as a rebuke to the Democratic leadership in Washington, particularly because they had taken no action following a similar raid in 1856 by proslavery forces in Missouri. It seems, however, that Brown had not yet revealed these intentions even to his closest followers from Kansas, let alone to potential recruits from Canada.

In 1859 the *Rochester Democrat* noted that Shields Green was connected with John Brown's "Provisional Government," which might be mistaken to mean that he had been among the thirty-four black delegates at the Chatham convention. However, Emperor was not among the Chatham delegates and was living elsewhere in Canada West at the time of the convention. The *Democrat*'s claim seems to have originated from a "list of the insurrectionists" published in the *Washington Evening Star* on October 20, 1859, which reportedly was based on an interview with John Brown. According to the *Star*, "Shields Green *alias* Emperor" had been taken prisoner along with Brown. The reporter added: "Capt. Brown stated that Green was a Member of Congress under the 'Provisional Government' he intended establishing."[24] Rather than suggesting that Green was involved in the Chatham meeting, Brown simply meant that Emperor had received his official field appointment according to the "Provisional Constitution."

* * *

Assuming that Shields Green was in Canada West at the time that Brown made his recruitment tour in 1858, Green likely had heard about his efforts despite having missed the opportunity to meet him. Perhaps too, Green heard about Brown's association with Frederick Douglass. Whether by newspaper or word of mouth, he quite likely had learned of Brown's interest in seeking out men from the black community. Finding this news irresistible, or so it seems, he determinedly made his way back to Rochester, perhaps with the hope of having Douglass introduce him to the famous Kansas veteran and militant abolitionist.

Even so, Green had to wait quite a while to meet Brown, since the Old Man had visited Rochester in April 1858 but did not return for a year to see Douglass. This gap of one year was due to the fact that Brown's plans had been jeopardized after the Chatham convention by the betrayal of Hugh Forbes, an English mercenary whom he had enlisted to train his men. Forbes, who turned out to be a whining money-grubber, began to leak information about Brown's mission to Republican leaders in the North, throwing most of his supporters into a panic. As a result, Brown was talked into creating a diversion by going back to Kansas, thus debunking any news of him moving upon Virginia. The diversion proved successful, but it kept John Brown out west from June 1858 until March 1859.[25]

According to Douglass, Brown finally met Shields Green at Douglass's home in Rochester, and even though he provides no date for their meeting, he placed it in his narrative just prior to describing how he and Green went down to meet Brown in Chambersburg, Pennsylvania.[26] Accordingly, the most likely date for Green's first meeting with Brown is April 10, when the latter made a brief stopover in Rochester en route to see Gerrit Smith in Peterboro, New York. We know of this hasty visit to Rochester—actually Brown's last visit to the Douglass homestead—from a letter the Old Man wrote to raider John Henrie Kagi the following week. "Had a good visit at Rochester, but did not effect much," Brown concluded.[27] By this he was expressing disappointment over Douglass's lackluster support of his recruitment efforts. Furthermore, it is quite unlikely that Brown met Green before April 1859, since the two did not meet in Canada, nor had Green returned to Rochester at Brown's previous visit. Likewise, Douglass wrote that when Brown met the fugitive, he "saw at once what 'stuff' Green 'was made of,' and confided to him his plans and purposes." In response, Emperor "easily believed in Brown," Douglass added, "and promised to go with him whenever he should be ready to move."[28] Had their meeting taken place earlier, Brown certainly would have summoned him to the Chatham convention.

By the time he met John Brown, Shields Green had relocated to Rochester, and had been operating a clothes-cleaning establishment on Spring Street since the previous summer. On August 10, John Brown Jr. met with Douglass in Rochester, alerting him to meet his father down in Chambersburg. John provided the orator with twenty-two dollars to defray the cost of traveling, and expected Douglass to arrive at Chambersburg the following week. At another visit to Rochester shortly afterward, John learned from Lewis Douglass that his father already had departed by train on Tuesday, August 15, traveling to New York City en route to Chambersburg. This left Emperor to make the trip from Rochester by himself, leaving the next day, Wednesday, August 16. Presumably, he took the same railroad line but made no stops along the way. He took "a more direct route," John concluded.[29]

That Douglass traveled a whole day in advance of Emperor to New York City is at least a point of curiosity. In his autobiography, Douglass passes over this detail, mentioning only that, "taking Shields, we passed through New York City," where together they called upon the Reverend James Gloucester and his wife in Brooklyn, and received ten dollars for Brown's war chest.[30] However, Douglass actually had the better part of a day and an overnight stay before meeting Shields Green in New York City.

Since Douglass neither reveals this gap in his story nor suggests that he had other meetings or appointments in New York City, it is likely that he had other reasons for leaving Rochester in advance of Green. Very likely, he went a day early in order to see his adoring German lady friend, Ottilie Assing, who lived in a boardinghouse in Hoboken, New Jersey, a ferry ride across the Hudson River from Manhattan. Assing was an attractive, savvy journalist who, according to David Blight, was "breathlessly" and permanently devoted to the handsome Douglass as an object of her literary endeavors, political admiration, and romantic desire. Blight points out that what is known of their extramarital relationship is based upon Assing's one-sided account. However, it is not hard to imagine that Douglass found her both intellectually appealing and sexually desirable. As Blight has observed, the Douglass-Assing friendship was an "on and off" affair that involved the intimacies of the mind as well as the flesh.[31] Nevertheless, the orator was a married man whose private conduct in this case not only contradicted his notable biblical pronouncements, but would have been regretted by friends and used against him by conservative critics on either side of the slavery debate. Consequently, his decision to leave for New York City one day ahead of Shields Green, presumably for an overnight stay in Hoboken, appears to have been an intentional measure to secure his privacy. Certainly, Douglass would not have wanted Emperor to know about such matters.

* * *

In a memoir published late in the nineteenth century, Lucy Colman, an antislavery activist, claimed that she was well acquainted with John Brown in her youth, and had conversed with Shields Green at Douglass's home just before he left in August 1859. Colman recalled that when Emperor walked her home afterward, she asked him whether he realized that by going south, he was exposing himself to the gallows, and that if taken he would surely be executed. He responded: "Yes, I shall probably lose my life, but if my death will help to free my race, I am willing to die."[32] Certainly, any notion that

Shields Green was lured, tricked, or otherwise ensnared into join-
ing John Brown is without foundation in the record. It was Shields
Green's own desire to fight slavery that brought him back from
Canada, just as it led him to John Brown's camp in 1859.

As history would have it, the only record of the meeting between
Brown, Douglass, Kagi, and Green in Chambersburg in August 1859
is that which was made available by Douglass many years later in his
Life and Times. Kagi, a journalist who might have left a brilliant narrative of Brown's intentions and activities, unfortunately was killed
during the Harper's Ferry raid. Of course, Brown and Green went to
their graves without so much as a passing remark about the meeting,
if for no other reason than not to betray Douglass into the hands of
the enemy. Besides evidence in the correspondence of John Brown
Jr. anticipating Douglass and Green's arrival in Chambersburg, the
only other reference to the confab is found in Osborne Anderson's
invaluable 1861 chronicle, *A Voice from Harper's Ferry*. Of the meeting, Anderson wrote: "* * went down to ———, to accompany Shields
Green, whereupon a meeting of Capt. Brown, Kagi, and other distinguished persons, convened for consultation."[33] Anderson used as-
terisks to redact the name of Douglass and a blank line to withhold
the place of the meeting, since he was writing when the raid was yet
recent and authorities in Virginia were still desirous of hanging the
famous black orator. Interestingly, however, Anderson used the plural
reference, "other distinguished persons," which leads us to inquire
whether Douglass was the only other participant in the company of
Brown, Kagi, and Green.

It is already clear that Douglass stylized his account of the
Chambersburg meeting, portraying it as if it took place only weeks
before the raid, when in reality it was convened two months prior, on
August 19, 1859.[34] Likewise, Douglass seems to have conflated a number of incidents of disagreement between himself and Brown into
one episode, as if he did not have certain knowledge of the Old Man's

plan to invade Harper's Ferry until the meeting in Chambersburg. As Douglass's final autobiography attests, he had long provided Brown a sounding board for his plan. However, it is clear that Douglass pulled back after learning that Brown had expanded his mountain-based plan to include an invasion of the federal armory at Harper's Ferry. In his autobiography, he writes that he learned about this innovation in Brown's plan only weeks prior to the raid. He padded this statement, adding that he had heard Brown speak of seizing Harper's Ferry "once in a while" but that Brown had "never announced this intention to do so." In fact, during a private meeting of black leaders in Detroit in March 1859, the two friends had strong words of disagreement over the matter. Nevertheless, Douglass struggled to remain faithful to his old friend without compromising his conviction that seizing Harper's Ferry was sheer folly. Indeed, the friends seem to have avoided a complete falling-out—Brown, by pulling back from his caustic and imperious approach, and Douglass, by meeting him more than once prior to the raid, including the confab at Chambersburg in August 1859. In the end, however, Douglass seems to have refused to encourage men to join Brown's movement, leaving the latter to conclude privately that Douglass was "unreliable."[35]

In describing the Chambersburg meeting, Douglass may have played down the presence of "other distinguished persons" at the quarry where the gathering took place. For instance, he mentions a local black leader, Henry Watson, whom he characterized as "simple minded and warm hearted," and who directed him to the secret site of the meeting. It is possible that Watson was present at the quarry at some point too, since the meeting lasted a day and a half.[36] Likewise, Hannah Geffert points out that the quarry meeting actually was arranged by another local black leader, Joseph Winters, known as "Indian Dick." Winters was a gunsmith, a leader in the St. James African Methodist Episcopal Church, and actually owned property adjacent to the quarry.[37] Given Douglass's popularity, it is reasonable to assume that both Watson and Winters might at least have been partial observers if not participants; and given Brown's eagerness to recruit black men, it seems unlikely that he would have excluded them.

As it pertains to Shields Green, however, the upshot of Douglass's narrative of the Chambersburg meeting rings true. According to Douglass, Emperor listened to an extended debate between himself and the Old Man and then made the decision to join Brown rather than return to Rochester with Douglass. "When I found that [Brown] had fully made up his mind and could not be dissuaded," Douglass wrote, "I turned to Shields Green and told him he heard what Captain Brown had said; his old plan was changed, and that I should return home, and if he wished to go with me he could do so." Brown persisted in his appeal that both Douglass and Green go with him, but the former continued to refuse. "When about to leave I asked Green what he had decided to do, and was surprised by his coolly saying in his broken way, 'I b'leve I'll go wid de ole man.' Here we separated," Douglass concluded, "they to go to Harper's Ferry, I to Rochester."[38]

In a published confession, raider John Cook reported that up until Sunday, October 16, the day of the raid, there were a handful of men who knew nothing of John Brown's "Provisional Constitution" or "the plan of operations." Cook included Shields Green among this number.[39] Taken of itself, this statement might appear to contradict Douglass, since presumably Green did not know about "the plan of operations," including Brown's intention of seizing the armory. However, Cook was mistaken in regard to Emperor, who not only knew about the Old Man's intentions but clearly supported them. According to Owen Brown, when "striking the first blow" at Harper's Ferry became a point of controversy among the raiders, Emperor and Kagi—who were with Brown at the Chambersburg meeting— defended their leader's objectives.[40]

With Douglass's departure from Chambersburg, Green would have to wait in town until he was brought down to John Brown's western Maryland headquarters, a rented farmhouse located about five miles from Harper's Ferry. Green might very well have stayed with either Henry Watson or Joseph Winters in Chambersburg. However, according to Owen Brown, his father was quite intentional about finding a family in Chambersburg "to whom he could confide his plans," particularly an underground railroad family, who would be willing "to board his men, black or white, temporarily, or stop over night until we could pilot them through to Harper's Ferry." Owen recalled that Brown initially spent a week or more in Chambersburg in June 1859, just "getting acquainted with black people."[41] Quite likely, blacks in town spoke favorably about Mary Welsh Ritner, the widowed daughter-in-law of former Pennsylvania governor Joseph Ritner.[42]

Mary, who was raising two daughters alone and supported the family by keeping a boardinghouse on East King Street, was a strong antislavery woman—"true to the cause," as Owen recalled, who supported the underground railroad.[43] Brown probably knew of the elder Ritner from his early years in northwestern Pennsylvania (1826–1835), when the latter twice ran unsuccessfully in the gubernatorial race on the anti-Masonic ticket. During his time in Pennsylvania, Brown had fallen out with the Lodge and became quite virulent in his opposition to Freemasonry, so probably he was quite pleased when he learned that Ritner's antislavery daughter-in-law kept a boardinghouse in Chambersburg.[44] The Ritner house became the Northern headquarters for Brown's operations, where he kept John Henrie Kagi stationed to monitor correspondence, receive clandestinely packaged weapons, and supervise the forwarding of both weapons and volunteers to the Maryland farmhouse.[45]

It is not clear from the record exactly when Shields Green was conveyed from the Ritner house in Chambersburg to Brown's

Maryland site, but certainly he was the first of the five black raiders to arrive. Following the Friday-Saturday confab with Brown and others, Douglass was invited to speak at the local town hall. The local *Chambersburg Times* expressed the surprise of the community as a whole, stating that Douglass had "appeared in town unheralded, and on two hours previous notice" had delivered a lecture on the "Slave Question" at Franklin Hall in Chambersburg. The speech had not been organized by Douglass, Brown, or black community leaders, although it served well as a decoy for his sudden appearance in town.[46]

As it turned out, when a local white Republican named Snively Strickler heard that Douglass was in town, he and Andrew Rankin, a local editor, had sought out the orator in the hopes of getting him to make an address to the community. Intimidated by the "colorphobia" of the day, Rankin later admitted, he and Strickler all but crept their way to the home of Henry Watson, where they arranged for Douglass's address on Saturday evening, August 20. Their mission completed, the two white men, fearful of being seen walking through a black neighborhood, took back alleys all the way home.[47] The difference between these specimens of the Republican Party and John Brown is worth noting. The Old Man freely moved within the black community and unabashedly sought fellowship and alliance, while the two Republicans in town deferred to the racist status quo despite good intentions. Not only is this an illustration of John Brown's undaunted Christian egalitarianism, but also it serves as a reminder that many "antislavery" whites actually were steeped in racial prejudice. As Douglass later observed of Abraham Lincoln, he was a white man who "shared the prejudices common to his countrymen towards the colored race."[48]

One local source says that both Brown and Kagi were among the large crowd that listened to Douglass at Franklin Hall, although Shields Green probably was in attendance as well.[49] Following his address, Douglass had no reason to extend his stay in town and probably departed Chambersburg on Sunday or Monday, August 21 or 22. Meanwhile, Shields Green remained in town at the Ritner boardinghouse with Kagi, John Brown, Jeremiah "Jerry" Anderson, and the Old Man's two sons Oliver and Owen. As the first of the "packages of freight"—Brown's code for the black raiders—to be secretly conveyed to his Maryland farm, the initial plan was to smuggle Emperor by covered wagon all the way to Maryland. However, Owen, who was to drive the wagon, was opposed to the plan because it involved staying at a hotel at Hagerstown, Maryland, while leaving Green covered up in the back of the wagon overnight. Instead, he suggested to his father that black recruits be conveyed in the wagon as far as Hagerstown and then be guided on foot the rest of the way through forest and thicket, hiding by day and traveling by night. Owen believed that despite the rigors of such a trek, it would be safer overall for Emperor and others since they would less likely be exposed to curious onlookers and proslavery citizens watching for blacks on the highway. As it turned out, Owen's idea proved far less practical than hiding in a wagon.

The exact date that the two left Chambersburg is not recorded in his reminiscences, and Owen mistakenly cited their trip as having taken place in July. However, the trip was made in August, perhaps no more than a day or two after Frederick Douglass had returned north. Owen's narrative is detailed in its description of their sojourn from Hagerstown, their passage through cornfields and thinly wooded areas, and the hilly landscape, as well as details like the sight of buildings in the distance and the torches of fishermen along the river.

One might well question whether Owen could retain such an accurate remembrance over two decades afterward, recalling their sojourn through the wild and along the periphery of small towns. The reservations of a discerning and careful scholar like Steven Lubet should not be taken lightly, particularly his contention that Owen's narrative is burdened by "highly improbable episodes" and implausible features. On the other hand, one might grant Owen the benefit of the doubt for a number of reasons.

First, his detailed remembrance of the sojourn, particularly the description of their movements across the terrain, might not have been so rare among nineteenth-century agrarians, who were far more attendant to the details of natural geography and could remember them in the way a modern urbanite might remember the layout of streets, buildings, and landscapes in the city. Second, some of the details that he questions, such as Owen tumbling forty feet while hanging onto a jug of lemonade, might seem like an improbability, but not necessarily so. Owen stated that he hurt his knee in this tumbling fall, but saving the jug seems more a matter of effort and good fortune. Likewise, Lubet finds it implausible that Owen improvised a makeshift raft by crossing six fence rails over six other fence rails, although the basis of this objection is not entirely clear. One can easily imagine an outdoorsman improvising such a contrivance for short-term use in crossing a broad but slow-moving river as Owen described it.[50]

What makes the raft account even more interesting is the reason for it. When the two travelers came to a river, Owen wrote, "I asked Green if he could swim, and he said he could not." That Shields Green could not swim might further attest to his background as an urban dweller who had little exposure to water nor need to swim throughout his life. Indeed, if there is a secondary theme in Owen's narrative, it is that Emperor was so much out of his element under the open skies of the Maryland countryside that his apprehensions finally got the best of him. "He had been brought up in the city," Owen recalled, "and was not used to being in the woods and felt rather disturbed through the day."[51]

As for the makeshift raft, Owen gives a fairly detailed description of how it was used: after bundling their provisions and weapons in a blanket, he had Green lie on his back on the raft with the bundle, bracing the raft with his legs on either side, which reinforced the structure. Owen then swam just behind the raft, pushing it across, which he found to be "very slow work," until he reached the muddy bank on the other side of the river.[52] It seems that Owen provided enough details to suggest why he was able to accomplish this feat, although not without great exertion on his part. He was in his mid-thirties and strong, and if the crossing was "very slow work," it is more likely because he had only partial use of one of his arms due to an accident in his youth.[53]

If Owen's narrative presents challenges, however, it is not so much for its physical plausibility as for what some might find to be an unflattering portrayal of Shields Green during the trek. From the onset, Green is uncomfortable with the experience of traveling in the wild and being subjected to its rigors and demands. At first it appears that he is "uneasy" and apprehensive, "afraid to stay in the woods, being unused to it."[54] However, it shortly becomes clear that the rustic circumstances alone are not what have begun to work on Green's nerves. It is rather the growing sense of vulnerability that he felt being out in the open. Furthermore, his apprehensions were only exacerbated because Owen, who had presumed that this course would be safer, could not avoid random encounters with whites.

Sure enough, not long after they had embarked on foot, they were spotted by three white men, who expressed curiosity about seeing Owen traveling with a "black boy." In the explicit manner of a racist society, these whites addressed only Owen in conversation, even when talking about Green. At this point, Emperor's defiance is clear in the narrative. According to Owen, when one of the whites mentioned to him that he had never seen this black man before, he acknowledged it, but Green boldly interjected: "No, you have never seen me before." This unsolicited response from a black man must have jarred them. "This looks a little particular, this business," one of the whites countered. "Which way are you going with him?" he questioned. Owen gestured toward the north but said nothing, and then abruptly asked them whether they would assist a runaway slave or keep him. The men differed among themselves, one saying he would let him go and another saying he would only let him go if he was a "darned mean nigger." The whites remained curious as to Owen's intentions with his black companion, but then assured him that they would not further disturb him. As they parted, Owen feared that they would assume that he had stolen a slave to sell him and was contemplating whether to take Green and hide in a cornfield or to retreat to the woods. Suddenly, Green tapped him on the shoulder, gesturing to him to look behind them. When Owen looked, he saw the same three whites following, not quite two hundred feet behind. More alarming was that two of them seemed to be reaching behind their backs, as if to pull their weapons. At this, Owen dropped to his knee and Shields hit the ground, lying flat in the weeds in case they opened fire. Instead, the three white men approached them again and solicited a drink from Owen's jug. As he offered the jug, Owen pulled his pistol on the drinker and asked, "Are you friendly?" Only two of them answered affirmatively, to which Owen responded, "You shall prove that you are friendly." Frightened, all three retreated, first walking, and then breaking into a run. Knowing that the incident would bring a response, the two hurried into a nearby cornfield, where they hid and watched as patrols on their trail galloped back and forth on horseback. While they hid, Green handed Owen his black woolen mantle, urging him to wear it because his white summer coat would attract attention in the field.[55]

The trip continued with twists and turns, falls and crossings, and at another point what seemed to Owen like an "eternal" cornfield. As the two continued their trek along the ranging landscape with its hills and slopes, Owen struggled at times for direction, awaiting nightfall so the stars above could lead them toward the mountains. In the meantime, however, it appeared to Owen that his companion was starting to come apart at the seams. "Green, by this time, was getting very tired," Owen recalled, "and I often got quite a distance ahead of him and would wait for him to come up." Worried and deep in thought, Emperor continued falling behind, to the point that Owen was afraid that they would be seen in open country. By the time Emperor finally caught up with Owen, the black man had become completely incommunicative. Owen now began to realize that his companion was overwhelmed more by the reality of his decision to return to the South than by their seemingly endless journey. "I talked to him frequently. He had escaped from slavery some time before and had volunteered to help father in his plan to free others," Owen recounted. "Now he was coming back into the slave country where if he were taken, he would have to endure great sufferings, as well as loss of liberty so dear to the heart of the slave."[56] Owen remembered Shields Green as a fugitive slave, and this may very well have been how Emperor described himself to the Browns and others, given the circumstances from which he had fled. Of course, he *had* escaped, and he had good reason for apprehension too, given that he was a black fugitive reentering the South.

Although the worst part of the trip was behind them, Green's anxieties were mounting. The sun was shining, and they were safely out of sight, but when they sat down under a large tree to eat, Green complained of not feeling well, eating with no apparent appetite. Staring down, he suddenly exclaimed: "O, what a poor fool I am! I had got away out of slavery, and here I have got back into the eagle's claw again." Owen says that he tried to encourage Green, assuring him that they were not in danger and would soon reach their destination. Perhaps, too, Owen offered, they could help hundreds of people out of the eagle's claw. None of his words availed to encourage the disheartened Emperor, who sat, bowed with head in hands, "looking as gloomy as ever." In retrospect, Owen believed that the existential reality of being once again in a slave state suddenly had cast a terrible shadow. "It was like a horrible night-mare to the poor fellow," he concluded.[57]

On the last leg of their journey, they passed along the "pike" through Roarersville, Maryland, and were now within ten miles of Brown's farm. But whereas his anxieties previously had imploded, Emperor was now growing visibly agitated and began bitterly complaining: "You don't know where you are going any more than a wild goose," he charged. "I believe it is forty miles to the Kennedy Farm!" Owen chided him for whining, but he recognized that he was speaking out of fear. "You'll never see your father or our folks again," Emperor exclaimed almost in a panic. "We are more than forty miles away, going in the wrong direction." Frustrated, Owen admonished him that they were not far from their destination, and the two spoke no more. Within about six miles of their goal, Green blustered: "This is the hardest tramp; this is the roughest siege I ever took in my life." Owen says that he responded, agreeing that it was rough, but then Emperor exclaimed: "I wouldn't have gone into this for all the wealth in Rochester"—an inadvertent admission that it was not money from Douglass or anyone else that had brought him back to a slave state. At this point, however, they were coming down the road to the farm, and the barking of a dog brought John Brown himself out to meet them at the gate. The Old Man, faintly smiling, expressed his relief, saying that he had feared that they had been taken and jailed in Hagerstown. Inside the farmhouse some of the raiders were gathered, waiting to greet them. Suddenly, it seemed to Owen that his traveling companion was delivered of every anxiety. "A happier man than Shields Green was never seen. He was like a new man," he concluded.[58]

While historian Steven Lubet does not doubt that Owen successfully guided Shields Green to Brown's Maryland farmhouse, he concludes of this episode that Owen intentionally rendered himself "the hero of his own story," portraying himself as solving problems quite remarkably and facing down hazardous situations during the journey. While he does not say that Owen demeaned Shields Green in his narrative, he does argue that the narrative reflects a larger inclination to protect the Brown family legacy and inflate his own legend as well.[59] Of course, these are two different issues, and each deserves consideration.

Owen Brown was among the eldest of John Brown's children and none can doubt that he was both an eyewitness and a brave participant in his father's adventures in Kansas and Virginia. Certainly, he was the most dependable of Brown's eldest sons, being the only one of the three to follow him to Virginia.[60] Yet if any of Brown's children assumed the role of safeguarding the family legacy and elevating himself at the same time, it was John Brown Jr. From the time of his father's death, John assumed the role of spokesman and apologist, enjoyed the prestige and companionship of leading abolitionists, and was not only sought out for interviews, but assertive in his own right in defending his father's name against posthumous opponents. Nor was John hesitant to blend his own unconventional political, social, and religious ideas into the Brown family discourse, even when they flew in the face of his father's beliefs.[61] If this were not enough, John did not hesitate to keep an inordinate amount of money donated to the Brown family after his father's execution—so much so that even his stepmother, Mary Brown, privately complained that the funds had been "unjustly" distributed.[62]

On the other hand, while Owen Brown was a passionate freedom fighter, his tendencies were neither assertive nor self-aggrandizing. Only a small number of his reminiscences were published in later life, and typically he had to be sought out by journalists. One such writer, Ralph Keeler, found Owen living in humble circumstances in 1874, and not at all eager to tell his story. In fact, Keeler had to patiently cultivate Owen's willingness to talk over a number of conversations, even when it came to obtaining an account of his dramatic escape from Harper's Ferry in 1859. The journalist concluded that "honesty and modesty" were "ingrained" in Owen Brown.[63]

As to the question of whether Owen dealt fairly with Shields Green, another example might be helpful. After the story of Owen's escape from Harper's Ferry was published in the *Atlantic Monthly*, apparently some criticism arose about how he had portrayed the conduct of some of the other escaping Harper's Ferry raiders. Owen was seemingly mortified that descriptions he had provided of his comrades were taken negatively. He quickly penned a letter to the editor of the same publication, complimenting the bravery and character of each raider he had named in his account. His narrative "was meant to be simply the history of our adventures and sufferings," Owen wrote, "and my opinions of my companions' characters were not so carefully expressed in it as they would have been if I had been speaking of what they *were* rather than what they *did* and *endured*." In his conclusion, Owen asserted his belief that the "courage of *all our men* has been sufficiently proved and acknowledged."[64]

The same conclusion may be drawn concerning Owen's unpublished portrayal of Shields Green. Just as he had no intention of elevating himself or fabricating an unreliable narrative of himself as a hero, neither was Owen endeavoring to diminish Emperor's courage by recounting moments of discouragement en route to Maryland. Like his published account about escaping from Harper's Ferry, Owen was only providing a frank account about their perilous and difficult trek. It is understandable that some might be irritated by the portrayal of Shields Green as being anything less than fearless throughout the entire narrative, from his flight from South Carolina to his enlistment by Brown, to the Harper's Ferry raid, and finally to his last hours of life. Some might see any suggestion at all that Emperor was fearful as racist subterfuge, the diminishment of a brave black hero by a white narrator. However, there are ample reasons to accept Owen's recollections as truthful, while doing so without lessening Shields Green's historical profile. First, it already has been pointed out that Owen himself proposed a distinction between what the raiders "did and endured" as men, and the unquestioned fact of their courage. There is no doubt in Owen Brown's mind that Shields Green was courageous, for in his letter to the *Atlantic Monthly* he explicitly stated that "all" of John Brown's raiders were courageous.

Second, within Owen's narrative, Shields Green's conduct is clearly decisive despite unnerving and difficult circumstances. Emperor was an urban dweller all of his life and had no experience in the wild, and it would be unfair to adjudge him less than brave because he was challenged and stressed when put into such untried surroundings. To the contrary, not only had he chosen to follow John Brown into the South, but when confronted by whites on the road, he asserted himself by speaking firmly on his own behalf, something considered improper and offensive within that racist context. Likewise, in this narrative, Green often is more mindful and alert of possible trackers than is his white companion, who is more focused on the journey itself. More than once in the account, Green was the one who spotted whites following them first, not Owen. Furthermore, he realized that Owen's white summer coat had drawn attention to them in the open field and insisted that he wear his black cloak instead. These details indicate that Green was observant and intentional, and did not take chances out in the open—all of which reveal a certain alertness and understanding that Owen clearly lacked. Despite the fact that this is Owen Brown's narrative, it is clear that his portrayal is honest in showing that they both had distinct forms of intelligence for the risky mission they were undertaking.

More importantly, in fairness to Shields Green, it is necessary that his story not be burdened by the imposition of any sort of political iconography that demands that he fit the profile of an antebellum superhero. What makes Emperor's story heroic is not that he was brave and fearless at every turn, but that he was courageous. For the most part, bravery—which is the ability to confront danger or pain without fear—is episodic and varied in human experience. Although often lauded for his bravery, John Brown himself was said to have believed that fearlessness in the face of danger was a matter of native temperament, not character.

Quite in contrast, courage—a willingness to undertake a challenge despite overwhelming fear or opposition—bespeaks moral strength, often the kind that enables one to oppose injustice. This is key to understanding the narrative of Shields Green, since courage "stems from a connection to a cause, and is driven by motivation, love, devotion, compassion, or passion."[65] Emperor was heroic because he determinedly gave himself to the struggle for freedom despite fear, not because he was consistently fearless and seemingly indifferent to every manner of threat and danger. As Anne Brown Adams later concluded, "Heroes are made out of men. People who never did a heroic deed themselves are very particular as to how heroes behave."[66]

3

Emperor among the "Invisibles"

Maryland, 1859

Nature is mourning for its murdered, and Afflicted
Children. Hung be the Heavins in Scarlet.

"A Declaration of Liberty," by John Brown

OHN BROWN entered the South in early summer 1859,
stopping first at Hagerstown, Maryland, on June 30. Along
with Jerry Anderson, the Old Man presented himself to
locals as Isaac Smith, a Northerner with an interest in mining. On
July 3, he and Anderson visited Harper's Ferry, Virginia, now joined
by his two sons Owen and Oliver. The party then crossed back over
to Maryland, passing the night at a small tavern in Sandy Hook, a
hamlet on the bank of the Potomac, about a mile away.[1]

The following day, a local slaveholder named John Unseld met
Brown and his companions traveling along a road that ran close to
the mountains. Unseld assumed that they were looking for miner-
als, but Brown, alias Smith, informed him that they were looking
for land. He explained that he also was a farmer from New York
State, and that his crops had been ruined by the frost. He told Unseld
that now he was considering relocating to the South as a result, but
that he wanted to rent a place until he became accustomed to the
area. Unseld informed him that the farm of the late Doctor Robert

FIGURE 3.1. John Brown.
From Robert DeWitt, ed., *The Life,
Trial and Execution of Captain John
Brown*, 1859.

Kennedy had been placed on the market by his heirs and that he
would be happy to show him the way. According to a nineteenth-
century description, the Kennedy farm was located near the mountain in a "shady and pleasant" place not far from a church on the
road to Boonesborough. The only drawback, Unseld explained, was
that it was a small farm and one could not do better than make a
living there. Brown told him that this was of no concern, since he
also dealt in livestock. Of course, the farm was precisely what John
Brown was hoping to find for his base in the South, a site close to
the mountains and away from well-traveled roads.[2] Informed that
Kennedy's widow and heirs lived in Sharpsburgh, Brown rode out to
see them and returned with a receipt for thirty-five dollars, the cost
of renting the farm through March 1860. The arrangement was more
than an expedient for Brown. By his reckoning, the rental provided

more than enough time to accomplish his goals in Virginia, before gathering the first fruits of his liberation harvest and disappearing into the mountains beyond easy reach of the army or local militia. It also safeguarded him from suspicion, assuring the landlord and neighbors that Isaac Smith was neither an opportunist nor a grifter from the North.

When John Brown occupied the Kennedy farm, it was a plain two-storied log house with a high, ground-level basement, located about three hundred yards from a sparsely traveled public road and surrounded by dense forest. Kennedy had enlarged the structure after purchasing it as a single-room cottage with a loft, although its renovated layout was awkward. The second story was only accessible on the ground floor from an outside stairway, and the kitchen had to be entered through a separate doorway on the front porch. The living area consisted of two rooms, one of which had a winding staircase that led to the attic. The front porch was accessible by a stairway from the ground level, and the space within the foundation walls on the same level was used for storage. There was also a smaller log structure on the property about six hundred yards from the farmhouse, situated on a swampy piece of ground with a good bit of shrubbery

FIGURE 3.2. Kennedy farm in Maryland. *Frank Leslie's Illustrated News,* Nov. 26, 1859.

surrounding it.[3] Brown and his sons may have considered the farm-house "perfectly adapted to their purpose," as Anne Brown Adams recalled; nevertheless, its peculiarities would pose certain challenges, particularly as the small residence would have to sequester a growing band of men over a good many weeks.[4]

In 1859 Washington County, Maryland, where the farm was lo-cated, was "a region of home-keeping, honest, dull country people." The total population at the time was just over thirty thousand, in-cluding nearly fifteen hundred enslaved people and more than an equal number of free blacks.[5] Of course, the apparent serenity of the area belied the same tragic undercurrent flowing just beneath the surface of other slaveholding communities. In a letter to his wife, Watson Brown thus reported that several enslaved people recently had lost their lives—another source confirming that they had died at the hands of their masters, "punished so that death ensued immedi-ately, or in a short time." Another enslaved man, named Jerry, had so despaired over his wife being "sold off South," Watson wrote, that he committed suicide, hanging himself in a nearby orchard. These harsh realities not only put the lie to slaveholders' claims about the sacred guardianship of the slaveholder, but also must have steeled John Brown and his men in their plans to attack slavery at the very gate-way of the South. Watson himself had left his young wife, Isabelle, and their infant son in North Elba. "I cannot come home as long as such things are done here," he concluded.[6]

Initially, the Old Man occupied the farmhouse with his sons Owen and Oliver, and Jerry Anderson, his trusted escort. Anderson had turned against the slaveholding legacy of his own family to fight proslavery thugs in the Kansas territory, where he became acquainted with Brown. Not long afterward, sometime in July, Brown dispatched Oliver to return to their mountain home in New York's Adirondacks to get Mary Brown and their teenage daughter Anne to join them in Maryland in order to set up housekeeping—a matter of both practicality and appearance. Very little family correspondence from this period has survived history. In late June 1859, just before Brown settled into the Kennedy farmhouse, Mary wrote him a short letter with some family details and only a veiled sense that her husband was preparing to launch a South-wide liberation effort. "I do hope that you will be blessed with health & success in the good & great cause you are engaged in," she concluded, signing pseudonymously, "Mary D. Smith."[7] Of course, Mary was quite intentional in making only minimal remarks, although her words also may suggest that she had no intention of involving herself in his Virginia plan and would oppose involving any other family members as well. Brown had enlisted sons Oliver and Watson, which left her only one son at home, twenty-three-year-old Salmon. More so, she found it unconscionable that her husband might consider involving any of the female family members.

According to Anne Brown Adams, her father was so confident that Mary would join him in Maryland that he had even told neighbors of her imminent arrival. On July 5, 1859, Brown wrote a letter that he sent with his son Oliver, whom he had dispatched home to retrieve both Mary and Anne. "I would be most glad to have you & Anne come on with Oliver, & make me a visit of a few weeks while I am preparing to build," he wrote. The Old Man felt it was "indispensable" to have some "women of our own family with us for [a] short time." Brown promised them that they would suffer no dangerous exposure and that they could return home "after a short visit." Typical of John Brown, he then provided detailed instructions of what she should and should not bring with her, admonishing Mary to come immediately without so much as mentioning her trip to the neighbors. Brown must have sensed that his wife might be displeased, which may be why he waited until the last minute to ask her. Hoping to sway her, he advised that her coming to Maryland would "prove the most valuable service" she could "ever render to the world."[8]

But when Oliver reached North Elba, he quickly learned that his mother had no intention of going south. Anne recalled that her mother "did everything in her power" to prevent her and Oliver's teenage wife, Martha, from going to Maryland.[9] In her discerning study of Mary Brown and her daughters, Bonnie Laughlin-Schultz dismisses any notion that the good wife's resistance was in any sense a dissent from her husband's plan. Nor does she believe that Mary Brown's protest was vociferous, although she was quietly uncooperative. As Laughlin-Schultz observes, Mary Brown probably was always passive-aggressive when her husband's demands became overbearing.[10] What Mary said in refusal was not put into a letter, and whatever resistance she demonstrated was neither pronounced nor dramatic. Quietly, however, she resorted to one last attempt at motherly subterfuge by hiding Anne's clothing in the hopes of thwarting her packing for the trip.[11]

However, there is no truth to the notion that Mary did not support her husband's plan, and she seems never to have protested when her sons were placed in danger for the sake of the antislavery cause. Although John Brown's older children (born to his first wife, Dianthe Lusk) had borne the brunt of the Kansas drama with their father, two of Mary's sons, Oliver and Salmon, were also swept up into the traumatic episode and were fortunate to return alive from "Bleeding Kansas" (where Salmon had nearly died from an accidental gunshot). With the initiation of the Virginia plan, Salmon stayed behind to run the farm, but Mary sent off Oliver and Watson to join the good cause, even though both were married men and Watson a new father. It was only the notion of traveling to the South with her teenage daughter that went beyond the limits for Mary, especially since it meant leaving two younger daughters behind at their Adirondack farm.

When Oliver returned south, he was accompanied only by his young wife, Martha Brewster Brown, and sister Anne, both teenagers being determined to assist Brown by sustaining a domestic front at the farm. The Old Man was visibly disappointed. "Your mother did not come?" he asked. Anne explained that Mary had stayed behind to care for little Ellen, their five-year-old daughter. "I felt sorry for him," she recalled, remembering the look on John Brown's face as he clasped her hand, standing amidst the coming and going of other travelers at the Harper's Ferry train station. "Whether he ever suspected that we were deceiving him or not, I do not know. . . . I never told him." That Mary refused to join him in Maryland "was a sorry disappointment to him," Anne recalled.[12]

Anne also described how she and Martha immediately began to set up housekeeping at the Kennedy farm, but after failing in their attempt to cook a meal of potatoes in the fireplace, her father promptly went over to Harper's Ferry to purchase a stove. In a short time, he made other purchases for the farm, such as a cow and a horse, a small wagon, and three hogs—none of which went unnoticed by neighbors. Perhaps it also did not go unnoticed that he bought neither seed nor farming implements. John Unseld, whom Brown had met at the onset, afterward recalled that the Old Man never cultivated the land.[13]

Domestic life at the farm was not entirely a façade, although conditions in the flea-infested house were spartan and minimal. Most housekeeping implements were brought from North Elba, and wooden crates containing weapons were covered and used for seats, the men sleeping on the floor in an upper room. Anne and Martha fared only slightly better, struggling to sleep on crudely stuffed mattresses. According to Anne Brown Adams, her sister-in-law Martha, the young wife of Oliver, cooked the meals and kept house, while much of the time she stood as "outside guard" to keep neighbors from entering the farmhouse. Her father demanded "constant watchfulness," Anne recalled, so she would sit on the porch or just inside, sewing or reading while keeping an eye on what was happening outdoors.[14]

One day, as Anne and her father sat at the kitchen table, she noticed two little wrens fluttering and tweeting, flying back and forth
from the door to their nest under the front steps. The noisy behavior
of the birds soon brought both father and daughter to their feet, the
Old Man going outside to investigate. Anne recalled that when her
father went outside, he observed that a snake was menacing the nest
with its little ones. Brown quickly killed the snake, at which point the
same wrens who had been fluttering about in alarm now alighted on
the railing and began to chirp in a manner almost joyful. "He seemed
very much impressed" with the scene, Anne remembered, "and asked
if I thought it an omen of his success." He was not a superstitious
man, she remembered, but her father had always believed that he had
been called by God to liberate the enslaved.[15] Indeed, John Brown's
strident Calvinism, centered as it was upon the doctrines of divine
sovereignty and providence, left little room for signs or omens. Yet
even the most orthodox of theologians cannot always account for
undeniable moments of visitation, presence, or "coincidence" that
push beyond the limits of understanding. All of his life, Brown had
lived among God's creatures in the field and the wild, and there was
little that he did not know about them. But in the peculiarity of this
episode, he felt its significance, discerning it as a kind of hopeful
metaphor for his mission.

Although unexpected guests defined Brown's experience in
Maryland, any sudden appearance by a visitor could expose his
sequestered little army and completely undermine his plan. Under
such circumstances, when the occasional guest happened to show
up at the door, the raiders had to quickly disappear to the upper
room or attic—newspapers and books, pens and paper, and dinner
plates and guns all whisked up with them as they fled.[16] Brown
could not hide his presence in the vicinity, but his friendly gestures
and conversations with neighbors were sparing and intended to
steer visitors away from the farm. In fact, throughout the summer

and fall, visits from the outside world were few and far between. Some of those visits could not be avoided, such as those from John Unseld, whom Brown had met when he first came into the area. Brown apparently tried to minimize Unseld's visits by stopping periodically at his house but never accepting his hospitality—perhaps as much for strategic reasons as the fact that Unseld was a slaveholder. When Unseld returned the favor of a visit, typically he remained seated on his horse while talking to Brown on the high porch of the farmhouse.[17] But not every guest could be anticipated, such as the time when kindly "Mother" Nichols made a sudden appearance at their front door. Nichols had hosted Martha and Anne at her boardinghouse when they first arrived in Maryland, and she wanted to call on the girls for a friendly visit. According to Anne, when the woman came to the door, the raiders—whom she called "invisibles," suddenly jumped up and quietly made it upstairs just in time to escape notice. At this moment, however, John Cook, Brown's infiltrator in Harper's Ferry, happened to be visiting and was completely caught off guard. While the girls took turns delaying Nichols, Cook was hustled into a back room on the first floor, where he escaped through a back window. Fearing that Nichols's curiosity might be aroused, Martha created a diversion, flying into a feigned, door-slamming tirade against Anne. The awkward ploy was successful, and the elderly Nichols was so overwhelmed by Martha's behavior that she had no idea of Cook's hasty exit from the house.[18]

Unfortunately for Brown and his "invisibles," it became impossible to maintain their desired secrecy because of one relentlessly nosey neighbor, Elizabeth Huffmaster, the thirty-three-year-old wife of a struggling laborer. The Huffmasters had four young children ranging from three to eight years of age, and happened to rent land on the Kennedy property to grow their own produce.[19] In every one of Anne Brown Adams's several reminiscences of life on the Maryland

farm, "this curious, little woman" figures prominently because of the
constant threat she posed by showing up at the door with disturbing
regularity, whether morning or afternoon. "Little Mother Huffmaster"
and her troop of young girls and a "big baby boy" on her arm frequently appeared, all barefooted and eager to get inside the house.
Huffmaster's "troublesome way of calling" not only was frequent on
a daily basis, but sometimes she returned more than twice a day, and
nearly always made it up the front steps and into the kitchen. This
was particularly disturbing to Brown's men when she appeared during mealtime, at which the "invisibles" were forced to "gather up the
victuals and table-cloth and quietly disappear upstairs." Most of the
time, Anne was able to delay the invasion of "the little hen and her
chickens" on the front porch, slowing their entry until her sister-in-
law Martha could usher the men upstairs and put aside any evidence
of their presence. But hiding a growing number of men in the house
was nearly impossible, especially with Elizabeth Huffmaster watching so closely, to the point of keeping track of the "smart lot of shirts"
hanging to dry on laundry day.[20]

Certainly, Huffmaster was more perceptive than Brown and company probably first assumed. Her home faced one side of the farmhouse, and the petite mother quickly developed a curious suspicion
that more was going on inside the Smith residence despite the domestic façade presented by Anne and Martha. Her constant, repeated
efforts to get inside the house took its toll. At one point, one of the
Huffmaster girls managed to slip through the door of the front room,
bounding her way upstairs. Had Anne not caught her at the last moment, the little girl would have discovered a room full of strange men,
white and black, quietly sequestered in the bedroom. As Huffmaster
pressed in, Anne began to "give her things, to keep her friendly." But
this seems only to have intensified her determination, and sometimes
she began to leave the children at home and show up at the door
alone with some or another excuse.[21]

Over the summer months, the number of occupants in the farmhouse grew with the arrival of Watson Brown and the brothers William and Dauphin Thompson, also from North Elba. By early August, more men arrived at the farm: Charles Tidd, a New Englander who had joined Brown in Kansas, followed by Aaron Stevens and William Leeman, two more Kansas veterans. They were in turn followed by four more willing Kansas enlistees, the Quaker brothers Edwin and Barclay Coppic from Iowa, William Hazlett from Pennsylvania, and Steward Taylor from Canada.[22] It is not clear when Dangerfield Newby arrived at the farm—no doubt smuggled in Brown's small covered wagon—probably at the very end of August or early September.[23] Newby, who was born from an interracial union and brought to Ohio to live as a freeman, joined Brown in the hope of liberating his enslaved wife and children.[24] As the number of residents in the farmhouse swelled to as many as twenty-one, Watson Brown, Jerry Anderson, and the Thompson boys moved out of the house at night to sleep in the small log cabin on the property that was still covered by thick brush and trees. This was not only an expedient intended to relieve the cramped upper sleeping quarters, but it was thought also that this would give them a strategic advantage in the event they were attacked.[25]

At sixteen years of age, Anne was all but saddled with the responsibility of keeping "the outside world from discovering" the presence of Osawatomie Brown and his militant raiders in the neighborhood, a burden made all the more difficult by her mother's absence and her father's insistence. "Father would often tell me that I *must* not let any work interfere with my *constant watchfulness*," Anne recalled. But the challenge of keeping the outside world from intruding was complicated by the problem of discouraging the "invisibles" from making themselves unduly visible. Most of the time, the hazards involved the men being exposed when a visitor like Huffmaster suddenly appeared, although as time passed, some of the raiders simply found it hard to be contained inside the small farmhouse. Albert Hazlett and William Leeman proved particularly feisty, and sometimes slipped out of the house at night to forage for apples and nuts or steal corn from the neighbor's field. Once or twice, the two even dared to travel down to Harper's Ferry during the night to see Brown's spy, John Cook. By September, it was increasingly difficult for the men to remain cramped up indoors, and when night fell, as Osborne Anderson put it, "we sallied out for a ramble, or to breathe the fresh air and enjoy the beautiful solitude of the mountain scenery around, by moonlight."[26]

To be sure, John Brown made good effort in keeping the men occupied throughout their residence at the farm. Going back to the late 1820s and early 1830s, he had experience in housing workmen in his tannery operations and knew how to stage activities like debates and forums as well as contests to educate and entertain them.[27] At the Kennedy farm, the men were furnished with an ample supply of newspapers, or they played checkers, cards, and other games, or indulged in storytelling and singing hymns or sentimental ballads. One of those songs, "Faded Flowers," a particular favorite of Tidd and Stevens,[28] seems almost prophetic in historical retrospect:

> The flowers I saw in the wild wood,
> Have since dropped their beautiful leaves,
> And the many dear friends of my childhood,
> Have slumbered for years in their graves;
> But the bloom on the flowers I remember,
> Though their smiles I shall never more see,
> For the cold chilly winds of December
> Stole my flowers, my companions, from me.[29]

Debate and discussion were favored by the men, usually beginning at mealtimes and spilling into the evenings as they debated religion, politics, and social topics. Brown, who was quite traditionally

Calvinist and evangelical in his view of the Bible, knew that he was surrounded by young men who were spiritualists, Quakers, and even agnostics. But he encouraged the free exchange of ideas on all religious matters, sometimes as a participant in debates and other times being approvingly observant as the young men went back and forth in their arguments. Contrary to the unfounded portrayal of Brown as a grim religious fanatic, his Calvinistic piety was never more insistent than the morning reading of a biblical passage, followed by a "plain, short, sensible prayer"—but certainly an abolitionist's prayer too. "I never heard John Brown pray, that he did not make strong appeals to God for the deliverance of the slave," recalled Osborne Anderson. Otherwise, as Anne remembered, "All questions on religion or any other subject were very freely discussed by the men, and Father always took an interested part in the discussions and encouraged everyone to express their opinions on any subject, no matter whether he agreed with them or not." When on occasion he believed that the fellowship of the men was blunted by his patriarchal presence, Brown would retreat to a stool by the stove in the kitchen, so as not to "spoil their enjoyment and fun by his presence in the living room."[30]

During the day, there were duties assigned to the men, such as studying a soldier's manual that Brown had had prepared for his movement, or they were quietly drilled under the training of Aaron Stevens, a former military man and Kansas veteran. In further preparation for the raid, the Sharps rifles were removed from wooden crates so the "invisibles" could apply a chemical for bronzing the gun barrels, or they would make belts and pistol holsters. Along with these weapons, other crates were opened so the men could assemble the pikes that Brown had specially ordered from a forge-master in Connecticut, requiring the raiders to attach the prefabricated spearheads to "fork handles"—a formidable weapon for a mountain-based campaign.[31] By mid-September, Osborne Anderson arrived at the farm, the only black enlistee directly recruited by John Brown in

FIGURE 3.3.
Teenage Anne Brown.
John Brown/Boyd B. Stutler
Collection, West Virginia
Archives and History.

Canada. Like Newby, Anderson was biracial, but he was born free in Pennsylvania, only afterward moving to Canada.[32] In almost any other context in the antebellum United States, Anderson invariably would have been distinguished from his white counterpart of the same surname by some sort of racial epithet, like "Black Anderson." Instead, the "invisibles" dubbed him "Chatham Anderson."[33]

But for a brief few months, the Kennedy farm, located in a slave-holding community, was dominated by both the spirit and the letter of equality, wherein one's humanity would never be reduced to mere skin color. Looking back at his several weeks at the Kennedy farm, Osborne Anderson thus wrote: "In John Brown's house, and in John Brown's presence, men from widely different parts of the continent met and united into one company, wherein no hateful prejudice dared intrude its ugly self—no ghost of a distinction found space to enter."[34] With regard to the equality of women, perhaps these young men were not on a whole yet where one would hope to find them, but even here John Brown was leading in the right direction. One evening during a debate after dinner concerning the "Woman Question," Oliver Brown made the case that women generally were not so intelligent and smart as men. Here the Old Man challenged: "I think my girls are quite as smart and intelligent as my boys. . . . Anne here succeeds quite well in holding her own in a dispute with any of you boys."[35]

As formidable women were concerned, over the last weeks of life at the Kennedy farm, Elizabeth Huffmaster evolved steadily from being a nuisance to "the plague and torment of our lives," as Anne recalled. This certainly was the case after the indefatigable neighbor caught sight of some of the "invisibles." Once, when Anne had gone with her father to a religious camp meeting, Huffmaster scurried over to the house without being noticed, making her way up the front porch stairs and passing through the doorway. Before she was noticed by Martha, Huffmaster had caught sight of two of the raiders, who had ventured downstairs. Much to the chagrin of all in the house, not only did she see William Leeman wearing a black cap, but also Shields Green, who had come down, stuttering out a proposal to Martha that he would iron the men's shirts if she would mend his coat. The teenage wife quickly interposed herself between the raiders and their unwelcomed guest, but the damage was done. In recounting this incident, Anne was much harder on Shields Green, portraying him in a manner far worse than she did the white raiders, some of whom were far more mischievous and careless. "He came near *be-traying* and *upsetting* the whole business, by his *careless*[ly] letting a neighbor woman see him," she wrote many years afterward.[36]

When John Brown was informed about the incident afterward, he urged Anne to intercede. "First you had better find out what she saw and what she thought of it," he told his daughter, "whether she has seen any one since she left here, and then tell her what you think best. It will not do to let it be known that a negro has been seen here with strange white men, so you will have to account for it some way." Brown apparently hoped that if Huffmaster, being poor, was not a proslavery woman, she might yet be bribed to stay silent. "I am short of money," he told Anne, "so if you can, induce her to take anything we can spare out of the house instead."

Fortunately, Brown's surmise seems to have been correct. Elizabeth Huffmaster was a Pennsylvanian by birth and perhaps felt no great affinity toward slaveholders, although certainly she had seen enough to jeopardize the whole plan. Taking some milk for the children, Anne went next door to speak to Huffmaster, confirming that she had seen both Leeman and Green and assumed that the black man was a fugitive slave. Anne assured her that these were friends and that they had moved on, pleading with her not to speak of the incident to anyone. She promised to remain silent, but neither Anne nor her father were confident that Huffmaster would remain quiet for long without being bribed. This concern overshadowed Brown and his men throughout the rest of the summer and into the early fall. To them, it seemed "like standing on a powder magazine, after a slow match had been lighted." What made matters worse for Anne was that the little farm wife now exercised a measure of power over her, so that "every time she thought of anything she wanted that we had, she made free to ask for things, and of course I gave them to her."[37]

Nor were they delivered of Huffmaster's unannounced visits. Following the incident when she saw Emperor and Leeman, she somehow managed to get even farther into the house, reaching the middle room where the wood crates containing rifles and pistols were kept. When she inquired about the crates, Anne concocted the explanation that the family was not ready to unpack their fine furniture until their mother arrived. On yet another day, raider Charles Tidd, who was something of a hardhead, insisted on reading a newspaper on the front porch while Anne stood on her watch. Complaining that he was tired of being confined to the indoors, Tidd refused to budge from the porch for a little while despite Anne's pleading. At this moment, Huffmaster suddenly came out from her yard, walking quickly down the path to the house. "Blast that woman," Tidd fumed. "What a torment she is!" and then slipped back into the kitchen, quickly ascending a ladder to the attic. Before Anne could do anything else, Huffmaster was upon her, declaring her need of lard, and then followed her quite determinedly into the kitchen. Afterward, Anne learned that not only had Huffmaster seen Tidd on the porch, but that she surmised that he had escaped to the attic upon entering the kitchen. Years later, Anne learned that prior to the raid, Tidd had unthinkingly gone over to the Huffmaster house to borrow an ax. He never told Brown and the others of his indiscretion, although in retrospect it could have undermined the whole plan had Huffmaster been so inclined to expose her Northern neighbors.[38]

Notwithstanding their worst fears, Elizabeth Huffmaster ultimately proved to be neither a spy nor an informer. Instead, it seems she was far more interested in taking advantage of the situation in order to get whatever she could for her family, from bacon to frying grease and household wares. It is also possible that she was sympathetic toward her neighbors, having concluded that they were Northern people willing to assist runaway slaves. Certainly, the Old Man had established himself within that agrarian community as a kind Christian man who attended local church meetings, shared veal and salted pork with neighbors in "country fashion," and offered his assistance if needed. In more than one of her reminiscences from this period, Anne spoke of her father doing "amateur surgery" on a poor neighbor—perhaps Elizabeth Huffmaster—who had an unsightly tumor on her neck, a condition that undoubtedly afflicted and embarrassed her, but which she was too poor to have remedied by a physician. Although Brown had no formal medical training, he was seasoned by life on the farm and the field and seems to have had a steady hand and good instincts for such matters. Nor was this the first time that he had laid a knife to flesh in order to help friend and family, or to remedy a problem with livestock. Being unable to pay for this medical treatment, the poor woman afterward offered Brown a large, young mastiff, already named "Cuffee"—an African name that often was used by whites in racist caricature. When Anne complained that the dog was brutish, her father responded, dryly teasing that he hoped she would not be prejudiced against Cuffee, "for you don't know what a good dog he may turn out to be."[39]

In a sense, Brown's surgical procedure on his Maryland neighbor is a kind of parable of his whole purpose for entering the South. Slavery was, in his thinking, a deep and abiding affliction upon the body politic of the United States. Slavery in Brown's mind was not synonymous with the United States, even though one might argue with him in retrospect that his view of the motivations and intentions of the Founding Fathers was too generous.[40] After all, the Constitution of the United States sanctioned and supported slavery, and the Declaration of Independence that he so revered was written by a liberal slaveholder. Still, to John Brown, slavery was not intrinsic to the identity of the United States, even though its presence in antebellum society had grown upon the republic like some horrid tumor—its roots going deeper and deeper into the flesh of the nation. As he showed to his Maryland neighbors, Brown held no regional prejudice against the whites of the South, believing that they were themselves the hapless progeny of slavery's brutal paternalism. According to one family tradition, it is recounted how in her youth, Brown's daughter Ruth made some harsh comments about Southerners. "Hush!" her father rebuked. "You would feel just as they do if you had been bred as they have. It is not their fault, but the fault of their training." There was in John Brown none of the regional bias and contempt that often was demonstrated by Union soldiers during the Civil War. It was upon slavery that he had declared war, not upon Southerners. "People mistake my objects," he told a Kansas associate. "*I act from a principle. My aim and my object is to restore human rights.*" Twenty years after his father's hanging, John Brown Jr. was hardly exaggerating when he wrote to a native South Carolinian: "My Father, brothers and their comrades who fell at Harper's Ferry, did not hate the *people* of the South. 'Twas only towards its *slavery*, that they cherished a 'sacred animosity.'"[41] Of course, the people of the South could not understand this in 1859, and unfortunately few Southerners think any differently of John Brown today. However, it was only slavery that the Old Man hated, and it was this—the tumor that had infested the nation's flesh—that he wished to excise "without very much bloodshed," as he wrote before dying.[42]

As an heir of the Protestant Reformation and the Puritans, and as a grandson of the Revolution of 1776, John Brown was invariably inclined toward text, particularly in the manner that texts provided a moral and legal platform for any movement, including his own militant antislavery efforts. Over a decade, from Massachusetts to Kansas, he had composed such founding documents, endeavoring to explain and vindicate his opposition to slavery, from his defiance of the Fugitive Slave Law to the defense of free state settlers in the Kansas territory.[43] It is evident that John Brown thought of his liberation effort not only as consistent with sacred scripture, but also as the correct and logical continuation of the founding of the United States, which had betrayed its commitment to freedom by enabling slavery to take root and flourish in the garden of republican liberty. Given this background, it was inevitable that he would find it necessary to draft documents of radical reform that he hoped would serve for the re-founding of the nation on consistent egalitarian and humanitarian terms.

The first of these documents was his "Provisional Constitution and Ordinances for the People of the United States," drafted in early 1858.

With the "Provisional Constitution," he intended to provide a legal and governmental framework for the armed guerrilla nation that he wanted to establish in the South—a transitional measure toward ending slavery under the flag of the United States. Over the years, the "Provisional Constitution" has been criticized by Brown's admirers and critics alike, although the best evaluations recognize that despite its flaws, it presents a correction to the United States Constitution, which implicitly condoned slavery. In contrast, Brown provided a framework for a society that protected the rights of all of those whom he referred to as the "proscribed and oppressed races" of the United States.[44] In forty-eight articles, his "Provisional Constitution" was "aspirational" in its quest for national reform. Even with its flaws and peculiarities (such as elevating his own role as commander-in-chief above the presidency), the "Provisional Constitution" nevertheless was "surprisingly concrete" at points, and seems "especially enlightened, even to the modern mind" by affording rights and protections.[45] This document, which Brown had composed while sequestered in the Rochester home of Frederick Douglass in early 1858, was shortly afterward approved by a convention of associates in Chatham, Ontario, Canada, and then printed and shipped to the Kennedy farm in Maryland.[46]

However, during the interim at the Kennedy farm, Brown completed another needful document, entitled "A Declaration of Liberty by the Representatives of the Slave Population of the United States of America." Like his first instrument, "A Declaration of Liberty" was quite evidently modeled on another founding document of the United States, the Declaration of Independence. As he also did in his constitution, Brown prioritized racial justice as a corrective to the Declaration of Independence, combining the mandate of liberation with the famous words of Jefferson:

> "When in the course of human events," it becomes necessary for an
> Oppressed People to Rise, and assert their Natural Rights, as Human

Beings, as Native and mutual citizens of a free Republic, and break that odious yoke of oppression, which is so unjustly laid upon them by their fellow countrymen . . . We hold this truth to be self-evident, that it is the highest Privilege & Plain duty of Man to strive in every reasonable way, to promote the Happiness, Mental, Moral, & Physical elevation of his fellow Man. And that People, or Clan[n]-ish Oppressors who wickedly violate this sacred principle, oppressing their fellow Men, will bring upon themselves that certain and fearful retribution, which is the Natural, & Necessary penalty of evil Doing.[47]

"A Declaration of Liberty" continues by stating that enslaved people had suffered a "most cruel bondage," and that it was necessary now to "Crush this foul system of oppression." The history of slavery in the United States, Brown continues, was not only a story of "injustice" and "barbarity," but it was worse than "cruel war" waged upon its victims. In addition to a recitation of the wickedness of slavery, Brown also argues in "A Declaration of Liberty" that the power of slaveholders had become so pervasive in the nation because their "Leeches" had seized power over the federal government, especially the military and the judicial system. Slaveholders had so effectively taken control that they now kept important information from the people of the country and shielded slaveholders and slave traders from justice with "mock trials." Since the slaveholding powers had proven "Deaf to the voice of Justice & Consanguinity," it was once more the time to make war on oppression, eighty-three years after winning independence from the tyranny of Great Britain. "A Declaration of Liberty" makes its appeal to the "unchangeable Law of God" and requests the aid of "all true friends of humanity."

"A Declaration of Liberty" was written out on large sheets by Owen Brown, who acted as his father's scribe, the pages being pasted consecutively onto a long sheet of cloth that was then rolled around a wooden dowel like a scroll. The work probably was not dictated, since the scroll version seems to be quite literally based upon John Brown's own peculiar style of writing.[48] Tony Horwitz compared the document to a Torah scroll, "Brown's Sacred Instrument, which he would bring down from the mountains to fulfill God's will and the destiny of his chosen nation." But this comparison is more clever than substantive.[49] First, the scroll format of "A Declaration of Liberty" was not as much an imitation of sacred scripture as it was an homage to the great documents of the English past, from the Magna Carta to the Mayflower Compact and the Declaration of Independence. Even in form, Brown wanted "A Declaration of Liberty" to look like the latest installment in the long narrative of freedom, and certainly wanted his movement to demonstrate continuity with the founders of the United States. Prior to the Harper's Ferry raid, Brown was even contemplating the design of some kind of field medal, perhaps to be worn by himself and his officers. When he consulted abolitionist Franklin Sanborn in the matter, the Concord schoolteacher presented him with rough sketches of the medals, including a military cross with an image based upon Jean-Antoine Houdon's life mask of George Washington.[50]

Second, "A Declaration of Liberty" is not presented as a document "from above," as if Brown were playing the role of Moses at Sinai. To the contrary, it is firmly a document "from below." Although the words of "A Declaration of Liberty" are undeniably John Brown's own sentiments, he wrote neither as a prophet nor as a radical "seeking to justify revolution."[51] Certainly, there is nothing revolutionary about the work, except that it demands that the goals of the Revolution of 1776 be extended to enslaved black people. There is no political intention within "A Declaration of Liberty" to overthrow the government, only to force an end to the system of oppression that had usurped power over the nation. Indeed, Brown clearly makes an appeal for help from the friends of "reform."

More importantly, "A Declaration of Liberty," while certainly being the words of John Brown, is not presented in his voice, nor

in the voice of white abolitionists, or even the antislavery people of
the North in general. Rather, it is presented on behalf of the enslaved, who then renew the words of Thomas Jefferson with prophetic
gravitas: "We hold these truths to be Self Evident; That All Men are
Created Equal." Understanding the intended voice of "A Declaration
of Liberty" is essential to grasping the purpose of its exasperated and
determined plaint—the witness of the enslaved and oppressed black
community against the tyranny of slavery in the United States.

This was not the first time that Brown presumed to take up the
voice of the oppressed, since his close association with black people
had presented one or two occasions where he felt sufficiently com-
fortable to do so, particularly in expressing concern for the improve-
ment and liberation of the African American community.[52] In this
sense, the precedent for "A Declaration of Liberty" was like the
document Brown had prepared for the United States League of
Gileadites (1851), an armed black resistance organization he founded
in Springfield, Massachusetts, in opposition to the Fugitive Slave
Law of 1850.[53] In this short document, "Words of Advice," Brown
wrote in what seems to be his own voice, dispensing tactical advice
for fighting off and even killing slave hunters if necessary. However,
the document concludes with a short agreement in which his voice
seemingly blends into the voices of the black resisters, enjoining each
other to arm themselves and their comrades, inviting other "colored"
people to join, and even impressing upon the elderly and the young
their duty to serve as lookouts.

By today's standards, John Brown's efforts to write for black people
might be attributed to the presumptions of white privilege, although
few if any African American commentators have ever made this
charge against him.[54] To the contrary, the overwhelming number of
black critics, including the most strident disputants of the white community, have credited Brown for backing up his words with militant
action, almost to the degree of turning white privilege on its head.

"I cherish old John Brown," wrote John Oliver Killens in the civil rights era. Killens, who could be even less sparing of white people's feelings than James Baldwin, took no issue with "winter soldiers" like Brown and the "too few" other whites who partook of black people's anti-racist dialogue.[55] "A Declaration of Liberty" thus is replete with such phrasings as "Regardless of *our* wishes," "invested with power to legislate for *us* in all cases whatsoever," "declaring *us* out of their protection, & waging a worse than cruel war upon *us* continually," "Slave holders *our* lords & masters, from which, Good Lord Deliver *us*," and finally, "We must therefore acquiesce in the necessity, which denounces their tyranny & unjust rule over *us*. Declaring that *we will serve them no longer as slaves.*"[56]

To be sure, it was Brown who provided the scope of "A Declaration of Liberty," and inevitably, as Robert McGlone points out, the document reflects "Brown's thinking as he matured his conspiracy."[57] As such, it reveals his purview of the political landscape of the United States as he had come to understand it by his own struggles against the proslavery element, especially in the Kansas territory. However, McGlone's reading of "A Declaration of Liberty" is problematic. First, he assumes that Brown's use of "et ceteras" and the fact that the document was unsigned suggest that it was unfinished. To the contrary, it was not unusual for Brown to use "et cetera" (which he preferred to render as "&c") to suggest that more could be said, not that his point was incomplete. Nor was this a document that required signatures, since it was written on behalf of the slave. Second, McGlone concludes that "A Declaration of Liberty" was "a failed call to arms" because he assumes that it was written at least in part by 1858, and possibly was slighted by Brown's black associates in his Chatham, Ontario, convention. This likewise is incorrect, since the document probably was not even completed until 1859, perhaps not until the last phase at the Kennedy farm. Since it was written late in John Brown's mission, it had no circulation whatsoever among either black or white associates, and its only real audience probably were his men at the Kennedy farm, since it fell into the hands of Virginia authorities after the Harper's Ferry raid. Immediately after Brown's defeat, Virginia governor Henry Wise dispatched Henry Hudnall, one of his staff, to travel from Richmond to inspect the documents seized at the Kennedy farm. Wise's interest in Brown's papers reflected his intention to find evidence of complicity between Northern Republicans and the Harper's Ferry raiders. To no surprise, "A Declaration of Liberty" was among the documents taken by Hudnall to be used as evidence against Brown. "Their Declaration of Independence," reported Hudnall, "bears strong internal proof of having been the work of Brown, parodied on the colonial Declaration, with some very original variations and interpolations by Brown himself."[58] Indeed, Hudnall thought the document so significant to Virginia's case that he prepared an exact and thorough transcription of "A Declaration of Liberty" for Wise and the prosecution.[59] It is possible that the document was acquired as early as the 1860s by a private collector, who filed it away among his holdings for another thirty years. It was finally rediscovered by Brown biographers after the collection was donated to the Historical Society of Pennsylvania in Philadelphia.[60]

On Sunday morning, October 16, John Brown and his men awoke for the last time in their Maryland headquarters. Anne and Martha had already returned home in late September, the farmhouse now having lost whatever semblance to a family homestead it had enjoyed. Brown opened the Bible as he had done every morning at the farm, first reading a passage of scripture and then praying before breakfast. No doubt, on that last morning, his prayer for the liberation of the slave resonated powerfully with the men. "The old man's usually weighty words were invested with more than ordinary importance," Osborne Anderson recalled. The gathering that Sunday morning was "impressive beyond expression. Every man there assembled seemed to respond from the depths of his soul, and throughout the entire day, a deep solemnity pervaded the place."[61]

After breakfast, Brown once more assembled the "invisibles," including those who had arrived the day before: Francis Merriam from Boston, and the last two black recruits, Lewis Leary and John Copeland from Oberlin, Ohio.[62] Shields Green, along with the brothers Edwin and Barclay Coppic, Copeland, Leary, and Merriam, were read the "Provisional Constitution" by Aaron Stevens, and then made a solemn oath administered by John Brown himself.[63] This was in keeping with Article XLVIII of the "Provisional Constitution," requiring every officer, whether civil or military, to make "a solemn oath or affirmation, to abide by and support" the "Provisional Constitution" and its ordinances.[64] It was in this final ceremony that Emperor received his assignment as a member of the Provisional Congress, a seat he would never fill. That evening, he and the others would don their ponchos, take up their arms, and march solemnly behind the Old Man as he drove his little wagon into the shadows, down to Harper's Ferry.

The Raid and the
Black Witness

Much has been given as true that never happened,
much has been omitted that should
have been made known.

Osborne Perry Anderson

THE controversy that once surrounded the Harper's Ferry raid may be a matter of the past, but there is not yet a consensus among historians as to the event itself nor its protagonist. The late Tony Horwitz, author of a popular narrative about the raid, *Midnight Rising*, put it quite succinctly that the Harper's Ferry raid was "poorly planned, badly executed, and probably doomed from the start, at least as a military campaign."[1] As to Brown, Horwitz thought him a high-functioning manic depressive with poor judgment.[2] In response to *Midnight Rising*, David S. Reynolds, the preeminent biographer of the abolitionist, responded in a review, concluding that "Horwitz's disdain for Brown comes through unmistakably," particularly in portraying Brown's whole plan to invade the South as a "manifest implausibility"—"even though," Reynolds writes, "it then seemed more plausible than any other plan, given the history of places like Jamaica and Haiti, where black populations had successfully driven out European colonizers by striking from mountain redoubts."[3]

Two years before the release of *Midnight Rising*, Horwitz laid the groundwork for his thesis in a *New York Times* op-ed observing the sesquicentennial of the 1859 raid. In his op-ed, Horwitz suggested viewing the raid through "the lens of 9/11," calling John Brown "the most successful terrorist in American history," and describing him as "a bearded fundamentalist" and the Harper's Ferry raid his "holy war." By 2011, when *Midnight Rising* was published, he had somewhat pulled back from his op-ed, admitting that "recent history also pro-vides a simplistic guide at best." Unfortunately, he still suggested to his readers that the Harper's Ferry raid might be viewed "through the lens of 9/11" as a kind of "al-Qaeda prequel" led by a "long-bearded fundamentalist." To these remarks, Reynolds responded in the *Wall Street Journal*, writing that an appeal to "the lens of 9/11" was "re-ductionism," although there was a certain irony in it that actually shows that Brown's plan was not as absurd as Horwitz assumed. "The past decade has shown what can happen when a determined splinter group wages war from hideouts—how disruptive it can be to the sta-tus quo," Reynolds explained. "Had Brown made it to the mountains before he was captured at Harpers Ferry, he too might have had a powerful effect on events—a positive one (unlike al Qaeda), since he aimed to free four million slaves."[4]

In fairness to Horwitz, he was not the first to appeal to "terror-ism" in discussing John Brown, since a number of writers (all of them white) preceded him with comparisons to domestic and foreign ter-rorism dating back to the 1990s, some of them using phrases like "homegrown terrorist" and "the father of American terrorism"—as if white people had never committed acts of terrorism until John Brown's controversial actions in Kansas and Virginia in the 1850s. In a brilliant article that every one of John Brown's presumptive judges should read, Paul Finkelman observes that the abolitionist did not fight against democratic institutions in a free society, but rather op-posed an unfree society that denied people basic civil liberties.[5] To be sure, Horwitz demonstrated the capacity to discern in the story what predecessors of the "terrorist" school did not. In concluding his prologue, Horwitz quotes the abolitionist William Lloyd Garrison in 1859, who declared that John Brown's invasion of Harper's Ferry had shown the nation that it was "high noon"—that the time had come to challenge slavery once and for all. *Midnight Rising* is not without other discerning moments, to be sure. Nevertheless, Horwitz did not entitle his book *High Noon*, and the title that he chose quite accurately represents the lens through which he viewed the Harper's Ferry raid and its leader.

It should be recognized too that *Midnight Rising* was written by a Civil War enthusiast with a notable following within that popular category. In the mid-twentieth century, Civil War scholars and writers enjoyed the prerogative to interpret John Brown and did so invariably with a certain contempt, and in a manner that privileged the great conflict and the rise of Lincoln, the "Great Emancipator." Of course, Horwitz was far advanced of earlier Civil War writers, many of whom were indifferent to black history and ham-handedly dismissed Brown as insane in their haste to elevate Lincoln. In 1950, Lincoln scholar Paul Angle confided to Brown aficionado Boyd Stutler, "No one among the historians we know seems to be particularly conversant with the history of the negro, at least for the Civil War period."[6] In contrast to his predecessors, Horwitz was quite masterful at interrogating history and culture as a journalist-historian, and was quite aware, for instance, that slaveholders in the Harper's Ferry raid actually were fearful despite their own propaganda of slave loyalty, just as he recognized that the murders of some enslaved people who had supported Brown were covered up afterwards.[7] Nevertheless, *Midnight Rising* bends toward the same "tragic prelude" notion insofar as it diminishes John Brown. As Reynolds observed, despite making qualifications here and there, Horwitz had all but refurbished "the grim Old Man of long-ago histories: bold, arrogant, sly, fanatical, murderous, muddle-headed and possibly insane."[8]

In keeping with its title, *Midnight Rising* certainly presents a narrative of the Harper's Ferry raid that privileges the white Virginians who were caught up in this dramatic episode. From Harper's Ferry night watchmen and a hotel clerk, a train conductor, and other local whites, to a prominent slaveholder, their experiences and testimonies are foundational in providing the reader's sense of the raid.[9] While this is consistent with Horwitz's style of "participatory journalism" brought to history, it is skewed against abolitionists and the enslaved community—who undoubtedly understood the raid as a liberation effort, not as an "al-Qaeda prequel."[10] Indeed, just as Brown and his men are viewed from the lens of frightened proslavery Virginians, Horwitz presents a nameless raider falling to his death in the street, gunned down by a sniper. The raider, Dangerfield Newby, is thus introduced to the reader postmortem, the same way the Virginians themselves came to know him.[11]

Beyond these observations, *Midnight Rising* underserves Osborne Perry Anderson's *A Voice from Harper's Ferry* (1861), a narrative written by the only black raider who lived to bear witness. All told, Horwitz refers to Anderson's narrative four times, and only once in describing the actual raid—particularly where the raider's testimony seems to reinforce the notion of Brown's incompetency, something that Anderson would never have permitted. Otherwise, Horwitz uses *A Voice from Harper's Ferry* like historical garnish. In another place, Anderson is quoted as saying that Brown had "dug the mine and laid the train" at Harper's Ferry that would "eventually dissolve the union between Freedom and slavery."[12] Yet this hardly diverges from the cynical "tragic prelude" version in *Midnight Rising*, since Civil War writers have always emphasized that Brown's blundering at Harper's Ferry helped to bring about the war that ended slavery. In fact, there is only a slight difference between Horwitz and Lincoln scholar Paul

Angle, whose backhanded salute to Brown in the centennial year of the Harper's Ferry raid entailed calling him a "strange, contradictory, aberrant throw-back to the days of John Calvin," while yet crediting him for doing more "to precipitate the Civil War than any other individual, except, perhaps, Harriet Beecher Stowe."[13] As Reynolds concludes, *Midnight Rising* reveals a "studied circumvention of a genuine reconsideration of Brown as an anti-slavery provocateur or as a pioneering spokesperson for civil rights."[14] Although Horwitz merits the reputation of being an unconventional writer in many respects, his treatment of John Brown and the Harper's Ferry raid is much more akin to an older school of Civil War scholars who were inclined to belittle Brown and overlook the black witness.[15]

* * *

Osborne Perry Anderson was twenty-nine years old at the time he joined John Brown's men at the Kennedy farm in Maryland. The son of a free black man, Anderson was born in Pennsylvania but moved to Canada in the mid-1850s, where he found employment as a salesman and printer's devil at the offices of the *Provincial Freeman*, a black-owned newspaper based in Chatham, Ontario. According to Eugene Meyer, the talented Anderson was contributing articles to the paper by 1857. The following year, John Brown came to Chatham with his "Provisional Constitution and Ordinances" and convened a secret convention there on May 8 and 10, 1858. Among the other black attenders, Anderson showed himself to be solidly behind Brown, voting for the passage of his constitution, and being elected as a member of the Provisional Congress.[16] Anderson writes that he declined a captain's commission offered "by the brave old man" because he believed that that role was better suited to those with military experience.[17] One local account says that Isaac Shadd, the publisher of the *Provincial Freeman*, opined that someone from Chatham's black community ought to join Brown in the event he succeeded in setting up

FIGURE 4.1.
Osborne P. Anderson.
Library of Congress
Collection.

"the kingdom of God in the south." Rather than find themselves in a
"mighty uncomfortable" place, it was decided that eligible candidates
would draw lots, and the fateful straw fell to Osborne Anderson.[18]

Anderson arrived at Chambersburg, Pennsylvania, on September
16, and stayed at the Ritner boardinghouse for several days before
meeting in counsel with John Brown, his son Watson, and John Kagi.
At this point, it was decided that he should wait several more days
and then set out for the Maryland farm on September 24. To avoid
raising suspicion, Anderson left Chambersburg alone and on foot, "a
necessary precaution" taken up after Shields Green's risky sojourn to
the farm. But the plan was painstaking, since Anderson had to walk
alone for nearly thirty-five miles to Middletown, Maryland, where he
finally rendezvoused with John Brown under the cover of night. "We

set out directly," Anderson recalled, "and drove until nearly day-break the next morning, when we reached the Farm in safety."[19]

Anderson reached the Kennedy farm on or about September 24, in the aftermath of a sharp conflict that had taken place not quite a month before his arrival. The dispute, led by the brash and hot-headed raider Charles Tidd, was in reaction to Brown's plan to seize the town and armory of Harper's Ferry. Tidd and others had be-latedly learned of the plan, perhaps when they were informed that their leader was going into Chambersburg with John Kagi to meet with Frederick Douglass, who actually knew about the plan already and was strenuously opposed to the invasion.[20] With this revela-tion, Tidd and others—including Oliver and Watson Brown—began to protest the plan, and the Old Man found himself outnumbered, being supported by only a few of his men, including Shields Green.[21] Although characteristically imperious, Brown privately confided to his son Owen that he was quite downcast over the objections of his men and was considering abandoning the undertaking at least on a temporary basis.[22] At its peak, the argument had actually gotten so bad that Kagi was brought in from Chambersburg, and John Cook, Brown's spy, came over from Harper's Ferry to defend their leader's strategy. This proved to no avail in appeasing Tidd, whose ire had grown so great that he went down to Harper's Ferry with Cook af-terward "to let his wrath cool off."[23] This is how the Browns remem-bered it, although Steven Lubet points out that Tidd's resistance was no mere temper tantrum. Not only did his opposition nearly break up John Brown's little army, but Tidd himself had packed his trunk and gone down to Harper's Ferry, probably with the intention of taking the train back home.[24]

This may explain why Brown went to such dramatic extremes as to resign, although by nature he would not easily have let go of the reins of command. According to Owen Brown, his father tendered his resignation and invited the remaining men to choose another leader,

promising that he would cooperate. Of course, anyone who knew
John Brown might have been skeptical when he promised to remain
on solely in order to "give counsel and advice" where he believed "a
better course could be adopted." Now, with Tidd's absence, the rest
of the men at the farm seem to have mellowed. None disagreed with
Owen, who told his father that it would be difficult to find another
leader "in preference" to him. Perhaps to no surprise, John Brown was
shortly reinstated.[25]

Although opposition to Brown's plan had quickly melted away,
it was left to Owen to win back the outraged Tidd, who was still
bunking at John Cook's place in Harper's Ferry. Acting as his father's
emissary, Owen finally went down to persuade him to come back to
the farm. On August 18, the faithful son sent his father a short note,
reporting that "all" had finally agreed "to sustain your decisions, untill
you have *proved incompetent*." Perhaps signaling Tidd's half-hearted
agreement, Owen added, "many of us will adhere to your decisions so
long as you will."[26] Tidd later claimed that Brown had offered him
a concession in order to win him back, even agreeing to modify his
plan, although he never did so. But this claim cannot be verified, and
more likely Tidd had yielded because of Cook's "unremitting enthusiasm" in favor of the Harper's Ferry plan. The latter—like Brown—had
carefully scrutinized the town and armory operation and knew how
easily they could be taken as long as the raiders did not linger.[27] This
seems to be borne out in the sorrowful aftermath of the raid, when
Tidd bitterly blamed Brown for the deaths of his men at Harper's
Ferry. However, in doing so he found fault only with his leader's delay,
not with the plan itself as he had previously done at the farm.[28] The
perceptive Osborne Anderson likely learned of this conflict after his
arrival, although tensions were considerably quieted by the third week
of September, and he makes no mention of it in his narrative.

But Anderson alludes to another episode that took place prior to the
seizure of Harper's Ferry, although it usually has been passed over by

historians. According to Anderson, less than two weeks before the raid, John Brown made a trip to Philadelphia, after which he debriefed the men at the farm, doing so "in the fullness of his overflowing, saddened heart."[29] Anderson provides no further information, but it is likely that he was referring to a last-minute visit with Frederick Douglass, a disappointment that the orator himself perhaps found too painful to include in his 1881 autobiography. In his memoir, the black leader William Henry Johnson recalled that Brown had looked forward to good support from blacks in Philadelphia. But Brown was quite disturbed when J. J. Simons, one of their associates, nearly exposed the plan in a public address made at Philadelphia's Shiloh Baptist Church in August 1859. In response, Brown, Douglass, and black community leaders had decided it was best to publish statements that contradicted Simons's remarks. While Simons's indiscretion jeopardized the plan, throughout the late summer and early fall Brown continued to hope that Philadelphia, with the support of Douglass, would yield some black recruits. However, in that final Philadelphia meeting with Douglass in October, Brown now realized that he had only doubled down on his opposition to the Harper's Ferry plan. The orator seems to have had the names of potential recruits, but steadfastly refused to enlist them on Brown's behalf, despite the urging of others in Philadelphia's black community. Douglass undoubtedly had his own reasons to pull back, but this left Brown to make a final, disappointed return to the Maryland farm, perhaps confiding to his men of "the forlorn hope of what might have been a grand expedition."[30]

Anderson wrote that by Saturday, October 15, people living in the neighborhood had become excited by reports of strange men about the Kennedy farm, and some were no longer confident "as to the real business" of their Northern neighbor. Anderson says that because of the close confinement at the farm, the raiders, no doubt led by Tidd, had gone "out about the house and farm in the day-time during the week, and so indiscreetly exposed their numbers to the prying neighbors, who thereupon took steps to have a search instituted in the early part of the coming week."[31]

Among Brown's biographers some discussion has been offered concerning the time of the raid's initiation, most tending to favor a letter written by John Henrie Kagi on October 10, in which the raider explained that it was the "right time" for the invasion to commence. As Kagi saw it, crops had been harvested and were "in the best condition for use"; the moon was "just right," being full in mid-October that year; local slaves were discontent; there was a religious revival taking place at the time that Kagi believed would work against pro-slavery sentiments; and Brown's financial resources were getting low. Still, Kagi's reasons for launching the invasion were circumstantial except for the last one he revealed—that the raiders could not "get along much longer without being exposed."[32] While some biographers have dismissed the notion that Brown's raid was hastened by external circumstances, Anderson's account states that concern over being discovered was real, and nearly came to a head just days after Kagi's report, a claim that Owen Brown also affirmed in retrospect.[33]

According to Anderson, suspicion about the goings-on at the Kennedy farm had ripened and there were murmurs in the neighborhood about an imminent investigation. Anderson attributed this suspicion to the impatience and carelessness among the men, something that is also verified by Anne Brown Adams. However, his testimony has been undervalued by historians even though it is a firsthand account. Anderson claimed to have been informed by a "tried friend" (perhaps a local slave) that the neighborhood was buzzing about Isaac Smith's "encampment," and some were even threatening to "search the premises." Over in Chambersburg, Kagi could not have been aware of this issue, particularly since it worsened after his last report on October 10.

Whether or not the date of October 16 had already been set by Brown for the start of the raid, it seems clear that he could not have waited much longer to make his move because the whole operation was in danger of being exposed.[34] However, Anderson adds that the federal government was preparing to move "several thousand stand of arms" from the arsenal "to some other point." This overlooked detail is important for a number of reasons. First, Anderson does not mention it as a reason for Brown to hasten his plans, but rather to provide a fuller sense of local anxieties heightened by news that the government itself was removing large holdings from the arsenal.[35]

Second, news of federal arms being moved from the arsenal to other points—probably south—would not have surprised John Brown, who already was aware of this inclination among proslavery leaders in the government. In early 1859, Brown told the journalist William Phillips that "a war was at that very moment contemplated in the cabinet of President Buchanan," and that the military "had been carefully arranged, as far as it could be on the basis of Southern power," including the best concentration of arms and troops in the favor of the South.[36] In late 1855, Brown could not have overlooked how proslavery forces had sacked a federal arsenal at Liberty, Missouri, and were never held accountable either by the Pierce or Buchanan administrations. Indeed, it was this proslavery violation that likely prompted Brown to make a preliminary "demonstration" (as he later called it) at the Harper's Ferry armory in commencing his intended south-wide liberation movement.[37]

Finally, the notion of the arms being removed by the government may have resonance in the false claim that Brown himself wanted to seize the Harper's Ferry weapons. In fact, this notion has become a mainstay for most narrators on the raid, from tour guides to scholars, even though it lacks historical warrant and is flatly contradicted by the evidence. The claim that John Brown wanted to seize federal arms is found in a few testimonies given after the fact, but more likely reflect the determination of slaveholders to cast Brown as a rank insurrectionist—something vital to Virginia's case against him in 1859, as well as the Senate investigation determinedly conducted by Virginia senator James Mason in early 1860.[38]

Brown himself made no mention of wanting the Harper's Ferry weapons before the raid, and in two important interviews with the *New York Daily Tribune* and *New York Times* after his arrest, he explicitly denied an interest in the weapons, pointing out that his Sharps repeating rifles actually were superior to the guns produced at Harper's Ferry.[39] Furthermore, there is not the slightest evidence that Brown tried to remove the weapons or even provided means to transport them from Harper's Ferry.[40] To the contrary, he brought only a small wagon filled with pikes and other useful implements to Harper's Ferry, and then posted guards at the arsenal entrance, apparently to keep Virginians from gaining access to them.[41]

In retrospect, Anderson's important observation suggests that notwithstanding their propaganda about loyal slaves, slaveholding societies in the South were fixated on weapons for their perceived survival against dreaded slave insurrections, and their anxiety over guns probably was projected upon Brown after the fact. As Edward House, the undercover correspondent of the *New York Daily Tribune*, observed at the time, Virginians were "forever handling" guns—the fixation of a people whose entire sense of security as slaveholders was based upon firearms. No wonder, as Anderson concluded, that "the fears of the neighbors" played a greater role in hastening on Brown to Harper's Ferry than any other factor.[42]

A Voice from Harper's Ferry merits recognition as a central source for studying the raid, but like any historical record, Anderson's account cannot be used uncritically. Although he was a participant in the raid, his account not only is based upon his own eyewitness, but also includes what he learned during the episode from others, and that which he gleaned from newspaper sources afterward. Quite certainly he had access to fellow raider John Cook's "Confession," which was published in the *New York Daily Tribune* in late November 1859,

after Anderson had escaped to Canada.[43] Clearly, in recounting
John Brown's "final charge" to his men on the evening of the attack,
Anderson included Cook's account even though he was himself an
eyewitness to the scene:

> And now, gentlemen, let me impress this one thing on your minds.
> You all know how dear life is to you, and how dear your lives are to
> your friends. And in remembering that, consider that the lives of oth-
> ers are as dear to them as yours are to you. Do not, therefore, take the
> life of any one, if you can possibly avoid it; but if it is necessary to take
> life in order to save your own, then make sure work of it.[44]

Anderson's succinct account provides an outline of Brown's plan to
seize the town and armory at Harper's Ferry: telegraph lines on both
the Virginia and Maryland sides were to be cut; several raiders were
assigned to seize both the Potomac and Shenandoah bridges and
hold the civilian night watchmen without violence if possible; and
the armory fire engine house (with an adjoining guard house) near
the entrance was to be seized and occupied until other buildings were
taken. Men were then stationed to guard the arsenal building and
the rifle factory throughout the occupation.[45] These first steps were
easily accomplished, placing John Brown in control of Harper's Ferry
and disproving the notion that the site was necessarily a "steel trap."
Both Brown and Cook had rightly concluded that a nighttime assault
would exploit the element of surprise and the lack of an adequate
guard, enabling a small number of men to take control of both town
and armory and attract a body of enslaved people to their ranks. A
short occupation and demonstration would have ensured that Brown,
his men, the first recruits of enslaved men, and their hostages would
have had access to escape routes.

However, the entire plan turned upon one hinge, the time factor.
In other words, had John Brown and his men entered Harper's Ferry

late on Sunday evening, October 16, and departed town within five or six hours, the Virginians would have been left dazed and defeated. Alexander Boteler, a congressman who witnessed the immediate aftermath of the raid and interviewed Brown as a prisoner, later acknowledged that had Brown gotten into the mountains, "there is no telling how extensive that raid might have been. Unquestionably a certain proportion of the slaves would have run away."[46]

With the town and armory under his control, Brown sent Aaron Stevens to proceed to the suburbs of Harper's Ferry to seize slaveholders and bring them into town, intentionally placing them into the hands of Osborne Anderson. Brown's purpose in doing this was clear, Anderson recalled, since he was black, "and colored men being only *things* in the South," it was only "proper that the South be taught a lesson upon this point." Along with charging Anderson to receive the arms of the slaveholder Lewis Washington, Stevens also selected John Cook, Charles Tidd, Lewis Leary, and Shields Green to take prisoners and enlist "any slaves who would come" with them to Harper's Ferry.[47]

Anderson writes that when they met "some colored men" on the road and informed them of their mission, they "immediately" agreed to join them. Their enthusiasm was clear, Anderson writes, and some of them said "they had been long waiting for an opportunity of the kind." Stevens then asked them to spread the news "among the colored people," and by this "many colored men gathered to the scene of action." After the arrest of slaveholder Lewis Washington, Stevens dispatched Green, Leary, and Tidd to the slave quarters, and afterward they went to the residence of John Allstadt, taking the slaveholder hostage and likewise gathering up his enslaved people "by their own consent." Anderson was clear that despite the hesitancy and unreliability of several free blacks they had encountered, Brown actually was "surprised and pleased by the promptitude" with which local blacks had volunteered, "and with their manly bearing at the scene of violence." As Anderson recalled, after their hasty work throughout Sunday night to alert the slaves, Brown remarked that he was quite taken by the enthusiastic response they had shown. The Old Man himself had not expected more than "one out of ten to be willing to fight."[48]

Understandably, then, Anderson was outraged by the propaganda of slaveholders after the raid, which he described as "a studied attempt to enforce the belief that the slaves were cowardly, and that they were really more in favor of Virginia masters and slavery, than of their freedom."[49] Shortly after Brown's hanging, Virginia governor Henry Wise announced that there was "no danger from our slaves or colored people," and all the black men who had followed Brown actually were "taken" by force, yet even then they "refused to take arms." It was not so much that their slaves had chosen to flee, he contended, but rather that they had been stolen by Northern abolitionists. "They prefer to remain," Wise concluded."[50] Indeed, the propaganda of slave loyalty was rife during the trials of the raiders, and ultimately found its chief expression in the report of the Senate committee led by Virginia senator James Mason, the premise of which was that Brown had failed solely because of "the loyalty and well-affected disposition of the slaves."[51] Even the slaveholder Robert E. Lee, who led the final assault on Brown in the engine house, afterward infused false claims of slave loyalty into his official report.[52] Ironically, however, if anyone did more to enshrine the fallacy of slave loyalty at Harper's Ferry, perhaps it was Abraham Lincoln, who accepted the conclusions of the Mason Report, decrying only the suggestion of Republican complicity in the raid. In his famous 1860 Cooper Union address, candidate Lincoln sought to exonerate his party, but dismissed "John Brown's effort" as "an attempt by white men to get up a revolt among slaves, in which the slaves refused to participate."[53]

Quite to the contrary, Anderson argued, when the raiders stopped at the plantations on Sunday night, "the greatest enthusiasm was

manifested by them—joy and hilarity beamed from every countenance." At the slave quarters, "there was apparently a general jubilee,
and they stepped forward manfully, without impressing or coaxing."
Anderson wrote that many of the colored men living in the neighborhood had assembled in the town, and many of them were armed.
One elderly slave, who had been given a shotgun and buckshot,
had even killed a prisoner when he refused to halt. Anderson thus
countered that if anyone had proven cowardly it was the panicked
Virginians—especially the hostage slaveholders, who broke down
into tears, "blubbering" pitifully.[54]

Some writers have mistakenly presumed that John Brown expected to rally hordes of slaves at the onset—a notion quite in keeping with the propaganda of the slaveholders, most notably expressed
in the official state record of Virginia. As Governor Wise proclaimed,
Brown had intended to place the arsenal weapons into the willing
hands of thousands of enslaved people. "The slaves were not to be
taken to be carried away, but they were to be made to stand by the
side of the robbers, and to be forced to fight to liberate themselves
by massacring their masters," Wise declared. Despite evidence to the
contrary, Wise proclaimed that the arsenal "was taken to supply arms
to servile insurgents . . . for the purpose of stirring up universal insurrection of slaves throughout the whole south."[55]

On the other hand, some have argued likewise incorrectly that
Brown barely alerted local enslaved people "either before or during
the attack."[56] But as Osborne Anderson attests, enslaved people in the
vicinity of the raid were adequately notified. Even setting aside claims
of Brown's interactions with certain free blacks and slaves in advance,
the abolitionist leader was confident that scores would quickly mul-
tiply into hundreds with the progress of the movement. In writing
about the Denmark Vesey conspiracy of 1822, Douglas Egerton has
discerned a similarity in John Brown's methods, and it is quite likely
that this is because the Old Man himself had made careful study of

the South Carolina liberator. Quoting Denmark Vesey in words that could just as easily have been those of John Brown, Egerton writes: "it was foolhardy to spread the word too widely. 'Let us assemble a sufficient number to commence the work with spirit, and we'll not want men, [as] they'll fall in behind us fast enough.'"[57]

Of course, quite famously, one black man in Harper's Ferry was dead set against being rescued by John Brown. Heyward Shepherd was the free black porter at the Harper's Ferry train station. Shepherd's reputation as a free black man in Virginia evidently was underwritten by a respected white ally, the town mayor, Fontaine Beckham.[58] The popular black porter was the antithesis of Shields Green—a strong black man whose loyalties lay with the slaveholding society that had granted him exceptionalism, property ownership, and a well-paying job. In an episode often cited by writers as a tragic irony, Shepherd was stopped by Brown's men and repeatedly warned to stay in his place after refusing their offer of liberation. Instead, he resisted, fuming and cursing the raiders, and despite repeated warnings, finally attempted to slip across the bridge to alert sleeping whites in Maryland. Upon seeing Shepherd's attempt at escape, one of the raiders raised his rifle and shot him, the bullet piercing his back and exiting from his chest. Shepherd struggled and finally died the following day, giving slaveholders and their segregationist heirs their first and perhaps only black martyr.[59]

Contrary to what both white and black writers have made of this episode, there actually was no great irony in the case of Heyward Shepherd, only in the man himself.[60] He had embraced money and exceptionalism to live amidst his people's suffering, even to the point of dying for those who kept them enslaved. Osborne Anderson was not present during the incident, but he learned from his comrades that Shepherd had been ordered to stop on the bridge, and having refused to do so, turned to go in an opposite direction. It was then that he was fired upon "and received a mortal wound." As Anderson considered the episode, Heyward Shepherd was "one foolhardy colored man."[61]

About the time that the black porter died the next day, neither Brown nor his men knew that a local doctor had become aware that something was wrong in town. Lewis Starry began to watch Brown's men and went so far as to speak with some of them, and afterward rode to the county seat of Charlestown around seven o'clock in the morning. Had the raiders known of Starry's subterfuge, his arrest would have bought them more time. But the doctor eluded suspicion and fled on horseback from town, and by mid-morning on Monday some local militia were making the eight-mile trek from Charlestown to Harper's Ferry.[62]

Despite Starry's role, however, it was John Brown's own decisions during the night that proved the most detrimental. First, when the temperature dropped to bitter cold, Brown suddenly abandoned the strategic position he had chosen at the Potomac bridge and moved his hostages to the armory engine house, where he started a fire to keep them warm.[63] Besides placing himself in this disadvantaged position, Brown then overestimated his ability to conduct a formal exchange of hostages for enslaved men—actually a needless formality that appeased his sense of propriety but proved yet another snare. Surrendering his strategic place at the bridge was perhaps his worst decision, since it had afforded the best route of escape if circumstances turned against him and his men. Placing himself within the armory grounds was a gross tactical error that sacrificed strategy to sentiment and ultimately cost the lives of Brown, most of his men, and an undetermined number of slave enlistees.[64]

Anderson shows that Brown's tactical judgment began to disintegrate at the very time when he needed to tighten the operation, gather his forces, and seek the advantage of the nearby mountains. By early Monday morning, panic was spreading in town "like wildfire," with men, women, and children running to their neighbors, their faces showing "sudden fear." Brown, whose own sons knew him to be ponderous to a fault, was increasingly caught between the expedience of the plan and the panic and tears of the Virginians, especially the captive hostage slaveholders with whom he was attempting to negotiate. Anderson recalled seeing Brown, describing him as "all activity" but "somewhat puzzled." After sunrise, Brown made another bad decision, permitting a train that had been held throughout the night at Harper's Ferry to move eastward.[65] But this was not merely a bad decision; it was also a demonstration that Brown had been overcome by the fears of the Virginians. In this awkward exhibition of double-mindedness, during the night Brown not only assured the train conductor of a safe departure, but even walked partway alongside the train as it moved cautiously across the bridge.[66] Then, to assuage some of the most pitiful of the weeping hostages, Brown granted them armed escorts to visit their loved ones.[67] These incredible allowances were hardly the actions of a terrorist. Indeed, as Brown's men understandably grew restless and concerned about overstaying in town, he dug in his heels, determined to conclude his parleying with the hostages as if he were a persistent statesman locked in negotiation rather than an abolitionist liberator. "Hold on a little longer, boys until I get matters arranged with the prisoners," Brown appealed.[68]

Lost to his own determination to carry out a negotiated exchange of hostages for slaves, and determined to show sympathy to the terrified Virginians, Brown thus passed the point of making a safe exit from Harper's Ferry by late Monday morning. "This tardiness on the part of our brave leader," Anderson recalled, "was sensibly felt to be an omen of evil by some [of] us, and was eventually the cause of our defeat." Anderson states that Brown's delays were "no part of the original plan to hold on to the Ferry, or to parley with prisoners," and by doing so his leader had created both the time and means of spreading word and rallying the forces that "surrounded us."[69]

The first real attack upon the raiders took place at about noon, when the Jefferson Guard, a militia group comprised of about one hundred untested fighters, attempted to push their way into town across the Potomac bridge from the Maryland side. The conventional narrative portrays the Jefferson Guard as easily pushing Brown's men back from the bridge and rushing into town, but this was the version of the story as told by the triumphant Virginians.[70] According to Anderson, however, the Jefferson Guard came across the bridge in "single martial column," not seeming to realize that they were going into combat, and "evidently expected we would be driven out by them without firing." Anderson says that Brown rallied his men from other posts, saying, "The troops are on the bridge, coming into town; we will give them a warm reception." Walking among his men, Brown advised them to remain cool and not waste their ammunition. "Take aim, and make every shot count!" he admonished. "The troops will look for us to retreat on their first appearance; be careful to shoot first." As Anderson recalled, the raiders then administered a crippling counterattack upon the panicked militia, wounding and killing several of them, and causing them to scatter in consternation, many of them falling back onto the bridge for cover.[71] As Robert McGlone states, up to the arrival of the Jefferson Guard, John Brown "could easily have fought his way out of Harpers Ferry and back into Maryland."[72] However, had he rallied his men *and* been willing to expose his hostages to danger, Brown and his raiders might at the last minute have intimidated the militia sufficiently to pull back from the bridge and open a way back into Maryland. Instead, he pulled back his men and shielded his prisoners, thus positioning himself for overwhelming defeat. Oswald Villard was at least correct in concluding that although Brown "kept perfectly cool and clear-headed," in this moment he "proved incapable of attempting anything aggressive" and "let slip the golden hours when escape was possible."[73]

According to Anderson, as they returned to their posts, the raider Dangerfield Newby fell under the sights of a sniper watching from a nearby building. Newby, an emancipated man with a white father, had joined Brown's raiders after all hope of purchasing his wife and children out of slavery were dashed.[74] Many narratives say that Newby was killed by a single sniper shot, but Anderson says that he was hit first by a shot that brought him to the ground. This is at least verified by another eyewitness narrative, which says that Newby was shot in the stomach.[75] Lying on his side, Newby tried to return fire but was already under the sights of another hostile, a sniper poised to shoot from a nearby window. The shooter had loaded his rifle with some sort of projectile in lieu of a minié ball, and the shot tore into Newby's upper neck, killing him instantly.[76] Afterward, some of the outraged Virginians demonstrated the extent of their depraved contempt for the black raider. Milling around Newby's body with grim delight, some began to dismember him, "slicing off his ears and cutting them into pieces as souvenirs."[77]

Despite the tragic death of Newby, the raiders had not yet seen the worst of it. There was yet "comparative quiet for a time," although the aroused citizenry was even more frenzied, "wild with terror," on the margins of town, some even scaling the mountains and climbing hillsides in fear. It was at this time that William Thompson, one of the raiders, was captured.[78] In the meantime, John Henrie Kagi had sent word from the rifle factory, urging Brown not to delay any longer lest they be overpowered. Brown, whose business was not yet satisfactorily conducted, sent a message back, telling Kagi to hold out a few minutes longer. This "proved disastrous," Anderson recalled.[79]

By noon, when the counterattack upon the raiders grew more intense, Brown and his men already were inside the engine house, but now were incapable of escaping without drawing fire. Realizing that circumstances had completely turned against him, Brown sent out flags of truce in the hands of his son Watson and Aaron Stevens,

apparently believing that the Virginians would respond to his representatives like a foe on the field. Instead, both men were treated as
contemptible insurrectionists and immediately fired upon, Watson
being mortally wounded and Stevens nearly so.[80]

It was now Monday afternoon and Brown's men faced the peril
created by their leader's needless delay. As heavy fire was exchanged
between the raiders inside the engine house and the Virginians outside, the town's mayor, Fontaine Beckham, carelessly placed himself
in sight of Brown's men and almost instantly was shot and killed.
In retaliation, two outraged citizens dragged the captured William
Thompson outside and shot him to death. Another raider, the young
William Leeman, was caught venturing out into the water while trying to make his escape. He was murdered outright by another armed
citizen, the killer's pistol placed at his head as he pleaded for his life.
Drunken, angry Virginians then used his remains for target practice,
leaving Leeman's bullet-riddled body sprawled out on a small islet for
hours. "This outrageous burlesque upon civilized warfare must have
a special chapter to itself," Anderson bemoaned, "as it concentrates
more of Southern littleness and cowardice than is often believed to
be true."[81]

If one episode reflects both the littleness and cowardice of the
Virginians, it is in the death of raider Lewis Leary, one of the black
enlistees from Oberlin. According to Anderson, Leary had been
sent with several other men to the rifle factory to support Kagi and
Copeland. However, with the arrival of an overwhelming force of
armed opponents, all of the men at the rifle factory were killed
except Copeland, who was captured and shown mercy only because
of the intervention of the same doctor Lewis Starry.[82] According
to the conventional narrative, Leary was mortally wounded during the fighting and eventually died from his wounds and, in the
words of Villard, was "in no wise molested."[83] Likewise, according
to Meyer, Leary was mortally wounded and carried into a nearby

cooper's shop, where he begged his enemies to write to his wife in Oberlin, his life slowly ebbing away for more than ten hours. "Reporters were among those witnessing his slow death," Meyer concludes. Unfortunately, in describing Leary's slow, painful death, Villard uncritically depended upon the testimony of Virginians, and Meyer provides no source at all.[84]

Certainly, even a basic familiarity with the outrageous behavior of the townsmen toward the raiders might leave one skeptical as to the notion that Leary, a wounded black man, was simply left aside for hours until he died. In fact, an early report in the *Baltimore Daily Exchange* reveals a more gruesome fate for the black Ohioan. According to a firsthand account, two men were seized alive from the Shenandoah River after being driven by a heavy force from the rifle works, their other comrades either being drowned or shot dead by the Charlestown Guards. One man was taken unharmed—clearly John Copeland, and another, an unidentified "mulatto" of about twenty-five years of age, was brought in wounded—this undoubtedly being Lewis Leary. The informant said that he propped up the wounded raider on his arm in an attempt to question him, but that the "mulatto" could barely speak, his "large eye" rolling and his head shaking. Suddenly, as the informant was questioning Leary, a white woman nearby "came up and struck him a blow in the face." Then another "one of the infuriated citizens" suddenly "came up and snatched the dying man from his arms, and with one gash of a knife cut his throat from ear to ear."[85] According to Richard Hinton, who was not always reliable as to detail, Leary's body was afterward abused and left to rot in the Shenandoah River, although it may have fallen prey to the rapaciousness of local medical students.[86] Osborne Anderson probably was never made aware of this deplorable scene because no other paper in Virginia or Maryland picked up the informant's account, while the slaveholder's tale of Leary's long, painful death has become part of the official record of the raid. That record, first presented in newspapers with reports skewed in favor of the slaveholder, was then officialized in a senatorial investigation report, and finally in various historical narratives. Anderson was not exaggerating when he wrote, "Much has been given as true that never happened, much has been omitted that should have been made known."[87]

The black witness of Osborne Anderson is both provocative and problematic, and doubtless for both reasons it has been too easily set aside by historians. It is provocative because Anderson, while the raid was yet a recent event, not only attacked the nobility and bravery of the slaveholding class, but also suggested that the Virginians had intentionally minimized the reported number of their fatalities at Brown's hands.[88] "Volley upon volley was discharged, and the echoes from the hills, the shrieks of the townspeople, and the groans of their wounded and dying, all of which filled the air, were truly frightful," Anderson writes. "The Virginians may well conceal their losses, and Southern chivalry may hide its brazen head, for their boasted bravery was well tested that day, and in no way to their advantage." Anderson claimed, at the time of writing, that only the funeral of the free black man Heyward Shepherd had been reported in the newspapers. "Had they reported the true number," he concluded, "their disgrace would have been more apparent."[89] In fact, the deaths of Mayor Beckham and two other citizens of Harper's Ferry were acknowledged in the report of the Senate investigation led by Virginia's senator James Mason, so Anderson was not entirely correct. However, the Mason Report portrayed two of the casualties, Thomas Boerly and George Turner, as noncombatants when in reality they were gunning for Brown's men at the time they were killed.[90]

Yet Anderson's concerns were not without basis, even if he was writing from the limitations of his perspective. "All this time, the fight was progressing; no powder and ball were wasted," he recalled. "We shot from under cover and took deadly aim. For an hour before the flag of truce was sent out, the firing was uninterrupted, and one and another of the enemy were constantly dropping to the earth."[91] Given the extent of the shooting that took place and the presence of many combatants, it was not unreasonable for Anderson to suppose that the list of mortally wounded was larger than commonly reported. According to a militia commander's report made to Governor Henry Wise shortly afterward, Brown's raiders had wounded ten combatants, some of them quite seriously, and killed two others.[92] Even the definitive lists published in popular histories today may not be the last word.[93] Certainly, the number of enslaved people who actually supported Brown, and the number of them who were afterward murdered, will never be known with certainty due to the self-interested claims of Southern leaders, slaveholders, and journalists. Indeed, the received version of the raid is so deeply embedded in our national memory that some highly problematic notions are still advanced without question in public forums.[94]

On the other hand, for all of its important insights, Anderson's narrative is hardly without errors and problems, particularly where he endeavors to speak beyond his own firsthand knowledge. For instance, Anderson quite erroneously states that raider Jerry Anderson was mortally wounded under fire and died "speedily" after he returned to the engine house, although in fact he was mortally wounded by the United States marines on the morning of October 18.[95] Yet errors in detail are not the greatest problem with Anderson's account, nor the basis of its easy dismissal by historians. In 1910 Oswald Villard thus complained that the central problem of *A Voice from Harper's Ferry* was its "misleading and exaggerated account" relating to Anderson's own claim that before escaping, he had witnessed the final marine assault on the Harper's Ferry engine house on Tuesday morning, October 18.[96] "Having captured our commander," Anderson wrote, "we knew that it was but little two of us could do against so many, and that our turn to be taken must come; so Hazlett and I went out at the back part of the [arsenal] building, climbed up the wall, and went upon the railway."[97] As Villard recognized, it was impossible for Anderson and Hazlett to have lasted in Harper's Ferry until Tuesday morning, let alone to have escaped unharmed after the invasion of the marines. To the contrary, Anderson had clearly escaped on Monday afternoon, October 17, a good many hours before the marines had even arrived at Harper's Ferry.[98] For this gross error, Villard presumed that Osborne Anderson's account was to be discarded as unreliable, a judgment that he seems to have bequeathed to other writers in the twentieth century.

However, had Villard been less inclined to brush aside the black witness,[99] perhaps he might have seen that the problem with Anderson's claim was only a confusion of what he had seen with what he had read about after the fact. Villard was correct that Anderson and Hazlett could not have witnessed the storming of the engine house by the marines, but Anderson very likely saw things from a distance that he associated with reports that he read about afterward. As Jean Libby has observed, on Monday afternoon the first militia group to push toward the raiders were the Jefferson Guard, whose uniforms were blue.[100] Another possibility is that Anderson had witnessed a group of Baltimore & Ohio Railroad men and other volunteers from Martinsburg, who attempted to storm the engine house on Monday afternoon using a ladder as a battering ram. Their attack was repelled by Brown and his raiders inside, who shot and killed two of the railroad men and seriously wounded eight others.[101] In light of these movements against the engine house, it was entirely reasonable for Anderson to assume that he had glimpsed the final marine assault on John Brown and his men inside the engine house. Responding to critics who afterward said that he had abandoned his leader at Harper's Ferry, Anderson wrote that they had never left their position until they saw, "with feelings of intense sadness, that we could be of no further avail to our commander" and "concluded it was better to retreat while it was possible." In his own defense, Anderson concluded that it was well enough for others "to talk flippantly about cowardice, and to sit in judgment upon the men who went with John Brown . . . but to have been there, fought there, and to understand what *did* transpire there, are quite different."[102]

But what of John Brown? How did Osborne Anderson explain his leader's failures, and what was his judgment for history? First, Anderson is clear that the catastrophe at Harper's Ferry was due not to a supposedly hopeless or suicidal plan on Brown's part, but rather to his inability to "[steel] his heart against the entreaties of his captives, or shut up the fountain of his sympathies against their families." If John Brown would have set aside his concerns for his opponents in favor of "adhering to the original plan" and "thus looked forward to the prospective freedom of the slave—hundreds ready and waiting would have been armed before twenty-four hours had elapsed." There was no doubt in Osborne Anderson's mind that John Brown's purpose at Harper's Ferry would have been both successful and eventful in history had "the noble old man" simply followed through on his own plan. Instead, he had become entangled in his own personal dilemma—not the lack of support shown by the slaves as many have supposed, but the same powerful ethic that had brought him to Virginia in the first place. As it turned out, for John Brown, Harper's Ferry had proven not so much a trap made of steel, but one of irony. His biblical devotion to the Golden Rule and the mandate to "remember them that are in bonds" brought him to Virginia, but the command to "love your enemy" had defeated him. Some historians have missed this explanation altogether. Others have dismissed it as unbelievable, preferring explanations of their own contrivance, such as the notion that Brown was following some secret plan that entailed martyrdom. But these cynical readings of the raid generally rest on speculative theories that raise more questions than they answer, and which also presume that Brown was untruthful and quixotic, even though afterward he repeatedly attributed his failure to his own fixations upon propriety in negotiation and sympathy for his prisoners.[103]

Despite this failure, however, Anderson believed that the judgment of Brown in history would be that his "mistakes were productive of great good, the fact of which the future historian will record, without the embarrassment attending its present narration. John Brown did not only capture and hold Harper's Ferry for twenty hours," Anderson concluded, "but he held the whole South." As to Shields Green, it was clear from Anderson's narrative that he was one of Brown's most loyal supporters and that he was a bold fighter, "the Zouave of the band."[104]

5

Alias Emperor

"Here, baby," he said to the child, handing her the
colorful fan stick before walking on to the jail.

O N Monday morning, Thomas Boerly, "a large and combative
man," attacked the raiders, blasting a shotgun at them as
they stood guard at the armory gates. In return, Boerly was
hit in the abdomen and bled out that afternoon. About the time of
Boerly's death, George Turner rode into town with the intention of
attacking the raiders, and positioned himself to pick off Brown's men
near a building on High Street, a main thoroughfare that ran above the
armory grounds.[1] But before he could pull the trigger, the slaveholder
was shot dead, as Anderson put it, "by one of the insurgents."[2]

Given the lack of conclusive information, historians have been
understandably hesitant to suggest which of the raiders shot the reported Virginians who were killed on Monday, October 16. A number
of narratives published in the late nineteenth and early twentieth
centuries put forth names, the best of them stating that Dangerfield
Newby shot both the belligerent tavern keeper Thomas Boerly and
the slaveholder George Turner, or that at least Newby had killed
Turner.[3] However, another self-identified eyewitness, the clergyman
Samuel Leech, claimed that Shields Green was the raider who had
killed Boerly.[4] Interestingly, the reporter "J.T.," who revealed that
Green was freeborn after interviewing him in late November 1859,
also wrote that he was charged with killing Turner. In response to
the charge, Green denied bearing any arms whatsoever, probably in

the hopes of winning clemency. But the writer concluded that "the fact is established otherwise."[5] What "J.T." meant here remains unclear, given the absence of trial transcripts and the general disinterest on the part of the press in covering the case of Shields Green. But whether or not Green killed George Turner, there is no reason to trust the flimsy claim made afterward that the latter was merely a noncombatant who had been handed a gun to protect himself.[6] To the contrary, the purported victim was an aggressive slaveholder, the kind that John Brown had previously battled in the Kansas territory.

George Turner was a Seminole War veteran and a graduate of West Point. Based upon the slave census for 1860, it appears that the forty-eight-year-old bachelor had six enslaved people at the time of his death. The eldest among them was a twenty-year-old female, and the youngest a three-year-old "mulatto,"[7] perhaps mother and child—and the latter perhaps also Turner's child by rape, a practice all too common in slaveholding households. Turner's enslaved people may have been relieved if not delighted by the news of his death, especially given his reputation as an abusive master. One source claims that Turner murdered one of his slaves and threw the body down a well.[8] Unfortunately, his death could only provide temporary respite because his slaves were shortly passed into the estate of his slaveholding brother, William Turner.[9] On the other hand, the Turner slaves, perhaps disappointed in the failure of Brown's invasion, may have taken action on their own. On the day of Brown's hanging or shortly afterward, the late master's estate was all but burned down, the flames then spreading to the property of William Turner. Frantic over the fire, Turner complained that a number of his horses and sheep had also died quite suddenly, and that he suspected they had been poisoned. While mysterious fires and livestock losses plagued other slaveholders at the time of Brown's execution, the Turner incidents may have been acts of retaliation as much as they were expressions of resistance prompted by the raid.[10]

Following the Turner shooting, however, events rapidly changed for the worst, beginning with the shooting of raider Dangerfield Newby. According to both Congressman Alexander Boteler and the Methodist minister Samuel Leech, a man named Bogert had taken a secret position at the window in a neighbor's home, but having no ammunition had loaded his rifle with a six-inch iron nail. Bogert took aim and fired at Newby, who already had been hit by another gunman and had fallen on the ground.[11] Boteler recalled that he had never seen a more hideous sight than Newby's corpse, his upper neck having been cut open "from ear to ear" by the projectile.[12] Osborne Anderson writes that in response to this ruthless act, Shields Green spotted the assassin and immediately fired back at him with his Sharps rifle, avenging Newby's death.[13] Green probably fired back at the sniper, but there is no evidence that his bullet found its mark.

* * *

As Robert McGlone observes, although Harper's Ferry was filled with militia by Monday afternoon, "every window, doorway, and rooftop commanding a view of the engine house harbored men firing as they pleased." As dusk approached, many had become drunken, whooping vigilantes, shooting their guns in the air or at the engine house.[14] Now, as the raiders were surrounded by hundreds of militia and subject to the constant and deadly harassment from armed, "reckless," and "half-civilized hordes," it was only a matter of time before they were defeated.[15]

Somewhat pitifully, Brown now began to try to negotiate with the surrounding forces in the hopes of gaining access to the Potomac bridge for his men and their prisoners, a route to which he had held easy access throughout the previous night and well into the morning. Sending along one of the hostages as a show of good faith, Brown conveyed a demand for access to the bridge to Captain Robert Baylor, one of the militia commanders. Baylor replied that if Brown handed over their citizens, "we will leave the Government to deal with you concerning their property as it may think most advisable." McGlone mistakenly concludes that in speaking of "government property," Brown was referring to the arsenal weapons.[16] But Brown clearly understood Baylor's intent: the local militia were only interested in rescuing their citizens, and had neither an interest in nor the authority to negotiate the consequences of his having seized the armory, which was a federal site. The Old Man and his raiders had not seized weapons, except to occupy the arsenal and guard it from entry, and the weapons themselves were not the point of concern for either Baylor or Brown.

Brown then replied that he wanted all of his men, at which point he would conduct them and the prisoners across the Potomac bridge into Maryland. Only after this was granted, he countered, would he "negotiate about the government property." Clearly, Brown wished only to regain some advantage by getting his party back across the bridge into Maryland. What made his reply even more notable is that he asked more of Baylor the second time than he had in his initial demand: he wanted *all* of his men—living, wounded, and dead, along with all of their own weapons, munitions, and even his horse and harness.[17] Brown's audacious demand suggests that he was hoping that his hostages would give him more leverage than he had in actuality, since the Virginians had no intention of letting him cross back over into Maryland. According to one of his hostages, these exchanges with Baylor continued throughout the rest of the day and into the night and "many propositions *pro* and *con* were made, looking to Brown's surrender and the release of the prisoners, but without result."[18]

At about one o'clock on Tuesday morning, October 18, a contingent of marines arrived, dispatched from Washington, D.C., by orders of President James Buchanan. Although the marines were led by one of their own, Lieutenant Israel Green, the president also sent Brevet Colonel Robert E. Lee and First Lieutenant J. E. B. Stuart directly from the capital to assume command. At first, Lee was of the mind to make an immediate attack upon the raiders, but then reconsidered out of concern for the hostages. Instead, he ordered that at dawn, if the demand for Brown's surrender was rejected, some picked men would storm the engine house, using bayonets to kill the raiders.

Sometime after seven o'clock in the morning, Brown received Lee's demand requiring that he surrender and "restore the pillaged property," meaning the several enslaved men who had followed him into the engine house. When his demand was refused, Lee ordered the attack to commence, the marines at first trying to batter down the doors with heavy sledgehammers. This proved ineffective, however, because Brown had secured the doors of the engine house with ropes in a manner that allowed them to sway without yielding to the blows. The marines happened to see the long, heavy ladder in the yard that had been used the day before as a battering ram by the Baltimore & Ohio Railroad men in their failed attempt to storm the engine house.[19] After several tries with the ladder, the marines broke through a lower panel in one of the doors, at which point they fired a volley into the engine house, and then the first marines slipped through the breach.[20] Lee had ordered no shooting, so the initial volley may have been intended only as a distraction to give advantage to the first marines entering the building.

In fact, the volley was probably needless. The raiders had already diminished their fire or altogether ceased firing in the moments prior to the entrance of the marines. Lee thus recalled that during the final assault, firing from the raiders was "harmless."[21] This was likely due to the fact that inside the engine house there was some discussion going on among the raiders about surrendering, and Brown himself had even relented from firing in order to call out to the marines that one of his men was surrendering. After his defeat, Brown told his interrogators: "There had been loud and long calls of 'Surrender' from us—as loud as men could yell—but in the confusion and excitement I suppose we were not heard."[22] To some degree, Brown probably was being diplomatic, for it seems unlikely that the marines did not hear the men yelling from inside, and this probably also explains what immediately followed.

The first marine to enter through the breach was the paymaster, Major William Russell, who was carrying only a rattan cane, followed by Lieutenant Israel Green, who was unarmed except for a light dress sword. Whether or not it was marine protocol for officers to enter a scene of conflict without appropriate arms, it is understandable why Brown and his men did not immediately fire upon them. They had been appealing for surrender and the first two marines who entered were officers who were all but unarmed. The notion, for instance, that Brown was "fumbling with a carbine" is baseless and misses the point.[23] He insisted afterward that the marine attack upon him and his men in the engine house took place, as he put it, "after I had ceased fighting and had consented to surrender, for the benefit of others, not for my own." His interrogators refused to believe him, but the Old Man was not lying. He was quite clear that he could easily have shot the cane-wielding Russell when he first entered through the door. "I could have killed him just as easy as a mosquito when he came in," Brown said politely, "but I supposed he came in only to receive our surrender."[24] Afterward, when Russell himself visited Brown along with a reporter from the *Baltimore Daily Exchange*, the Old Man likewise told him: "I could have killed you, but I spared you." Had this not been true, Russell likely would have disagreed, but instead he bowed and thanked John Brown for having spared his life.[25] Over against the conventional notion of the raid, Brown's testimony makes sense. If the raiders were not in a posture of surrender, how could the first two marines have entered the engine house without being fired upon?[26]

Nevertheless, the marines had no notion of receiving John Brown's surrender, and the second to enter, Lieutenant Israel Green, was

specifically intent on killing the Old Man. Green was a native of
Vermont, an adopted son of the South, and an admirer of slaveholders like his friend Lewis Washington, one of Brown's hostages. No
doubt, these loyalties fueled his malice, for once he was through
the breach, the marine lieutenant sprang upon Brown—at first attempting to run him through with his dress sword, although the less
durable blade probably bent double against Brown's accouterments.
Green afterward cursed and lamented that he had not killed Brown,
something that amused J. E. B. Stuart in retrospect.[27] Gripping the
bent blade in his hand, Green then began to beat Brown over the
head, the Old Man falling backward, his scalp cut open and bleeding profusely. Unsatisfied with Brown's defeat, the wild-eyed marine
continued to beat on him in a murderous rage, something that has
been overlooked in the conventional telling of the episode.[28] Then, to
add barbarity to injury, another marine made a number of stabs into
Brown's prone body, perhaps only to ascertain whether he was dead
or alive, since none of the wounds were lethal. Afterward, looking
"grim and grizzly" with his bloodied scalp and face, Brown told his in-
terviewers: "These wounds were inflicted upon me—both sabre cuts
on my head and bayonet stabs in different parts of my body—some
minutes after I had ceased fighting."[29]

Along with Israel Green's attack upon Brown, the marines began
to come through the breach with bayonets drawn, the first being
killed by one of the raiders, and another wounded. It is not clear
who shot the marines. One of the hostages later testified that Brown
killed the marine, but two others contradict this in their testimonies,
and it is unlikely that he did so, being in a posture of surrender.[30] It is
more likely that the shots came from raider Edwin Coppic, who was
in a fighting posture and had discharged his weapon, notwithstanding some misfires.[31] In reaction—and quite against Lee's orders—the
marines outside began to fire in upon the raiders, giving the impression to some reporters that a battle was taking place, although the

struggle was all but over.[32] Probably due to panic and ambivalence, the two raiders closest to the breach, Jerry Anderson and Dauphin Thompson, were overwhelmed in the close conflict. Thompson was a young man with no combat experience and was the first to express a desire to surrender by laying down his rifle. Anderson followed him in laying down his weapon too, but when the marines burst in, their instinctive reaction was to take up their weapons again, although it is not certain whether they discharged them. Outraged at the sight of their fallen comrades, the marines viciously bayoneted both raiders and nearly attacked one of the hostages by mistake. Young Thompson was so run through that others nearby could hear his teeth gnashing in agony.[33] As Osborne Anderson concluded of the episode, the conduct of the marines at Harper's Ferry was "deserving of severest condemnation" as "one of those blood-thirsty occurrences, dark enough in depravity to disgrace a century."[34]

In the final moments, Shields Green already had surmised his fate as an armed black man facing an onslaught of uniformed white men acting at the behest of slaveholders. At the battering of the engine house doors, he quickly pulled off his hat and dropped his rifle, knife, and gun belt, and then quickly stood aside the several enslaved men in the engine house.[35] Knowing that the marines were charged with recovering the "property" of the slaveholders and divested of his weapons, Emperor rightly discerned that the marines would assume he was a slave upon first sight.

In his biography of Brown, Oswald Villard dismissed Emperor's maneuver as cowardly, citing the opinions of "several reliable prisoners in the engine house." Villard's reading—which privileged the perspective of the Virginians instead of Shields Green—was apropos of one whom David Levering Lewis has described as a "haughty" paternalist with a Southern wife who typically barred both black and Jewish visitors from their home.[36] Quite to the contrary, Emperor was no coward. Prior to entering the engine house with Brown, he had distinguished himself, according to Osborne Anderson, as the "Zouave of the band" and as "the most inexorable of all our party, a very Turco in his hatred against the stealers of men."[37] Outside the engine house and during the final struggle, Green had shown himself a warrior, firing his weapon "very rapidly and diligently."[38] His decision to lay down his weapons and blend in with the enslaved men in the engine house reflected the same alertness of mind and adeptness at self-preservation that he had shown when he and Owen Brown were threatened with discovery on their way to the Kennedy farm.

Similarly, Green showed the same "inexorable" nature toward the Virginians in the engine house that he had shown in answering back to whites on the road to Maryland. According to one narrative, he was "conscious of his own extra importance in the enterprise," something that Brown's hostages in the engine house probably found disturbing, Green being "a Negro of the blackest hue, small in stature, and very active in his movements."[39] The hostage Lewis Washington clearly resented Emperor's boldness, describing him as "rather impudent" in the way he had spoken to his white prisoners. His resentment was an aspect of the slaveholder's particular narcissism, as Steven Lubet observes, since he "was accustomed to enforced deference from black men" as a slaveholder. However, in a white supremacist culture, resentment toward self-confident, outspoken black men was an infectious problem among whites in general, especially in the South. As one Baltimore journalist thus described him, Shields Green was a "somewhat notorious character," meaning that his ample sense of dignity and self-assuredness as a man had offended their white racist sensibilities. In the engine house, Green had gone so far as to correct his white hostages while waving his rifle in their faces. "Shut that window, damn you," Emperor commanded. "Shut it instantly."[40]

To no surprise, even before the smoke had cleared, the slaveholder Lewis Washington made sure to point out Emperor to the marines.[41]

He was immediately hauled out and placed in the guard house, a separate office that adjoined the engine house. Edwin Coppic, who seems to have survived similarly by dropping his weapon at the last minute and standing with the white hostages, was also brought in unharmed.[42] Stretched out on a bench nearby was the mortally wounded Watson Brown, whose life was slowly ebbing away. By Tuesday morning, October 18, the armory grounds were thoroughly covered by journalists, including a number of Baltimore reporters who had come in on the train with the marines. Among them was Clifton Tayleure, a native South Carolinian who had witnessed the climax of the marine assault and even assisted John Brown "as he stumbled forward" out of the engine house and was stretched out nearby on the grass. After helping the Old Man, Tayleure wandered into the guard house, where he found Emperor, Edwin Coppic, and the suffering Watson Brown. Sympathetic to the latter, Tayleure brought him a cup of water and rolled up someone's pair of overalls as a pillow for the dying man. "What brought you here?" Tayleure asked young Brown. "Duty, Sir," he replied. Tayleure tried to interrogate him further but Watson put him off. "I am dying," he muttered. "I cannot discuss the question. I did my duty as I saw it."

Writing about this incident in 1879, Tayleure remembered the two forlorn raiders also looking on, attributing "perfect equanimity" to Edwin Coppic but "uncontrollable terror" to Shields Green. By that time, however, the South Carolinian had changed his opinion of John Brown, now believing that he "was an elected instrument for the commencement" of slavery's destruction. But although Tayleure had come to renounce slavery and reverence Brown, his memory of Shields Green was frozen in time—yet the product of a mind "deeply imbued with the political prejudices" of a racist, proslavery society.[43] To be sure, probably both Emperor and Coppic were frightened, for they—along with their wounded leader—were being threatened by angry mobs in Harper's Ferry that surely would have lynched them were they not protected by the same marines who had defeated them.[44] Still, there is a certain irony in the fact that Shields Green had fled from South Carolina and its flagrant white supremacy, only to be held captive within the memory of a white Carolinian who could only see black men either as docile, faithful servants or as cowering, fearful slaves.

* * *

The raiders were under guard at Harper's Ferry until the following day, when they were transported by train to the county seat of Charlestown, where they would receive a preliminary hearing, then a trial, and then await execution. The local jail was originally a large house, but it had been renovated to serve as both jail and jailer's residence. Often it was also used to hold enslaved people awaiting transport after being sold farther south.[45] The jailer, John Avis, was a veteran of the Mexican War and was by trade a shoemaker and had done well for his young family in attaining his new position. Avis, despite having been among the militia that had pushed back Brown's forces, was kindly toward the Old Man and his raiders as inmates in his jail.[46] Throughout his captivity, the abolitionist spoke highly of his jailer as a brave and noble man. Avis was doubtless a proslavery man, but he was no slaveholder, and he impressed Brown to the point that the Old Man wrote about him to a friend: "*The Jailor* (in whose charge I am) *& his family; & assistants* have all been most kind: & notwithstanding he was one of the bravest of all who *fought* me. . . . So far as my observation goes: *none but brave* men are likely to be *humane.*"[47] However, it is not clear whether Brown knew of Avis's side job, which was acting as an agent for the sale of slaves to buyers farther south. In fact, from the summer before the Harper's Ferry raid and well into the end of the year, Charlestown's brave jailer ran an advertisement in the local *Virginia Free Press* that read: "I have been authorized to buy for a gentleman's use on his own

Plantation 50 NEGROES. Persons having likely Negroes to dis-
pose of can get the highest cash price by calling on or addressing the
undersigned at the Charlestown jail."[48] Among the Virginians, jailer
Avis is the most kindly and sympathetic figure in the story of John
Brown's last days. However, his willingness as a "humane" Southerner
to participate in the theft of black labor, the trafficking of human
bodies, and the normalizing of black oppression only verified John
Brown's final analysis—that slavery would never end without "very
much bloodshed." To no surprise, then, when secession came in 1861,
John Brown's kindly jailer joined the slaveholders' rebellion.

After disembarking from the train, Brown and his men were escorted under guard to the jail, and their presence immediately drew
a gathering of curious townspeople. As the prisoners passed by one
house sitting close to the street, Emperor noticed a little white girl
standing on a box so that she could observe the spectacle along with
the adults. When his eyes suddenly fell on a "pretty broken fan stick"
lying on the road, he promptly stooped and picked it up with bound
hands. "Here, baby," he said to the child, handing her the colorful fan
stick before walking on to the jail. It was a peculiar moment—a show
of kindness that might very well have been captured in a painting to
be displayed aside Hovendon's *Last Moments of John Brown*, where
the Old Man is portrayed as kissing a black baby. However, the episode remained a private memory to the girl and her family for many
years, and only found its way into the record by chance of a single
interview in 1908—and then was forgotten in the archives for more
than a century.[49]

After spending several days in the Charlestown jail, Brown and his
men were led by the sheriff over to the courthouse on Tuesday morning, October 25, for a preliminary examination before a Magistrate's
Court, a unique feature of Virginia law. The local correspondent for the
proslavery *New York Herald* described "Old man Brown" and Edwin
Coppic being handcuffed together as they entered the courtroom,

followed by the badly wounded Aaron Stevens, who had to be held on his feet by others throughout the hearing. Last were "the two unmanacled blacks," John Copeland, described as "a bright mulatto, about 25 years of age," and Shields Green, "a dark negro, aged about 30."

The purpose of the Magistrate's Court was to determine whether a case would come to trial according to the determination of the seven presiding judges, all of whom were slaveholders. "In all," writes Brian McGinty, "the magistrates who were now to examine the charges against Brown owned 105 slaves."[50] No doubt, in this case it was a foregone conclusion that the raiders would go to trial, just as it was assumed that they would hang. But neither Brown nor his men were aware of this feature of Virginia law, nor had they yet been provided attorneys, so the Old Man concluded that the hearing was a pretext for immediate execution. "There are mitigating circumstances that I would urge in our favor if a fair trial is to be allowed us," he interjected. "But if we are to be forced with a mere form—a trial for execution—you might spare yourselves that trouble." His ill-informed protestations annoyed the Virginia correspondent, who concluded that Brown "cast a hasty and rather defiant look around him."[51]

Discerning the preliminary nature of the hearing, Brown was no less assured by the manner in which he was assigned two Virginia attorneys, one of whom actually declined the appointment. The attorney's demur worried Brown, for it seemed to him that the trial would yet prove a farce. "I wish to say that I have sent for counsel," Brown protested. "I wish for counsel if I am to have a trial; but if I am to have nothing but the mockery of a trial, . . . it is unnecessary to trouble any gentleman with that duty." At this point, an attorney for the state intervened, assuring Brown that he would have a fair trial. Brown responded that he was a stranger, did not know the character of the lawyers being discussed, and preferred to wait for his own lawyers to arrive, "if I am not, as I said before, to be hurried to execution before they can reach me." When the attorney insisted that he either accept or decline the court-appointed lawyers, Brown put him off, dismissing the examination and saying that he should have at least had an opportunity first to consult with the Virginia attorneys. Turning away from Brown, the state attorney then addressed each of the raiders separately, including the black raiders, "and each stated his willingness to be defended by the counsel named."[52]

The matter of legal representation aside, the Magistrate's Court heard a number of witnesses, including slaveholders and armory employees. Under oath, Armistead Ball, one of the armory staff, made the dubious claim that Brown had told him that he intended "to free all the slaves in the vicinity" and that he was going to put the arsenal weapons "in the hands of black men." Ball's testimony was alarmist and reactionary, but it served the interests of the prosecution. In fact, Brown had only intended to gather as many people as would join him and arm them with his own weapons—the pikes he had had manufactured in Connecticut for his black enlistees. However, Ball's testimony is not without value insofar as he described the conduct of the raiders within the engine house. Ball testified that Shields Green had fired his rifle repeatedly.[53]

Beyond the legal purpose of the hearing, however, the political narrative of the raid was an unspoken mandate set forth at the conclusion of the Magistrate's Court when Judge Richard Parker addressed the newly impaneled grand jury that would be charged to hand down an indictment of Brown and his men. As McGinty observes, Parker came "perilously close to prejudging" the raiders in his address by speaking of "the enormity of the guilt" of Brown and his men, although he immediately shifted his argument, reminding the jury that as "a minister of justice," he was obligated to hold the prisoners innocent until proven guilty.[54]

Despite the judge's brush with legal peril, he was quite successful in assuring that the desired political narrative of the Harper's Ferry raid was embedded in the record. John Brown and his men were confident that they would be "joined by our slaves and free negroes and [unfurl] the banner of insurrection," the judge declared, although the raiders were "unable to obtain a single circuit," meaning that Brown's men had not been able to attract groups of local slaves to join them.[55] Judge Parker—who was also a slaveholder—had not only declared the raiders insurrectionists from the onset, but also laid the cornerstone deception of the official narrative of the Harper's Ferry raid by charging that Brown had elicited no response from the enslaved community.[56]

* * *

Although the trials of Brown and his men may be studied through the lens of legal due process, they should also be viewed as the formality of a slaveholding society that was hostile toward any effort to undermine slavery. This is evident in the insistence of Governor Henry Wise that the raiders be tried by Virginia rather than by a federal court, where they likely would have been sentenced to prison rather than hanging. While Virginia had a legitimate legal claim upon the raiders, the Buchanan administration also had more than a sufficient legal basis for remanding Brown and his men to federal custody after the raid. However, the conservative Buchanan administration was completely passive in the matter, while Wise, with all the audacity and defiance of an antebellum slaveholder, openly stated that he would never have handed over the raiders to the federal government even "if the President of the United States had so ordered." His rationale for this defiant attitude was that "Virginia and the other slave-holding states must rely on themselves."[57] Beyond this, the denial of Brown's actual appeal to the enslaved community, and the haste with which he and his men were brought to trial reflect how the legal process actually was functioning to appease the wrath of the slaveholders. As McGinty has concluded of this episode, "*dignity* and *decorum* do not translate to fairness when the accused is rushed to judgment," effective counsel is denied, and verdicts are not sustained by evidence.[58]

On November 5, the *Daily National Intelligencer* of Washington, D.C., reported that the trial of "Shields Green, *alias* Emperor, negro, is now going on." The report stated that Green would be represented by one of John Brown's lawyers, Hiram Griswold. But if this was the case at all, the latter had proven so controversial for having taken money from Brown for his services that perhaps Brown's abolitionist friends in the North had decided to secure another attorney. The *Intelligencer* report also surmised that Green's case would follow a similar pattern to the cases previously argued for Brown and Coppic.[59] This also proved incorrect.

Instead of Griswold, George Sennott was dispatched from Boston to represent the black raiders. Sennott, who was a portly man, was repeatedly mocked in Charlestown's newspapers, but he quickly set the Virginians straight by his rigorous and brilliant arguments in the courtroom. Like Ned House, the *Tribune*'s undercover reporter in Charlestown, Sennott was an abolitionist affiliated with the Democratic Party. Abolitionist Democrats were a minority in the North and unheard of in the South, but Sennott was unabashed in his antislavery views, arguing in court that slavery was an "illogical and absurd" system, and claiming that his role as the attorney for Brown's black raiders was an honor. In spite of their mockery of his obesity and contempt for his abolitionism, even the Virginians were at points dazzled by Sennott's powerful arguments.[60] Most notably, he effectively contended that Shields Green could not be rightly charged with treason in light of the *Dred Scott* decision (*Scott v. Sandford*, 1857), in which the chief justice of the Supreme Court had ruled that black men were not citizens of the United States.[61] As Steven Lubet observes, "It was nearly impossible for an abolitionist to find any redeeming virtue in the Dred Scott case, but Sennott had sensed a way to turn it to his clients' advantage."[62] Despite his sympathy for the prosecution, even Judge Parker had to acquiesce to Sennott's argument that if a black man could not be a citizen, he could not commit treason against the Commonwealth of Virginia.[63]

It is not clear whether the *Tribune*'s Ned House knew Sennott from his days in Boston, but he was clearly thrilled by his arguments. "Mr. Sennott, however, went on with an infinite variety of objections," House delightedly reported, "scattering them all over the indictment with unflinching persistence. The spectators listened, then laughed, then fell to whispering, and then unbridled their irritation. . . . The general idea was that of complete amazement at the utterance of 'Abolition sentiments' in a Virginia Court of justice." In another report, House added that the court "was hardly prepared for so much acuteness as he showed."[64] As far as Shields Green was concerned, however, the local press saw him as an unworthy beneficiary. Sennott was "doing his [damndest]" for his unfortunate client, but the Virginians saw him either as a pitiful, "regular out-and-out tar-colored darkey," or as a defiant black man with a "very roguish aspect of countenance."[65]

Lubet also observed that "almost none of the local or national newspapers devoted significant space to Green and Copeland . . . typically limiting their reports to one or two perfunctory paragraphs." As for dark-skinned Emperor, no reporter seems to have been interested, "other than to disparage him as appearing 'so woe-begone that there was small room for his looking worse.'"[66] But if Shields Green was disparaged by some as pitiable, at one point during his trial he was attacked and excoriated as a threat to the sexual hegemony that white males held over their enslaved women. In this case the attack came from the prosecuting attorney, Andrew Hunter. Although there are no court transcripts and very little press coverage of the trial, one particular incident survived in the record because of the indefatigable reportage of Ned House, who continued to smuggle his correspondence to Greeley's *Tribune* until Brown's execution.

According to House, Hunter was a "sort of modern Caesar, who would rather be the first man in a village than the second in an empire." At fifty-five years of age, he was well established in Jefferson County as a leading figure and a successful lawyer with all the appropriate political, business, and social connections. His appointment as the prosecutor of the Harper's Ferry raiders came directly from Governor Wise, who preferred him over the local commonwealth attorney, Charles Harding. Harding was a drunk who was observed, during the trial of Shields Green, to have fallen asleep in court and then "woke very suddenly, and called out for tobacco, at which everybody around him laughed." Quite in contrast, Hunter was ambitious, "the man of this occasion," as House called him. His influence upon the court was obvious enough to the journalist, who even noticed how Judge Parker looked to Hunter's "gesture of assent or dissent before determining a disputed point."[67]

In other circumstances, Hunter might have recused himself from serving as the state's prosecutor. His wife was the niece of Mayor Fontaine Beckham, who was killed by the raiders, and his son was one of the murderers of raider Henry Thompson, who was killed in cold blood in retaliation for the mayor's death. But as McGinty pointed out, Hunter shared Governor Wise's impatience with the process of trying the raiders. On October 22, prior to the Magistrate's Court, Hunter wrote to Wise that Judge Parker was "for observing all the judicial decencies. So am I, but at double quick time." He was "straining every nerve" to have the raiders "condemned and executed next week," Hunter added, "but fear it may be delayed somewhat longer." As for the badly wounded raider, Aaron Stevens, Hunter concluded that he would "probably die of his wounds if we don't hang him promptly." This impatience was impelled neither by legal nor temperamental necessity, but rather manifested the appetite of slaveholders for revenge, as if killing Brown and his men would vindicate their cause. After Brown and Coppic were convicted on November 2,

Hunter dashed off another letter to Governor Wise. "I think we will put the two negroes through this week," he wrote.[68]

In retrospect, Hunter portrayed his prosecutorial role as one of dignity and propriety, writing in 1887 that the trials of all the raiders were "perfectly fair from beginning to end."[69] However, the trial of Shields Green demonstrated not only, as McGinty writes, that he "was subject to a host of legal incapacities under the laws of Virginia" as a black man,[70] but also that Green would have to bear the brunt of the slaveholder's jealous outrage, and this was nowhere better portrayed than in his treatment by Andrew Hunter.

Despite the lack of a record of the trial's proceedings, one episode was preserved in the pages of the *Tribune* by Ned House, who recounted how during Green's trial, the prosecutor "turned upon the negro," animated by outrage and exhibiting "a wonderful acquaintance with the vocabulary of invective," hurling insult and accusation at him, merely because he had shown interest in a "mulatto" woman on one of the plantations. Hunter thus charged that it was only "guilty passion" that had inspired Shields Green "to join the expedition." House observed further that Hunter's outrage inflamed the courtroom, and "the crowd that filled the hall blazed with fury and clenched fists in agonies of virtuous indignation." Up to that point, House thought that Hunter's remarks in court had been "careless and ineffective, though usually to the point." But in the moment when Hunter accused Shields Green of making "advances" toward the "mulatto" woman, his denunciations of the black man were spirited and incessant. To his credit, however, Emperor, as ever, played the fighter, quietly resisting Hunter's abuse without so much as batting an eye. "How the negro ever sat so stolid under it," House concluded, "I cannot understand."[71]

Fortunately, Green's determined lawyer did not allow the prosecutor's accusations to go unanswered and had the "mulatto" woman summoned to testify on his behalf. As it turned out, the woman testified that Emperor had merely kissed her baby, while raider Aaron Stevens had put his arm about her shoulder, asking her to come along with them. Dissatisfied with this testimony, observers quickly started a new rumor to the effect that Stevens had "offered violence" to the woman because she would not join the raiders.[72] The episode was particularly revealing of Andrew Hunter, for whom the attack seems to have been quite personal. After all, the prosecutor was himself a slaveholder, and among the several enslaved people listed in the 1860 census as his own property was a female, thirty-five years old, and a male "mulatto," six years old. His outrage not only revealed the basic hatred that slaveholders felt toward anyone who wished to deprive them of their "property," but the possessiveness that privileged white masters often felt toward the women they kept in bondage.

On Friday, November 4, Shields Green's trial was concluded, and he stood before Judge Parker with lawyer Sennott to hear the verdict of the court. Sennott had indeed done his "damndest" on Green's behalf, and if he could not save him, he had at least beat the charge of treason. As Ned House put it, the hefty lawyer's "struggle with the prosecution was a sort of guerilla warfare," and he had "attacked the indictment [of treason] on all points," including the argument that since Green was evidently black, according to the state of Virginia, he must have been considered a slave unless proven otherwise, and as such could not be charged with treason. As the *New York Herald* reported, the treason charge had to be abandoned because "it was not proven that the prisoner was a *free* person."[73] Consequently, following a brief deliberation, although the jury returned verdicts of guilty on the charges of treason, murder, and conspiracy, they finally "consented that the prisoner should be considered 'not guilty' of the first, which charged him with treason."[74]

Little is known about the last days of Shields Green apart from a few vignettes and illustrated newspaper sketches (see chapter 6). On the afternoon that Green received his guilty verdicts, a correspondent stopped in the jail to visit Brown and the other prisoners. When he came to Green's cell, he found him looking quite sad. The reporter asked Green why, if he was free in Pennsylvania, he had gotten involved in coming to Virginia. The reporter claimed that Green responded that "he had been completely deceived and taken in in this business," and "wished he had been more cautious." When an onlooker blurted out that he deserved his fate, jailer Avis told him to keep quiet. The trustworthiness of this description of Emperor may be open to question. Possibly, the reporter captured him in an episode of despondency and regret; but it is also possible that his words about having been deceived were an interpolation of the *Herald*'s local correspondent, the likes of whom were not above tainting the record to suit Virginia's expectations.[75] Several days later, perhaps the same correspondent paid another visit, this time finding Green, Copeland, and Coppic standing together at a single barred window, the view of which afforded them "the only prospect of the world beyond" that they could hope to see "till brought out for execution." This time, when the reporter tried to speak with them, they showed almost a "repugnance" toward speaking. At least they seemed "resigned to their fate," the journalist concluded.[76]

Although a guilty verdict was handed down in his case on November 4, Green's sentencing was deferred until the trials of the other raiders were concluded. Accordingly, prosecutor Hunter pushed through the trials of Copeland and Cook, and on Friday, November 11, four of the raiders stood before the judge for sentencing. When asked whether they wanted to speak, both Green and Copeland declined, perhaps in an expression of protest. According to the *Herald*, the white prisoners Edwin Coppic and John Cook lamented that they had no knowledge of their leader's intention to seize Harper's Ferry until that previous Sunday, "when they were called upon to take the oath of obedience to their commander. They expected to be punished," they said, "but did not think they should be hung." Coppic, who denied committing treason and the other charges, admitted that trying to "run off slaves into a Free State and liberate them there" was a crime. But "the punishment for that offense would be very different from what you are going to inflict on me now," he appealed.[77]

It was now time for Judge Parker to pronounce sentence. First, he decried their "mad inroad upon this State" and their attempt to "raise in our midst the standard of servile insurrection." Then once more came the slaveholder's claim that the raiders' mission had been a complete failure because they had "obtained no support from that quarter whence you so confidently expected it," and not a single "slave united himself to your party." Indeed, Parker boasted, the slave had run from his would-be liberators back to "the care and protection of his owner." Despite the sorrow and sympathy that he felt for them, Parker concluded his "sad duty," declaring: "The sentence of the law is, that you and each one of you, John E. Cook, Edwin Coppic, Shields Green, and John Copeland, be hanged by the neck until you be dead," setting the date and time of their executions as Friday, December 16, 1859. The black raiders would be executed first in the morning, the white raiders in the afternoon, but they would all be hanged in public. According to a reporter for the *Alexandria Gazette and Virginia Advertiser*, both Judge Parker and a large number of spectators wept.[78]

* * *

In late November, according to the *Baltimore American*, both Copeland and Green had "made professions of conversion" under the pastoral care of the Reverend J. Hoffman Waugh of the Methodist Episcopal Church. Emperor may have had a background in the church in South Carolina, but there is no evidence that he attended church or otherwise showed an interest in religious matters in later years. George Leech, an associated clergyman in the Methodist Episcopal Church from Baltimore, recalled Green's spiritual transformation in condescending terms, saying that "he saw visions—heard voices, [and] soon professed conversion." The two black converts, who tolerated a proslavery clergyman in deference to the concerns of their own spiritual formation, stood quite in contrast to their pious captain. For his part, the Old Man repeatedly turned away any proslavery clergyman from his jail cell—not for lack of an orthodox faith, but because, for Brown, praying with a proslavery clergyman was unconscionable heresy. The *Baltimore American* journalist thus noted how Brown was approached by a Presbyterian minister a few days before, the clergyman expressing a desire "to advise him spiritually." The Old Man "repelled it," the reporter concluded. John Brown dismissed him, saying that he did not worship the same God because the minister was a slaveholder.[79]

On the morning of Friday, December 2, jailer Avis escorted Brown to visit his men for the last time. According to the *New-York Illustrated News*, he "ascended with easy steps to the room of the colored men, Green and Copeland, in the upper story of the jail, shook hands with them, and expressed his regret that they should have said things about his history which was not true."[80] Brown had not been able to communicate freely with the raiders held in other cells, but evidently there were some issues between the Old Man and the raiders, primarily with John Cook, who had provided "a stream of information—not all of it truthful—for the convenience of Andrew Hunter and Governor Wise."[81] However, John Copeland had made a statement to the authorities too, answering a number of questions that included identifying John Kagi as the one who had "induced" him to join Brown's movement. Copeland knew already that this had displeased the Old Man, and apparently had made a number of attempts to send notes of explanation down to his cell on the first floor of the jail. When Brown could finally speak to the raiders, he expressed displeasure to Copeland about him having named Kagi, to which Copeland responded that Kagi was already dead and beyond injury. "No matter," Brown retorted, "never betray your friends or bring obloquy on their memory, for beyond all other things, it will bring upon you the contempt of mankind." Reaching out to both men, Brown handed them each a quarter—a little more than five dollars by today's standards—and concluded: "I came in to see you, and to bid you farewell, and to give you some small change which I have left, but have no use for any longer. All I ask of you is that you will die like men; let there be no flinching on your part." He shook hands with them and left the room.[82] Outside the jailhouse, a yellow furniture wagon was waiting, its cargo being a large crate that contained his coffin. With his arms pinioned behind him at the elbows, the Old Man mounted the wagon and sat down on the crate. As the wagon rode away from the jailhouse toward the site of the gallows, he relished the winter sun on his face for the last time.

The following day, December 3, several black leaders from Philadelphia composed a letter to Governor Henry Wise, requesting leniency toward Green and Copeland. If not, they appealed, the governor might then at least hand over their bodies. The letter was signed by abolitionist Alfred M. Green, Jabez P. Campbell, a churchman (and later bishop) of the African Methodist Episcopal Church, and Jeremiah Asher, pastor of the Shiloh Baptist Church. Despite the impulses that led these black men to Harper's Ferry, they wrote, "they are one in identity of interest, complexion, and of national proscription with the men whose liberty they sought to secure." The letter asked that the bodies of Green and Copeland be "transmitted to us for a respectable interment," then went on first by pleading for mercy, and then turning into something of an appeal in their defense. Following the same line of argument employed by lawyer Sennott, the writers appealed that Green and Copeland could not be rightly convicted of treason against the state of Virginia, since they had "no part nor lot" in the blessings of the nation, "save by sufferance, not by right." All else failing, they concluded by requesting that Wise "grant to us, their friends and brethren, the privilege of paying them the last sad tribute of respect" to their memory.[83] There is no evidence that Governor Wise ever answered their letter, and no reason to think that he would have done so.

* * *

The night before they were to be executed, John Cook and Edwin Coppic tried to escape. Evidently, they had been working for at least a week, secretly laboring with a saw they had made from an old knife. Prying off their shackles so that they could be removed at any moment, they improvised a chisel from an old bed screw, with which they removed wall plaster and then the bricks, until they had an opening to the outer bricks of their first-floor jail cell. They kept a bed in front of this work, hiding the loose bricks in the drum of the potbelly stove in their cell, and concealing loose dirt and plaster under their bed sheets.

When the hour came for escape, the two raiders slipped through the opening and into the snowy back yard of the jailhouse. The yard was enclosed by a high wall, so they improvised a means of mounting the wall with some of the timbers from John Brown's disassembled scaffold. However, as they mounted the wall, they were spotted by a sentinel, who fired off his rifle. Coppic surrendered first and slipped back down into the yard, but Cook hesitated. Coppic said afterward that if he could have gotten to the guard and overpowered him, they could have fled into the night and reached the Shenandoah mountains in ten minutes. But the guard was out of reach, a warning shot had been fired, and Cook was held at the end of a bayonet.

After they were returned to their cells, all the prisoners were placed in handcuffs and extra leg irons, and guards were now posted inside the jail. This extra security remained until the last two raiders were executed in March 1860. The failed attempt at escape was only possible in the first place because the raiders were yet living on the entitlements that had been won by John Brown's conduct. The Old

Man had promised jailer Avis that he would never escape and there-after earned the complete trust of the jailer, his family, and many of the guards. Now, Virginia authorities held Avis chiefly responsible and placed a military guard within the jailhouse, something that ir-ritated local authorities. Many people in the community were already disturbed with Avis for what they perceived as his excessive kindness toward the prisoners, all of these factors finally resulting in him los-ing his position the following year. Coppic afterward wrote a letter in explanation of the escape in which he mentioned that Shields Green had provided them a knife blade with which they were able to cut saw teeth into another blade. According to one report, the black raid-ers, perhaps fearing retaliation, expressed concern that they might be blamed as having knowledge of the desperate escape plan.[84]

On the same day of Shields Green's execution, James Gordon Bennett, owner and editor of the *New York Herald*, published an edi-torial entitled "Execution of the Harper's Ferry Traitors To-Day." It was not a flattering title because Bennett was an ultraconservative Democrat who despised abolitionists, defended slavery as "neither an evil nor a crime," and commonly employed the basest racial epithets in his newspaper.[85] In this case, he was not really concerned for the fate of the two black raiders, but was simply taking a swipe at the ab-olitionist movement, which he despised. Bennett was the antebellum version of a right-wing media mogul, having established a successful newspaper that drew upon affiliates and correspondents across the nation and around the world. By the time of the Harper's Ferry raid, his paper had the largest national circulation of all the major New York publications. The *Herald* offered titillation, but its wide range of reportage, information, and human interest stories still makes it a no-table resource for historians and researchers.[86] Despite all the "wild fanaticism" raging over the Harper's Ferry raid, Bennett thus opined, "the bodies of the two unfortunate free negroes have no friends at the North to claim them and lay them decently in mother earth." Instead, they would be buried under the shadow of the gallows. "Where are the friends of the afflicted colored race now?" Bennett mocked. "Where are Wendell Phillips and Lloyd Garrison, and Ralph Waldo Emerson, and the other advocates of human freedom? Alas!"[87]

However, there was a measure of truth in the editor's mockery. Compared to the enthusiasm and interest shown for John Brown, there was considerably less concern for his men in general, but particularly for his black men. As Bennett had pointed out, apart from the expressed concerns of some black churchmen, certainly the leading white abolitionists had paid little attention to Green and Copeland in life, and probably would likewise overlook them in death. On December 8, a little more than a week before their executions, the white abolitionist J. Miller McKim had given a eulogy at the burial of John Brown, honoring the Old Man and his two sons slain at Harper's Ferry. "The world will yet acknowledge itself debtor to them and history will embalm their memory," McKim declared. Then, he reminded the gathered mourners that some of Brown's men still awaited execution, and "that they too are not unworthy of a tribute on this occasion." In particular, McKim continued, they had heard nothing negative about Shields Green and John Copeland at Harper's Ferry. "This was eulogy," he concluded. "If they belong to the oppressed and hated race, and if anything could be said to their disadvantage, we should have had it ere this." McKim's remarks were at once both salutary and desultory. It was true enough that the imprisoned raiders had done nothing to bring shame upon themselves or the antislavery cause. However, his comment also seemed to suggest that as black men, Emperor and Copeland were to be commended for meeting a minimal level of expectation. But at least McKim had remembered the two black men awaiting death in a Charlestown jail cell. As Bennett surmised, Wendell Phillips, who followed McKim with a magnificent eulogy for the dead, said nothing about the doomed black raiders.[88]

Fortunately, Bennett's political enemy and rival in the newspaper business, Horace Greeley, was somewhat mindful of Green and Copeland—at least to the extent that the *New York Daily Tribune* featured a brief article about what would become of their bodies following the executions. Published on December 16, the day of their hangings, the *Tribune* piece reported that its correspondent expected them to be interred "near the gallows" because their remains "probably would not be claimed." The *Tribune* writer was ignorant of whether the condemned men had relatives and seemed to think that the Virginians might hand over their remains if family were to claim them. Apparently, some efforts had been started by African Americans in New York to claim the bodies, but these relented upon discovering the letter written to Governor Wise by churchmen in Philadelphia. The *Tribune* writer correctly predicted that Wise would disregard the request of the black Philadelphians, "but it should be understood that the free colored people of the North are not wanting in the proper feeling which is natural to them under the circumstances. Green and Copeland, however obscure and unknown, were still of African blood, and die on behalf of the freedom of their race."[89]

At daybreak on Friday, December 16, the reveille was sounded, arousing the encamped militia, and soon all of Charlestown was astir. From the time of Brown's incarceration, the town had been bursting at the seams with a military presence, and although this lessened after his hanging on December 2, the town was once more filled with a good many militia companies—the Wythe Guards, Mountain Guards, Richardson Guards, Petersburg City Guard, Washington Guards, Petersburg City Grays, and others.

No doubt, all four of the doomed raiders had awakened early too, but Emperor and Copeland were scheduled to die first, at eleven o'clock in the morning—although one would think the white raiders had died first, given the priority that their executions received in newspaper reports. At nine o'clock, the entire military force was formed on the main street in Charlestown, and then marched to take their places on the gallows grounds, but it would take another ninety minutes before General Taliaferro (an Italian name that the Virginians tended to pronounce like "Tolifer") ordered his staff of twenty-five officers to prepare "the negro prisoners" for execution. The assigned militia then formed a hollow square around the jail, and an open wagon pulled to the front of the building—the transport for the raiders, loaded also with their coffins and accompanied by another carriage for the sheriff and his deputies.

While the execution of John Brown was a closed event, attended only by military and select citizens, politicians, and newspapermen, the executions of his raiders were treated as public events. Naturally, as the reporter for the *Richmond Dispatch* observed, there were at least five times as many people present to see Green and Copeland die than had watched their old captain ascend the gallows two weeks before. The correspondent for the *New York Herald* likewise concluded that there was a "great influx of strangers and citizens" in town, which obligated local residents to venture out early to the scene of the execution to make sure they were not crowded to the margins by "foreigners." In the early morning hours, clouds still darkened the horizon, but now they were dispersed with the appearance of another bright winter sun, just as it had on the morning of John Brown's hanging. The snow that had covered the ground only the day before quickly melted, leaving the ground somewhat soft and mushy for the gathering crowd. Green and Copeland, who had followed Brown to Harper's Ferry, would now follow him to the same field and scaffold.

As the troops made their "evolutions with great skill," they were reviewed by Taliaferro, who was mounted on an impressive steed. "Everything conspired to make the display a grand one," the *Herald* correspondent wrote gleefully, as if he were observing a parade. "The bright bayonets and gay uniforms of the soldiers combined to perfect the picture." At a quarter before eleven o'clock, the raiders appeared at the door of the jail in the company of the sheriff and the Reverend N. Green North, the same Presbyterian minister whom Brown had previously turned away from his cell after the clergyman made the mistake of telling the Old Man that Saint Paul was not opposed to slavery.[90] The two black men "seemed downcast, and wore none of that calm and cheerful spirit evinced by Brown under similar circumstances," an observation that perhaps gave the Virginians a sense of satisfaction. According to the *Herald* reporter, the raiders' despair was even a point of barroom conversations the night before, "and so firmly had this conviction settled in the public mind," that it seemed to some that the finale had already been reached. The reporters present observed as Emperor and Copeland, their arms pinioned behind them at the elbows, were assisted as they climbed up into the wagon and took their seats on their coffins in the wagon "without scarcely looking to the right or the left." Then the wagon and the carriage behind slowly moved forward to the field of execution, flanked on either side by a company of riflemen, marching "double file, in lock step."

The procession reached the gallows' field only minutes before eleven o'clock, "and the prisoners cast a shuddering glance towards the gallows erected on the rising ground in its center." As the two men ascended the gallows with a "firm step," the military escort took their positions in the field. Before they fell, the raiders bid "an affectionate farewell" to the several clergymen who had prayed with them on the scaffold, especially their Methodist Episcopal advisor, the Reverend Beverly Waugh. Now, as the men stood upon the scaffold, caps were drawn over their heads. Copeland remained quiet, but reporters could hear as Emperor "was engaged in earnest prayer up to the moment the trap was drawn and they were launched into eternity."

All available accounts say that Emperor died quickly, his neck having broken in the fall, while Copeland "seemed to suffer very much, and his body writhed in violent contortions for several minutes." The editor of the *Richmond Dispatch*, however, was pleased to provide an additional description of their deaths. In the second account, while Shields Green had "scarcely made a struggle," Copeland's death was far more disturbing to observe: "For several minutes, he endeavored with his pinioned arms to grab at the rope around his neck; he raised his knees almost to a level with his body, swung to and fro, and in fact, gave every indication of dying the most agonizing death imaginable." After hanging for a half hour, the bodies were put into the poplar coffins provided for them and carried back to the jail. But as most of the local observers probably knew, the coffins were more or less props to the Virginians. The press reported that the bodies were to be interred the next day on the spot where the gallows stood. However, proslavery journalists, having no apparent concern for human feeling as it pertained to black people, could not resist adding that there was a "party of medical students here from Winchester" that would probably not allow the bodies "to remain there long."[91]

Emperor Seen

Image and Identity

Historical enquiry must match the depictive
content of the art-work.

Sarah Barber

I n early November 1859, while John Brown and his men sat in
their jail cells awaiting execution, the Boston sculptor Edward
Brackett arrived in Charlestown on a mission to capture the
Old Man's image in a bust. Brackett was financed by one of Brown's
most generous supporters, George Luther Stearns of Medford,
Massachusetts, but the task was an unpleasant one because of the
hostility of the Virginians toward their prisoners. When Brackett
arrived in town, he was cordially greeted by community leaders
but soon began to realize that their courtesy belied a determined
opposition. Finding himself sent back and forth between the judge
and the jailer to no avail, Brackett became increasingly disturbed at
getting the runaround by his hosts. When he finally complained to
authorities, he was curtly informed that he was suspected of being
an abolitionist spy. As coincidence would have it, Brackett found a
secret ally in Edward "Ned" House, the undercover *New York Daily
Tribune* journalist with whom he was acquainted. House duly relayed
Brackett's frustrations in the pages of the *Tribune*, lamenting that it
appeared the sculptor would be "obliged to return without accom-
plishing his object, for it is wholly impossible to satisfy the jealous

Virginians that there is not in his visit here a great deal more than meets the eye."[1]

Amidst these frustrations, Brackett found fleeting hope when he discovered that a daguerreotype operator—a man with a camera—was accessible, his idea being that he might at least depart from Charlestown with a photograph of John Brown from which to work. However, as House reported, the notion of the camera also "was met with opposition" by leaders in Charlestown. The *Tribune* journalist noted that the daguerreotype operator was a "traveling" photographer, but it may be that he was introduced to Brackett by a local artist named Lewis Graham Dinkle, who may also have had a facility for photography.[2]

The idea of using a camera perhaps came to Brackett when he learned that ambrotype images were being made of some uniformed militia men near the site of Brown's incarceration. The extant ambrotypes show cheerful young Virginians in uniform, one of which often was presented as a Civil War photo during the twentieth century.[3] According to another researcher, the ambrotypes were made at the instigation of some of the Richmond Grays, a militia unit that included the actor John Wilkes Booth, later the assassin of Abraham Lincoln.[4] Outraged by the attack on Harper's Ferry, Booth had abandoned his performance role at a Richmond theater and went to Charlestown in the guise of a Virginia Gray so that he could participate in the execution of John Brown.[5]

Despite Brackett's efforts and the proximity of a camera to the jailhouse, history was deprived of photographic images of Brown and his men in their jail cells, the only reason being the prejudice and resentment of the Virginians. Notwithstanding opposition from officials in town, however, Brackett did finally manage to steal a meeting with Brown. While the abolitionist himself had no interest in modeling for a bust, he sat cooperatively when he learned that it was the desire of his friend Stearns, who was Brackett's patron.[6] After a sketch was made and skull measurements were taken to complete the preparations for the work, Brackett expediently left town. His friend House now de-lightedly reported to the *Tribune* that the Boston sculptor had departed Charlestown with his mission accomplished. "While everybody was looking after him as a suspicious object," House wrote triumphantly, Brackett and a helper had "spent an agreeable half hour with Brown in noting down everything that was needed."[7]

Despite naysaying conservatives who despised John Brown for having upset the status quo of white supremacy, Brackett's bust won acclaim in the North. In early 1860, only two months after the Old Man was hanged, the abolitionist Lydia Maria Child wrote a descrip-tive piece in the *Tribune* about the bust. Not only was it an "excel-lent likeness," she opined, but a Boston aficionado had pronounced it "singularly like Michael Angelo's Moses." She added, to underscore the point, that one particular critic of Brown had even been put to silence in the presence of the image.[8] George Hoyt, the young at-torney from Massachusetts who served initially as Brown's lawyer in Charlestown, also examined Brackett's masterpiece, concluding that not only was it "a true reflection of his external features," but an admirable display of "his irresistible manhood."[9] Three years later, Harriet Tubman chanced to come upon the bust during a visit to Boston. According to the *Boston Commonwealth*, the deeply spiritual hero of the underground railroad was quite moved when she beheld the image of her old associate. "The sight of it, which was new to her, threw her into a sort of ecstasy of sorrow and admiration," wrote Franklin Sanborn. As she gazed at the marble rendering of the Old Man, she concluded that it was not John Brown who had died at Charlestown. "It was Christ; it was the Savior of our people."[10]

But if it was Christ who had been hanged on the scaffold in Charlestown, then Shields Green had shared his bitter cup. Indeed, Green had literally made it possible for Tubman to gaze with rever-ence upon Brown's image. In reality, Brackett the sculptor was nearly defeated in his hopes of seeing the prisoner and was almost forced to leave Charlestown a failure. Even Brown's sympathetic jailer, who was willing otherwise to risk harsh criticism for his kindness to the prisoners, had bluntly refused to permit Brackett to enter the jailhouse. As the sculptor told House of the *Tribune*, the jailer had lectured him that "there was an immense opposition" to his gaining access to Brown, and that scores if not hundreds of people had complained that "no such thing should be permitted" to honor the man who had invaded Virginia and attacked Harper's Ferry.[11]

However, after Brown was found guilty and his trial concluded, a door of opportunity was opened with the trial of Shields Green. When the black man was escorted across the street to the courthouse, the sculptor—aided by one of Brown's attorneys—slipped into the jailhouse under the watchful eye of a sympathetic guard. True to his promise not to enter Brown's cell, Brackett then asked him to pull his chair up to the doorway. Seated on the other side of the threshold, he sketched his likeness while Brown's attorney, under instruction by the sculptor, took careful measurements of the subject's head. This was made possible because, across the street in the Jefferson County Courthouse, all of Virginia's attention was focused upon venting its legal wrath upon the lonesome Emperor. Of all the raiders to stand trial in Charlestown, Shields Green was the most notably harangued, maligned, and browbeaten by the vindictive prosecuting attorney—the harshest words being reserved for the darkest of the Harper's Ferry raiders. As a follower of John Brown, Emperor was inevitably doomed to share his scaffold, although it seems clear that the darkest one, to Virginia, was also the blackest villain among his men.

But what of Shields Green's image? Unlike John Brown, whose visage actually survives in twelve different photographic images,[12] no photographic image of Green has survived, if one was ever made at all. Even Brown's men, including the other four black Harper's Ferry raiders, left daguerreotype images of themselves for history. Only the man who called himself Emperor left no such image in a time when daguerreotype photography had made camera portraits accessible to common people.

Fortunately, several sketches of Emperor were made of him as a prisoner in Virginia—rendered by professional artists working for the three leading illustrated newspapers of the day, all of them based in New York City. However, even apart from the necessary discussion as to the technical precision of these sketches, there is the question of their portrayal of Green's humanity and our ability to find it through the only images bequeathed to us. Historians cannot "make art incidental illustration," writes Sarah Barber. "The work must be illustrative but the historical enquiry must match the depictive content of the art-work."[13] While the "irresistible manhood" of John Brown, a controversial white man, could be sacralized in a sculpted bust despite negative reportage and hostile caricature, what happened to the humanity of black Shields Green under the observing eye of the leading white artists of the antebellum era?

Perhaps it may be ventured that the Harper's Ferry raid was the first major press event of the modern era in the United States. Just as the first contemporary newspaper interviews seem to have been born from the Harper's Ferry episode, it is no surprise that some of the leading illustrators of the day were sent to Charlestown to capture the scenes of John Brown's last days. Representing *Frank Leslie's Illustrated Newspaper* were its chief artist, the German-born Alfred Berghaus, and his capable associate, William S. L. Jewett. The latter was all but run out of Charlestown prior to Brown's hanging because he was erroneously suspected of being the sleuth who was filling the pages of the *New York Daily Tribune* with embarrassing and revealing vignettes of Charlestown and its leading citizens. Of course, Ned House, the actual *Tribune* journalist, was delighted to provide a report on the entire episode while hidden in plain sight from his Virginia hosts.[14]

DeWitt Hitchcock of the *New-York Illustrated News* was also on the ground in Charlestown, representing the newest of the rival weekly publications. Finally, *Harper's Weekly* was perhaps the most comfortably received in Charlestown because the reporter and artist covering the scene was the talented David Hunter Strother, a Virginian. Despite his opposition to any notion of Virginia seceding from the Union, Strother was both proslavery and hostile toward John Brown for having invaded his beloved Virginia. Strother's sketches, which still survive in great number today, reflect his ability to make refined, lifelike sketches of his subjects, including black people. However, as his work in *Harper's Weekly* shows, he was quite ready to use racist caricature and the exaggerations of the political cartoonist in attacking John Brown. Fortunately, among Strother's surviving sketches of the Harper's Ferry episode there are examples of his abilities as an artist as well. Taken together, all four of these artists—Hitchcock, Berghaus, Jewett, and Strother—made sketches of Shields Green that have saved him from going facelessly into the historical record.

Like the other illustrators, DeWitt Hitchcock visited the prisoners in Charlestown jail and sketched Shields Green in his cell along with John Copeland, the other black prisoner, and Albert Hazlett, a white raider who was captured after escaping with Osborne Anderson (see figure 6.1). Hitchcock shows us Emperor seated on his bed in the jail cell with ankle chains. Copeland is nearby, also in chains, seated despondently in a chair with his hands in his pockets; and Hazlett is standing to the right, also in chains and smoking a pipe. The artist's treatment of Shields Green shows him as a dark-complexioned man, with hair untrimmed and a slight mustache and chin whiskers. In this sketch, Emperor seems compact in build, but one can imagine also physically strong for his size—what John Brown might have called "pony built" in the agrarian vernacular of his day.

Alfred Berghaus was the senior artist for *Frank Leslie's Illustrated News*, the chief rival of the preeminent *Harper's Weekly*. Initially, Berghaus was dispatched to Harper's Ferry, but shortly returned to New York City and was replaced by Jewett to cover developments

FIGURE 6.1. DeWitt Hitchcock's sketch of Shields Green in the Charlestown jail with Copeland and Hazlett. *New-York Illustrated News*, Dec. 10, 1859.

in Charlestown, where the prisoners were taken for trial and incarceration. However, by mid-November 1859, bitterness and suspicion against Jewett, along with Brown's young attorney, George Hoyt, obligated both men to make a hasty retreat from Charlestown, Hoyt returning to Massachusetts and Jewett to New York. In response to this setback, Berghaus returned, accompanied by the respected journalist Augustus Rawlings, to cover the final days of Brown in Charlestown.[15] Given these circumstances, *Leslie's* actually featured sketches of Shields Green done by both artists. The first, by Berghaus—the one most used by historians—is a sketch of Emperor sitting next to Edwin Coppic shortly after capture, seated under guard at Harper's Ferry on October 18 (see figure 6.2). This portrait gives an impression of Green's reported description, including his powerful build.

FIGURE 6.2. Alfred
Berghaus's sketch of
Shields Green under
arrest at Harper's Ferry
with Coppic. Detail of
Shields Green shown
above. *Frank Leslie's
Illustrated Newspaper*,
Nov. 5, 1859.

Quite in contrast with the Berghaus sketch is the treatment by
William S. L. Jewett, whose version of Green, Copeland, and Hazlett
in jail actually appeared in *Leslie's* on December 10 (see figure 6.3).
In his sketch, Jewett presents Green with shorter hair and a slender
facial and bodily form. Interestingly, there is significant variance from
Hitchcock's portrayal of the same scene in the *New-York Illustrated
News*, including the appearance of Copeland and Hazlett, as well
as certain features of the jail cell itself. In this light, Jewett's sketch
seems less likely to have been made from life—probably rather from
a preliminary sketch or even the artist's memory after his obligatory
departure from Virginia in mid-November.

Interestingly, just beneath the great blanket of political controversy
over the Harper's Ferry raid covered by the national press, there was a
thin sheet of controversy reflecting the competition of illustrated newspapers in their coverage of the episode. At first, Frank Leslie, proprietor
of *Frank Leslie's Illustrated News*, considered it beneficial to his paper's reputation to attack the preeminent illustrated news publication

FIGURE 6.3. William S. L. Jewett's sketch of Shields Green in the Charlestown jail with Copeland and Hazlett. *Frank Leslie's Illustrated Newspaper*, Dec. 10, 1859.

Harper's Weekly, the self-proclaimed "Journal of Civilization." During Brown's incarceration, Leslie unleashed an attack on *Harper's* under the heading "Bogus Illustrations" and dubbing it rather "The Journal of Demoralization." Leslie further charged that *Harper's* featured contrived, "fancy" pictures and that its publisher "preposterously" exaggerated its circulation.[16] But if Leslie was vying for first place among illustrated publications, he was also quite intentional about demeaning ambitious upstarts like the fledgling *New-York Illustrated News*. The latter had all but made its debut in the immediate aftermath of the Harper's Ferry raid and the hangings of John Brown and his men. The publisher, J. Warner Campbell, issued an editorial on December 17, the day after Shields Green and his compatriots were hanged, claiming that his paper had "quite unsettled" the indolent Frank Leslie, prompting him to "do a little more than he has done heretofore." According to Campbell, *Leslie's* had published "the unblushing falsehood" that *New-York Illustrated News* illustrations "were the fruits of a highly prolific

imagination . . . fancy drawings and a gross imposition upon the public." To the contrary, Campbell countered that it was "Master Frank"
Leslie who had used illustrations that were "feigned and bogus."

Two days later, Leslie returned fire, publishing a rebuttal in the
New York Herald, insinuating that *New-York Illustrated News* artists were "imitators" who had published "bogus illustrations." Leslie
boasted of having both superior "advantages and facilities"—implying
that his illustrations were superior to both Campbell's *New-York
Illustrated News* and *Harper's Weekly*. The whole country should be
cautioned, Leslie concluded, lest it be "imposed upon by bogus pictures" in other publications. To no surprise, Campbell published a
rejoinder in the same issue of the *Herald*, under the title "Enterprise
and Truth versus Laziness and Lying; The New-York Illustrated
News versus Frank Leslie's Newspaper." In particular, Campbell
defended the authenticity of *New-York Illustrated News* drawings
of the raiders' executions, declaring that *Leslie's* artists actually had
left Charlestown prematurely. Furthermore, Campbell argued, his
sketches were acknowledged by military and civil authorities, and
his artists had a special train on the Baltimore & Ohio Railroad
and even gave room to other journalists. Frank Leslie was "afraid of
our new paper," Campbell concluded. "And that is why he resorts to
shabby tricks to prejudice the public against us."[17] To what extent
either Campbell or Leslie was telling the truth is difficult to discern,
although it does seem that Frank Leslie's attacks upon other publications may have been meant to distract from deficiencies in his own
paper's coverage. Certainly, the *Leslie's* sketch of Shields Green in his
jail cell was something of a "fancy drawing."

The last works featuring Emperor come from the pen of David
H. Strother, who sketched and reported for *Harper's Weekly* under
the pseudonym Porte Crayon. Strother was born in Martinsburg,
Virginia, in 1816, and attended college in Pennsylvania, afterward
studying the art of wood engraving illustration in New York City. At

the outbreak of the Civil War, he not only opposed Virginia's secession, but served in the Union army, attaining the rank of brigadier
general.[18] As for the black people who appear in much of his work,
Strother was a paternalistic racist who held to gradual emancipation according to the prerequisites of white society. His contempt
for John Brown, whom he referred to as "the old felon" at the time
of the Harper's Ferry raid, is evident in his *Harper's Weekly* entries.[19]
However, following the war his attitude toward Brown underwent
something of a change. For a time, Strother even tried to bring a
revised, more sympathetic portrayal of the abolitionist to the speaking circuit. In 1868, in a speech made in the heart of Brown's own
Western Reserve, Strother told an audience in Cleveland, Ohio:

> When a bold man, in advance of opinion attempts to maintain that
> Truth in Action, he usually falls a victim to his devotion. . . . And
> now, the World, regretful and half repentant turns back to enquire
> more curiously concerning that Old Grey Man, who from Obscurity,
> ignorance and poverty (as if imbued with Divine inspiration) foresaw
> the designs of Providence, and zealously rushed to death in advance
> of the inevitable conflict.[20]

In his remembrance, Strother mentions Shields Green twice, but
only passingly as a background figure in his recollections of the raid
and its aftermath.

However, what he did not recall in word, Strother provided in the
witness of two sketches he made of Emperor—one with the other
raiders in court in October, and the other rendered on the day of his
execution in December—the latter largely having been overlooked
by historians. Strother's first sketch of Green with Brown and his
raiders was made while they were hearing their indictment in court
on Wednesday morning, October 26. In preparation for a published
sketch, however, Strother prepared studies of both Brown and the

FIGURE 6.4. David H. Strother's preliminary study of Shields Green and John Copeland. West Virginia and Regional History Center, West Virginia University Libraries.

two black raiders, the latter providing an even better perspective of Green and Copeland (see figure 6.4). The completed sketch, showing Brown and his men as a group, appeared in *Harper's Weekly* on the cover page of the November 12 issue (see figure 6.5).

Reporting clandestinely from Charlestown, Ned House proudly observed that the *New York Daily Tribune*—by which he meant his own correspondence—had "fed the flames of Virginia fury" even though the banned antislavery paper could only reach the Virginians surreptitiously. As for the illustrated newspapers, he added, both

Harper's Weekly and *Leslie's* were well received, although the "effect of *Harper's Weekly* upon the public mind was much more favorable, the prisoners all wearing, in that paper, the most approved cut-throat air, and having mostly the appearance of relationship to lower than human grades of animals, as gorillas or ourang-ontangs." Nor was it overlooked in Charlestown that "the artist of *Harper's Weekly* is a true Virginian." Strother's illustrations and correspondence featured "the rarest rhetorical ferocity upon the subject of the invasion," House concluded, something that was quite pleasing to the Virginians, who were "jealously sensitive" of their portrayal in Northern newspapers.[21]

Whatever House's view of Strother's sketches, the Virginian's two images of Green seem to reflect a frank side of his artistry. The *Harper's Weekly* sketch of November 12 (figure 6.5) is a lifelike portrayal of the raiders who were taken alive at Harper's Ferry and carried to Charlestown, the seat of Jefferson County: from left to right, John Copeland (still wearing the poncho worn by all of the raiders), Shields Green, John Brown, Edwin Coppic, and the seriously wounded Aaron Stevens, who had to be held up by others in order to stand before the court.

While the portrayal is unflattering, Strother captured Brown with a certain authenticity—his slightly stooped posture, cropped beard, bird-of-prey profile (as his sons described it), and an upward shock of hair that is also evident in his daguerreotypes.[22] As to the sketches of Copeland and Green, Strother seems to have provided a fairly lifelike portrayal. Emperor certainly fits the written physical description of a solid, dark-skinned man of moderate height. His hair and chin whiskers in particular are reminiscent of the Berghaus and Hitchcock sketches. This is a reasonable portrayal of Shields Green, although the published sketch lacks the quality of the original study that Strother made on site. Compared to the sketch published in *Harper's*, the preliminary study that Strother made of the standing figures of Copeland and Green is superior. Here each man is quite distinct, not

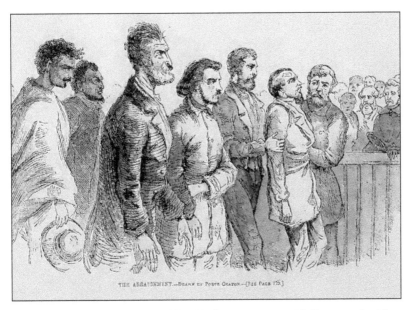

THE ARRAIGNMENT.—DRAWN BY PORTE CRAYON.—[SEE PAGE 722.]

FIGURE 6.5. Strother's sketch of Shields Green in court with Brown and raiders. *Harper's Weekly*, Nov. 12, 1859.

only in looks and stature, but even in skin tone. In the published version, their complexions are less nuanced, while in the study, Green appears darker in hue, as described by eyewitnesses. Both men appear gaunt, as one would expect after hours of sleepless effort and struggle, but Green's facial features are distinctive.

Strother's other sketch of Emperor was made on the very day of his execution, December 16, 1859, when he was being conveyed to the gallows (see figure 6.6). The image has never been published and often has gone unnoticed by writers and students of the Harper's Ferry raid. Perhaps this sketch provides the closest and fullest view of Shields Green's face. Of course, it is the haggard, drawn face of a man who has spent over six weeks brooding inside a jail cell with little of either sunlight or appetite. His somber appearance is poignant and moving. His receding hairline certainly suggests that he is a man well beyond his twenties in age. As one facing death within the hour, his arms are

FIGURE 6.6. Strother's
sketch of Shields Green
riding to execution, Dec.
16, 1859. West Virginia
and Regional History
Center, West Virginia
University Libraries.

restrained while his hands are clasped in prayer. His eyes gaze upward, as it were, into the world to come. Taken together as bookend
studies—one made on October 26 and the other on December 16—the
Strother sketches may provide the most detailed portrayal of Shields
Green available to us in the record. Yet if they are the best in one sense,
the question remains as to which is the most like the man who lived.

* * *

It must be remembered that the historical sketches of Shields Green
have a particular context, and this is especially important for us

because these sketches are the only images of him that have survived. As such, it must be asked which of these images, if any, come
closest to representing Emperor according to the witness of the historical record. As Sarah Barber has observed, "art is not privileged as
a source with special status," as if it provides a window onto history
that should not be examined and interrogated by historians in the
way they would a written record.[23]

While one might prefer to have even one photograph of Emperor
instead of several sketches, both types present an interpretation of
the subject and must be subjected to examination in historical terms.
To be sure, the photograph radically differs from sketch portraiture "in its ability to produce objective images of the visible world
by purely mechanical means." In the words of Derek Sayer, at least
the photograph is the "trace or footprint" of reality, what "*was once
there*."[24] Thus, when the leaders of Charlestown denied the camera's
access to John Brown and his men in jail, they were doing more than
expressing contempt and jealously guarding their own self-interest
as slaveholders. They also were slighting the historical reality of what
the Harper's Ferry raid actually meant to slavery and to a slave state
like Virginia. In short, they had misrepresented history by means of
image in the same way that they had skewed the written record of
the Harper's Ferry story by banning antislavery journalists, and by
using the proslavery press to manufacture a version of the raid that
secured their agenda. "Then the liberty of the press was for the first
time practically destroyed in this country," Henry Steel Olcott recalled of Virginia's suppression and manipulation of reportage during
John Brown's last days.[25]

Of course, they could not maintain absolute control over images
any more than they could keep Charlestown under an airtight journalistic seal. But just as historians should use evidence to check the
slaveholders' version of the Harper's Ferry raid and its aftermath, the
images of John Brown and his men must be considered in light of

every other kind of evidence available. Given that Shields Green is
the least endowed by history with either image or description, then
how his images are understood is particularly important.

In contrast with photography, sketches are the *likeness of reality* at
most, and at least the product of the artist's imagination—"artefacts
of the human hand whose resemblance to their subjects is entirely
dependent upon the artist's knowledge and skill in manipulating materials."[26] For instance, David Hunter Strother's sketches of Shields
Green may be the most appealing for their apparent precision and
quality of realism in lieu of a photographic image. But it cannot be
overlooked that perhaps they are also the ones in which he is rendered in a manner least like himself, since he is portrayed—by a proslavery artist—not only as a prisoner (as do all the sketches), but as a
black man seemingly brought low by the superior power and right-
ness of a slaveholding society. As Barber concludes, "portraits imply
something about the era which generated them, the attitude of the
artist towards the sitter, and the role of the sitter in their society."[27]
Consequently, how we view the sketches of Emperor requires us "to
decipher the intention of the artist, the possibility of a whole range of
meanings, either implicational or overt, but period-specific and lost
to modern audiences."[28]

One means of evaluating the images of Shields Green that have
come down to us is a consideration of the artist's "cultural circuit," the
continuous interrelationship between the artist's memories of events
and his or her awareness of cultural representations of events, past
and present.[29] What was the cultural circuit of those who sketched
Emperor's face and form? Certainly, at a basic level, all of the artists
were white men who shared similar ideas about race and the preroga-
tives of white society based upon their understanding of the nation's
past. Albert Berghaus, a German immigrant, most likely held antislavery sentiments,[30] while David Strother, a Virginian, was explicitly defensive of slavery. Yet despite differences over slavery between

Strother and Berghaus (and the other two Northern artists), it is likely that they all tended to see the Harper's Ferry raid as an unfortunate occurrence. Given the norms of white privilege and prerogative that prevailed in the United States, the three white artists from the North probably saw John Brown's effort as an act of extremism even if they opposed slavery. In varying degrees of sympathy, most Northern "antislavery" people would agree with Abraham Lincoln's conclusions at the Cooper Union the following year, that John Brown was a brooding "enthusiast" who fancied himself "commissioned by Heaven," and who had attempted an unfortunate and "peculiar" liberation effort in Virginia. Even Horace Greeley, in the pages of his sympathetic *New York Daily Tribune*, declared of the Harper's Ferry incident, "we deeply regret this outbreak."[31]

In other words, whatever their view of slavery, all four of the artists who sketched Emperor at least assumed that white society had the right to determine the most appropriate means and time of granting black liberation. As such, a dark-skinned black man held captive in Virginia could only be perceived variously as inferior, unfortunate, or pitiable. On the other hand, given that Green had taken up a weapon and used it against whites in a supposed insurrection, they might very well have viewed him as troubling—better confined than free. Arguably, the cultural circuit from which reporters and sketch artists functioned could never produce a portrait that corresponded to the manner in which Shields Green was seen by those who knew him best. At most, then, he must be discerned by a careful consideration of the descriptions provided—a proverbial reading-between-the-lines of the historical record, in image as well as text.

As Steven Lubet has observed, "almost none of the local or national newspapers devoted significant space to Green and Copeland" as prisoners in Virginia.[32] From the time of his arrest at Harper's Ferry, Green was particularly disdained by whites. The two Baltimore journalists who first encountered him as a prisoner at Harper's Ferry had nothing good to say about him. The reporter from the *Sun* identified him as "a somewhat notorious character," while Simpson Donavin of the *Daily Exchange* described him first as "a bad fellow" and a liar, and again as "a large man, with a very bad countenance and expression, and a most arrant coward." Donavin claimed, too, that Emperor cringed and begged every person who approached him.[33] These journalistic descriptions are neither kind nor free of bigotry, although they may be useful if correctly understood.

First, the descriptions of Green being a "notorious" and "bad fellow" undoubtedly reflect how his indignation and defiance as a militant black man were perceived—that is, something white society generally resented, and slaveholding society in particular both loathed and feared. Even a description of Green in the *Rochester Democrat* declared that he was reportedly of a "reckless disposition" in the North, which probably means that he was known to have answered white bigotry with a bold reply if not a fist.[34]

During the raid, when Brown and his men still held dominance at Harper's Ferry, Emperor was bold and even threatening in the way he spoke to an uncooperative white prisoner, something that one slaveholder perceived as an "impudent manner."[35] Virginians and slaveholders in general thrived on the mythology of loyal blacks. In the reportage that accompanied his sketches in *Harper's Weekly*, David Hunter Strother quite certainly lied when he reported that enslaved blacks at Harper's Ferry actually had run away from Brown when he came to liberate them. At the same time, however, Strother asserted quite incredibly that these supposedly timid blacks would have arisen boldly to defend their masters if need be, even to the point of killing Brown and his men.[36] Not content with such written duplicity, Strother fabricated images that conveyed the same propaganda in the pages of *Harper's Weekly*. In one issue published before the executions, he submitted caricatures of blacks who were either cowardly, stupid, or loyal (see figure 6.7).

FIGURE 6.7. Strother's caricatures of fearful and loyal enslaved people. *Harper's Weekly*, Nov. 19, 1859.

In the same issue, however, was a very realistic sketch showing a slaveholder and his family surrounded by loyal, protective blacks whom he has armed with weapons to fight against the abolitionists (see figure 6.8). The master and his wife appear stately and dignified, and an elderly "uncle" stands nearby holding the master's young heir in his arms.[37]

Viewed in the context of a racist society, the negative manner in which Emperor is described by whites actually coincides with how he was described by fellow raider Osborne Anderson. As Anderson remembered him, Shields Green was "the most inexorable of all our party, a very Turco in his hatred against the stealers of men."[38] By the use of "Turco," Anderson was alluding to the African American version of the popular Zouaves, fearless warriors who performed daring feats and fought according to the traditions of Asiatic Muslim and African Zouaves.[39] "I shall probably lose my life," Emperor told an antislavery friend before the raid. "But if my death will help to

A SOUTHERN PLANTER ARMING HIS SLAVES TO RESIST INVASION.

FIGURE 6.8. Strother's sketch showing loyal slaves. *Harper's Weekly*, Nov. 19, 1859.

free my race, I am willing to die."[40] Considering the racial phobias and coded language of white society, unflattering descriptions from journalists in the North and South actually affirm Shields Green's confidence and pride as a black man, his contempt for racism and slavery, and his defiance of white supremacy.

What of the charge by Donavin of the *Baltimore Daily Exchange* that Green, while still under arrest at Harper's Ferry, was an "arrant coward" who cringed and pleaded with his captors? Given that Donavin was one of the first journalists on the scene at Harper's Ferry, it appears that he witnessed Emperor's ruse, which had begun at the breakthrough of the marines. According to the slaveholder Lewis Washington, who had been taken captive by Brown and his men, when the marines began their final assault on the engine house, Emperor had "thrown off his hat and all his equipment and was endeavoring to represent himself as one of the slaves." Washington himself had made a point of informing the marines afterward of his identity, at which point he was put under arrest with raider Edwin Coppic in the guard house that adjoined the engine house.[41] It was during these first moments of his arrest that Green made desperate appeals to anyone who might listen to him, no doubt in the hopes of finding some recourse to escape. The charge of cowardice did not stick to Emperor's legacy, although unfortunately some writers have been inclined to trust the accusation of white Southerners over the witness of raider Osborne Anderson.[42]

Interestingly, though, after Emperor was arrested, Donavin published one last description in the *Daily Exchange*, describing him in a different mood. "He spoke glibly and good-naturedly of the occurrences through which he had passed," Donavin concluded, "as if it was a matter upon which he should pleasantly congratulate himself."[43] Donavin, who was perhaps too young and insular in his racist perceptions, mistook Emperor's attitude for ignorance. However, it is more likely that having failed in his ruse to portray himself as some white man's frightened and dislocated slave property, Shields Green now portrayed himself as the man he was in actuality, confidently resigned as a prisoner and showing no apprehensions about what lay ahead.

When Emperor had played the role of a frightened, pleading slave in the hope of escaping, he was considered bad and deceitful by whites. Afterward, when he spoke honestly, showing a pleasant confidence before his captors, he was dismissed as ignorant. Some white visitors, discerning that he was neither stupid nor a coward, simply chalked him up as being "stubborn as a mule" or as having "brute courage." The tendency on the part of white journalists to variously impute fear, stupidity, or insolence to black men in crisis says much more about their racist orientation than it did in describing their subjects. Similarly, when Brown and his surviving men were taken to the railroad for transport from Harper's Ferry to Charlestown, another reporter described Green and Copeland as having wild, twitching eyes, "almost bursting from their sockets," while the white raider Coppic seemed "calm" despite being "evidently much frightened."[44]

FIGURE 6.9.
Detail from Hitchcock's
sketch of Shields Green
in jail *New-York Illustrated
News*, Dec. 10, 1859.

Furthermore, quoting the proslavery *New York Herald*, Steven
Lubet observed that no reporter appeared "to have been particularly
interested in Shields Green, other than to disparage him as appearing
'so woe-begone that there was small room for his looking worse.'"[45]
Another report in the *Herald* described Green and Copeland as appearing "utterly hopeless" in regard to their trial.[46] It is no surprise,
then, that this was also how Green was portrayed in most of the
sketches that preserve his image for history—perhaps with the ex-
ception of the one made by DeWitt Hitchcock for the *New-York
Illustrated News*. In the other sketches, Green seems to have no claim
over his own body—either as captured and crestfallen at Harper's
Ferry, or as standing meekly before a Charlestown tribunal, or in the
surrendered final moments of his life en route to execution. However,
in the Hitchcock sketch, it seems that Shields Green—not the

artist—has recovered something of himself despite his circumstances (see figure 6.9). Indeed, in this single sketch, one may grasp something of the man as he was, for here he reclaims a regal air despite imprisonment and a death sentence.

Placing his hand inside his jacket in the manner of pre-photographic portraiture, Emperor snatches dignity back from the oppressive world that surrounds him by striking a determined, even defiant, pose for history. It is singularly in Hitchcock's sketch, then, that we finally glimpse the "irresistible manhood" of Shields Green, Emperor inexorable. "Death from the hands of the law for no offense save for believing in liberty for myself and my race, would not be a degradation."[47]

Epilogue

Legacy, Relic, Legend

He was lying on his back—the unclosed,
wistful eyes staring wildly upward.

James Monroe

CERTAINLY, even before Green and Copeland were hanged, some Virginians already were determined to have their bodies. According to Eugene Meyer, on December 12, four days before the execution, the director of the medical college in Winchester, Virginia, wrote to Governor Wise, requesting that the bodies of Green and Copeland be donated to the school for its museum of anatomy. Two days later, Wise responded positively, granting the two bodies "absent any demand 'by their proper relatives' for the remains."[1] This seems to have been deceitful on the part of Wise, who probably had already received a letter from the father of John Copeland in Oberlin, Ohio, written on December 4. "I write to crave the body of my boy after execution," the broken-hearted father pleaded, "that I may bury it by the side of his friends." Hoping to strike a chord of mercy within Wise, the elder Copeland further sought to assure him that he knew nothing of his son's involvement with Brown. But Wise ignored the appeal of Copeland's father, just as he had ignored the letter from the black clergymen of Philadelphia. Desperate, Copeland then sent a telegram to Wise on the same day that the director of the Winchester Medical College had taken up his pen. "Will my Sons Body be delivered[.] Please answer by tele-graph."[2] Wise responded coldly, "Yes: to your order to some white citizen. You cannot come to this state yourself." But once more, Wise showed his racist contempt by telling his staff not to reply to any fur-ther inquiry from Copeland, and then passed the matter to General Taliaferro in Charlestown, who simply ignored it. When Copeland wired once more on December 14, asking that the body be delivered to an associate in Philadelphia, Wise once more ignored the grieving father. Meanwhile, Taliaferro ordered that the remains of the black raiders be interred at the site of execution, almost as if there was an unspoken agreement among authorities that the bodies of these black men would be better stolen than returned to loved ones and admir-ers. Shortly after the interment on December 16, eager students from the Winchester Medical College dug up the bodies while an armed classmate stood guard over the morbid proceedings.[3]

Hoping that the governor's cold cooperation would yield up the body of their son, the Copelands back in Ohio proceeded to en-list James Monroe, a white faculty member from Oberlin College, to act as their agent in retrieving the remains. Monroe, whose trip was funded by local abolitionists, obtained a letter of introduction for Judge Parker in Charlestown from John Brown's former lawyer, Hiram Griswold, and made his way to Virginia. Given the openly hostile attitude of the Virginians toward antislavery Northerners, the venture was risky, but Monroe at first presumed success. After Parker arranged for him to meet with the faculty of the Winchester Medical College, he was promised the body of Copeland and even paid to have it prepared by the school's mortician. But Monroe's success quickly dissipated when he was visited later in the day by a contin-gent of angry medical students. Their spokesman threatened Monroe with "all sorts of trouble" and plainly told him that Copeland's body belonged to them. Despite this bullying, Monroe made another ef-fort the following day, reaching out to one of the faculty whom he had taken to be sympathetic. Instead, he found that the professor was now reluctant and unhelpful, and was made to know that Copeland's body had been stolen away by the students and hidden, even beyond the reach of the faculty.[4] His family and friends back in Oberlin would have to be content with a memorial marker.

Before making his return to Ohio, Monroe was shown around the school, including the dissecting rooms. Whether out of guilt or in some sense as an offering of consolation, a faculty member brought him finally into a cold dissection room, where he was surprised to see the body of Shields Green. Otherwise defeated and disappointed, Monroe departed Virginia empty-handed. Since he had failed to obtain Copeland's body for his family, it probably had seemed too hard a thing for him to claim Green's remains too. The trip may have been made in vain, but had Monroe not gone to Winchester and taken that last walk through the school, history would not have had a last glimpse of Emperor.

Monroe's first description of the remains of Shields Green was relayed only a year after the executions, appearing in the New York–based black publication the *Weekly Anglo-African*. "Our messenger to Virginia," goes the report, "saw him as he lay in a garret, naked, frozen and bloody; his dead eyes open and looking straight to heaven."[5] Many years later, when Monroe published his own reminiscence of this sad episode, his description of Emperor's body was little changed: "A fine, athletic figure, he was lying on his back—the unclosed, wistful eyes staring wildly upward."[6]

However, these morbid final glimpses of Shields Green are significant not only in themselves, but also in the manner that the two vignettes are framed by the writers. The first description, provided by Monroe but relayed by James Mason Fitch of Oberlin, reflects an almost apocalyptic yearning for divine judgment to fall upon the South, apropos of the climaxing antebellum period and the coming of the Civil War. To Fitch, who had himself spent time in jail after participating in the Oberlin-Wellington rescue of 1858, Green's "dead eyes open" had gazed heavenward, "as if he would say, 'How long, O Lord, holy and true, dost thou not judge and avenge our blood,'" thus paraphrasing a martyrs' plaint from the book of Revelation. In contrast, the description offered by Monroe himself nearly forty years later portrays Emperor's eyes as staring "wildly upward, as if seeking, in a better world, for some solution of the dark problems of horror and oppression so hard to be explained in this [world]."[7] Here, Shields Green is no longer a martyr whose body seems to invoke divine retribution upon the slaveholders of the South, but rather a figure of anguished longing. His upward gaze now represents the long-drawn-out disappointments of an aging generation of abolitionists who had lived long enough to see Reconstruction undermined and the rise of Jim Crow segregation in the South. The first glimpse, rendered in 1860, anticipates vindication through divine judgment; the latter, published in 1897, disappointedly longs for a better world.

* * *

In June 1870 the *Charleston Daily News* included a brief line entitled "Crumbs" under "City Affairs." The entry reads passingly, "A son of Shields Green, colored, who was hung with John Brown, lives in this city."[8] Despite careful research, this appears to be the only independent reference to the son of Shields Green that has survived in the pages of history. No doubt, this unnamed son was the small boy whom Emperor left behind when he had stolen his way northward on a sailing ship so many years before. City directories for Charleston at this period are irregular. In some years, "colored" citizens are designated, and in other years the directories provide no racial reference—and perhaps exclude blacks altogether. The 1869 directory lists a handful of black men named Green, among them a wheelwright, a gardener, and a drayman. Were one of these men the son of Shields Green? Or was S. C. Green, who ran an "ice cream garden" on King Street, his son? Moving five years ahead to the 1875 Charleston directory, there is a Primus Green listed, a Charleston city detective who lived on King Street, and a Stephen Green, who was a brickmason residing on Wentworth. Or perhaps Emperor's son was suitably named Prince Green, a longshoreman who lived on Queen Street.[9] With so little to go by in the record, any one of these men might have been the son of Shields Green—or none of them were, and we have only found him to lose him again.

Whoever Emperor's heir is in the historical record, we know that he was left an orphan after the Harper's Ferry raid. Perhaps family members or guardians told him the story of his father as they knew it. In some quarters of Charleston, it may even have been that Emperor's story was well known, even celebrated. Certainly, it was familiar enough in that city for his son to have been a point of interest to the editor of the *Charleston Daily News*. Still, if John Brown's invasion had made him an orphan, then in a real sense the raid also had enabled him to come of age in a society free of slavery—in no small way because of the enlistment of black men in the Union cause.

W. E. B. Du Bois writes that "to win the war America freed the slave and armed him"—something that John Brown had sought to do and something that Shields Green had personified.[10] David Reynolds argues quite convincingly that Brown's influence actually was found in three factors that led to the Union's victory and the defeat of slavery: "emancipation, black enlistment, and Sherman-like fighting." Further, by 1864, President Lincoln "*was* like Brown in his vision of a unified America that had rid itself of slavery through violence."[11] Although President Lincoln initially had feared the impact of emancipating slaves in the South in the style of John Brown, as the war dragged into years, the president began to think more seriously of the Old Man's intention of liberating and arming enslaved people.[12] As Frederick Douglass recalled, Lincoln eventually even considered using black scouts "whose business should be somewhat after the original plan of John Brown, to go into the rebel States, beyond the lines of our armies, and carry the news of emancipation, and urge the slaves to come without our boundaries."[13]

For his part, throughout the Civil War years Douglass repeatedly invoked John Brown and Shields Green as among the forerunners of liberation, also including Emperor in a short list of the most militant black freedom fighters like Denmark Vesey and Nat Turner.[14] In a real sense, then, the legacy that was received by Shields Green's son was the legacy of the Civil War as an extension of his own father's struggle against white supremacy and for black liberation. Emperor's legacy thus presumes an understanding of the Civil War that has been largely impalpable to the white community, awash as it is in what David Blight calls "the politics of forgetting" and the priorities of white reconciliation in the late nineteenth and early twentieth centuries. As Blight so powerfully concludes, the "master narrative" that came to define the Civil War so emphasized the reunion of Northern and Southern whites that it also enabled the reassertion of white supremacy.[15] As a result, the war and the reasons for it were obscured even as they were sentimentalized by notions of the conflict, such as "the War between the States," "the Blue versus the Gray," or "brother fighting against brother." Consequently, the master narrative, as Du Bois also observed, required that chattel slavery be viewed "so impartially, that in the end nobody seems to have done wrong and everybody was right. Slavery appears to have been thrust upon unwilling, helpless America, while the South was blameless in becoming its center."[16] Within such a narrative, it is no surprise that a proslavery thug like Jesse James became a beloved cultural icon, and the slaveholding "land monopolists" (as Brown would have called them) who died at the Alamo became legendary heroes in the imagination of white society. Within such a narrative, too, the Harper's Ferry raid could only be understood as an unfortunate precursor to the Civil War, and as a quixotic effort led by an unstable Old Man and his doomed followers, white and black.

* * *

In 1882 the *Gazette* in Huntsville, Georgia, published a brief note under a column entitled "News and Sentiment." The piece noted that "the skull of Shields Green, colored, one of John Brown's band, who was hanged at Harper's Ferry, is on exhibition at Lyndon's drug store, in Athens, Ga."[17] Nearly a quarter of a century after his body had been stolen and dissected by Southern medical school students in Virginia, Emperor had somehow reappeared, if only as a historical curiosity on display. This peculiar news item appeared here and there in newspapers throughout the South, but nothing more seems to have come of the exhibition, and the relic itself appears to have been lost from the reach of history. What path had Emperor's cranium taken from the Winchester Medical School in 1859 to Lyndon's drug store in 1882? Had it been kept by one of the same students who had bullied James Monroe, preventing him from returning John Copeland's remains to the tender hands of his loved ones? Or was it hastily removed during the Civil War, when the Winchester Medical College was burned down by Union forces? Where had the skull been since 1859, and why was it on display in Athens, Georgia? Once more, it seems, any light that penetrates the shadows surrounding Shields Green's story is never more than a glimmer.

Perhaps, at the level of the mundane, Emperor's skull was displayed merely as a point of pedestrian historical interest—a mere relic of a recent and interesting episode, just as the furniture wagon that carried Brown and his raiders to the gallows may be observed today in the Jefferson County Museum in Charles Town, West Virginia (no longer rendered as "Charlestown," no longer part of Virginia). To be sure, even at the level of the mundane it might seem strange to modern thinking that Emperor's skull was exhibited at a "drug store." However, in the late nineteenth century in cities like Athens, Georgia, the drug store was different from the contemporary pharmacy in certain respects. As a business, Lyndon's establishment in Athens not only sold drugs at retail, but also at wholesale. Lyndon's also sold paints and solvents, garden seeds, oils, medicinal rye whiskey, and doubtless many other goods and services, including watch repairs.[18] But according to local historian Steven Brown, in the 1880s it was also not unusual to see people passing through Athens "with a craft or a skill, saying they can be found at Lyndon's Drug Store." Indeed, the nineteenth-century drug store in Athens, and perhaps in many other cities throughout the South, "was rather loose and could be a community center." This may suggest that whoever had possession of Emperor's skull at the time had gotten permission from the proprietor to place it on exhibit for a time at the Lyndon establishment. Apparently, the grim exhibit was not advertised in any local newspapers, perhaps because word of mouth was more than sufficient to draw townspeople and others from the area to see the skull of John Brown's black raider.[19]

Arguably, however, the display of the skull of Shields Green as a relic of the past bespeaks more than curiosity and human interest; it was significant to the reigning narrative at the time. Annabel Jane Wharton writes that a relic "is the remnant of a history that is threatened by forgetting. . . . It offers reassurance that the past retains its authority." As a "sign of previous power, real or imagined," the relic "promises to put that power back to work."[20] That Emperor's skull appeared in post-Reconstruction Georgia suggests that it was of interest to a society that saw it not as a morbid reminder of death but rather as a connection to a time of absolute authority over black people—a connection that was quite consistent with the political, social, and economic depredations made upon blacks in that era, all of which promised to put that former power "back to work."

The proprietor, Edward S. Lyndon (1839–1917), was considered "a most worthy citizen, a highly educated physician, an excellent druggist, and a Christian gentleman."[21] Yet his profile seems to suggest likewise the reclamation of previous power after the demise of Reconstruction—which many white Southerners then referred to as "Redemption."[22] Lyndon was the son of a plantation owner and had his own slave from the age of eight. Although he seems to have been in every respect a benevolent master who broke the rules by having his slave educated alongside him, Lyndon faithfully served as a medical doctor for the Confederacy. After the war, he moved away from medical practice, purchased a drug store, and maintained a plantation and a foundry, perhaps by using cheap black labor.[23] That Lyndon was willing to display the skull of Shields Green in his establishment suggests that it was a kind of relic of "Redemption" to its viewers—an exhibition suggesting their reclamation of control over black people in the defeat of Reconstruction.

* * *

During the years of tragic reversal and the decline of Reconstruction, whenever Frederick Douglass was asked to recount the story of John Brown, he invariably spoke of Shields Green too. For instance, in a speech delivered in Charlestown, Massachusetts, in late 1873, the orator recalled Emperor's role in the Harper's Ferry episode, concluding: "If a monument is erected to John Brown, and one ought to be, the name and figure of Shields Green should have a conspicuous place upon that monument, for he was true to the 'old man,' when his cause was most desperate, and in the face of a death upon the gallows."[24] None in the audience doubted the depth of Douglass's feeling, and one journalist from the *Boston Globe* observed that he had "eulogized" Emperor with "rare pathos."[25] With such notices of Douglass's speeches being republished in newspapers across the country, perhaps even the son of Shields Green had read of this

FIGURE E.1.
Frederick Douglass in
later life. Library of
Congress Collection.

tribute. More prominently, in May 1881, Douglass repeated his tribute, almost word-for-word, in a memorable address at Storer College
in West Virginia, an African American school located close to the
site of the Harper's Ferry raid.[26] Among those present were former
Virginians who once had called for his death, especially Andrew
Hunter, who had so vigorously and—in the case of Shields Green—
spitefully prosecuted the trials of the Harper's Ferry raiders in 1859.[27]

In his third autobiography, *The Life and Times of Frederick Douglass*
(1881), the orator writes that he met raider Osborne Anderson
after his escape from Harper's Ferry and asked him about the demise of Shields Green. Douglass specifically inquired how it was
that Emperor had not escaped. As Douglass relayed this account,
Anderson responded: "I told him to come; that we could do nothing more, but he simply said he must go [down] to de ole man."[28]

As Douglass told the story, Shields Green finally had chosen to join John Brown in the engine house rather than make good his escape from Harper's Ferry.

Douglass's meeting with Osborne Anderson in Canada can be verified in the record. Having fled the United States to evade arrest because of his association with Brown, Douglass had opportunity to meet Anderson before leaving for England in November 1859. The orator conferred with the Harper's Ferry raider, briefly alluding to their Canadian meeting in a letter that appeared in his publication, *Douglass' Monthly*. In that notice, Douglass was careful not to reveal Anderson's identity, referring to him only as an "eyewitness, and a prominent actor in the transactions at Harper's Ferry, now at my side."[29] Despite their meeting in 1859, however, Douglass's account, written in 1881, actually is contradicted by what Anderson himself had written much earlier in *A Voice from Harper's Ferry*. In his account, Emperor had not chosen to go with "de ole man." Rather, Anderson writes, "when we were ordered by Captain Brown to return to our positions, after having driven the troops into the bridge, [Shields Green] *mistook the order*, and went to the engine house instead of with his own party." Anderson thus concluded that if Emperor had stayed with him and Hazlett instead of entering the engine house, he might very well have escaped too. Quite in contrast to Douglass's account, there was no reiteration of Emperor joining "de ole man." Shields Green may have been loyal to his leader, but neither would he have intentionally put himself in jeopardy if it could be avoided.

Certainly, there is no reason either to doubt Osborne Anderson's testimony or privilege Frederick Douglass's later version. Anderson had no desire to demean Shields Green, and he probably would have been quite disgusted by Oswald Villard's later insinuation of Emperor's cowardice.[30] To the contrary, Anderson wrote that "a braver man never lived than Shields Green."[31] Indeed, Emperor had proven his bravery throughout the episode, and it would have been the better part of wisdom for him to have fled from Harper's Ferry had he not misunderstood his orders. However, the more interesting question is how Douglass's tale became the dominant narrative despite Anderson's firsthand account of Green's unfortunate turn toward the engine house.

Following the publication of Douglass's tale in 1881, it was appropriated by Richard Hinton, the English journalist, abolitionist, and associate of John Brown. As a work of history, Hinton's *John Brown and His Men* (1894) is uneven and sometimes unreliable, but it was an influential work for decades. In this case, not only did Hinton ignore Anderson's narrative and accept Douglass's fabrication, but he garnished the account further with his own racially caricatured narrative. In a contrived conversation inspired by Douglass's story, Hinton reinvented the conversation of Emperor with Osborne Anderson and Albert Hazlett at Harper's Ferry:

> "You think der's no chance, Osborne?"
> "Not one," was the reply.
> "And de old Captain can't get away?"
> "No," said both men.
> "Well," with a long look and slow utterance, "I guess I'll go back to de old man."

Hinton relayed the story of Anderson's own escape, yet it appears that he intentionally omitted what Anderson had written about Shields Green's fateful error, writing only that he unfortunately "returned" to Brown in the engine house.[32]

Despite having access to Anderson's narrative testimony, W. E. B. Du Bois became the next influential author to relay Douglass's fictive account in his lyrical *John Brown* (1909). Du Bois, too, refurbished the tale, portraying the narrator apparently as the white raider Albert

Hazlett: "'I told him to come,' said the white man afterward, 'that we could do nothing more,' but he simply said, 'I must go down to the old man.' And he went down to John Brown and to death."[33] Du Bois's biography was criticized in no small part because he had used certain sources that proved to be historically inaccurate, including Hinton's book. Yet Du Bois had access to Anderson's account and still overlooked what he wrote about Shields Green in favor of the Douglass tale.

Despite his claim to have written the definitive biography, Oswald Villard also continued the Douglass tale in his *John Brown* (1910), quite carelessly using Hinton's rendition and mistakenly attributing it to Anderson's account. "O. P. Anderson, however, speaks of Green's bravery," Villard wrote, "and declares that Green could have escaped with him, but that the former slave protested that he would go back 'to de old man,' even if there was no chance of escape."[34] Over a half century later, the otherwise astute Benjamin Quarles apparently failed to see the conflict between the original account by Osborne Anderson and Frederick Douglass's later narrative. In his quintessential *Allies for Freedom: Blacks and John Brown* (1974), Quarles portrays raiders Osborne Anderson and Albert Hazlett as seeking "to persuade [Shields Green] to join them in their planned escape." In keeping with the Douglass fabrication, Quarles mistakenly concludes that "Green declined, much in the manner in which he had done at the old stone quarry meeting of Brown and Douglass [in August 1859]."[35] Yet in the larger scheme of the story of Shields Green, perhaps the Douglass tale itself is not as interesting as the question of why he chose to fabricate it in the first place. During their Canadian meeting in 1859, Anderson probably told Douglass what had happened to Emperor at Harper's Ferry. Certainly, by the time the orator wrote his autobiography twenty years afterward, he had enjoyed sufficient time to have read Anderson's account closely. So why did he invent the story of Emperor's decision not to flee from Harper's Ferry?

In the 1880s, Anne Brown Adams wrote to one of her father's admirers, "I never could have the respect for [Douglass] that I should have had, if he had told the plain honest truth, of how he hired Shields Green (Emperor) to go in his place."[36] Nor was this the only time that Anne made this claim. Some years later, in writing to Richard Hinton, her claim grew even more audacious: "[Shields Green] *told me* Frederick Douglass hired him to go in his place and brought him to Chambersburg. He was to receive his pay when he returned, a sum of money and the daughter of Douglass." In an interview in 1908, Anne reiterated this claim without mentioning Douglass's daughter, but with other details. According to Anne, Steward Taylor, one of the fallen Harper's Ferry raiders, had stopped in Rochester and had visited Douglass's printing office before joining John Brown in Maryland. Anne claimed that, according to Taylor, some young men working in the printing office had expressed amusement over the fact that Douglass had employed Emperor to go in his place to join John Brown. They allegedly were quite amused by "Douglass's foxiness in promising to pay Green on his return from the raid." Then she repeated the claim that Shields Green himself had told her the story.[37]

As David Blight points out, however, Douglass was no stranger to rumors and accusations, and it is unwise to take these outlandish claims at face value. Among the allegations leveled by Anne Brown Adams, Blight examines her claim that Shields Green was the "paid substitute" for Douglass. He argues that this claim reflected "much more ex post facto bitterness than reality," perhaps the blaming of others for John Brown's failure at Harper's Ferry.[38] Anne Brown Adams is one of the most important sources for the narrative of 1859, especially the raiders' weeks at the Kennedy farm.[39] But Blight's argument is substantive, especially in light of the fact that Anne perhaps was first among a number of Brown family members who held a grudge against Frederick Douglass throughout their lives, believing that the orator had failed to support their father.[40]

FIGURE E.2.
Anne Brown Adams
in later life. John
Brown/Boyd B.
Stutler Collection,
West Virginia
Archives and History.

To be sure, not every criticism of Douglass's conduct in 1859 can be dismissed as malicious gossip.[41] Indeed, Anne never actually blamed Douglass for her father's failure at Harper's Ferry. Despite her relative ignorance of what had taken place in the raid, in later life Anne fashioned herself as her father's confidant, even relaying the old canard that Brown had grossly overestimated the support of enslaved blacks.[42] Likewise, it is simply untenable that Douglass, after repeatedly opposing Brown's plan to seize the armory, and after doing all that he could to prevent Brown from invading Harper's Ferry, would have paid a "substitute" to take his place. The notion that Douglass somehow recruited Shields Green while refusing to endorse Brown's plan simply makes no sense and depreciates Douglass's character, which unfortunately is what Anne was trying to accomplish with these stories. Similarly, her claim that the orator had promised his daughter—twenty-year-old Rosetta Douglass—to Emperor seems like gossip, perhaps the jealous blather of some of the young men in Rochester who were vying for her hand. To be sure, Douglass himself wrote that Green was with his family in Rochester, so it is possible that Emperor had shown some interest in Rosetta. Of course, regardless of whether Douglass thought Emperor was good enough for Rosetta, he hardly would have bartered her in any sense, let alone promise her to Green as an incentive. Whatever passed between the two men regarding John Brown, the notion that Emperor was enticed into going to Harper's Ferry by Frederick Douglass simply has no substance.

Yet in looking back over the years, perhaps Douglass had some quiet regrets regarding Shields Green. In a letter written in the 1890s, Anne opined that Douglass should have "put up a monument for Shields Green, for an act of penance, or conscience easer."[43] Did Douglass regret not having pushed back harder when Emperor expressed his determination to follow John Brown? If he was so stridently opposed to Brown's intention to invade Harper's Ferry, why then did he facilitate the meeting of Brown and Emperor in his Rochester home, and then escort the latter to Chambersburg to join "de ole man"? In the retrospect of years, did Douglass have regrets over having facilitated Shields Green's enlistment with John Brown after having used his influence to restrain so many other black men from joining him? Did he feel like a shepherd who had protected the flock at the cost of a single sheep? Even setting aside most of Anne Brown Adams's cranky stories, then, perhaps there was some truth in her contention that Frederick Douglass should have "put up a monument for Shields Green." Indeed, perhaps this is what he did—not one carved in stone, but rather fashioned as legend.

Acknowledgments

I WOULD like to thank Lisa Hayes, researcher at the South Carolina Historical Society, for her excellent assistance in my quest to find some record of Shields Green in Charleston. Thanks also go to Molly Silliman, the librarian at the South Carolina Historical Society, for her kind assistance. Likewise, in correspondence, I was assisted by Bernard Powers Jr. of the history department at the College of Charleston, and Harlan Greene, the head of special collections at the College of Charleston. Harlan was particularly patient, enduring a number of emails from me and offering very thoughtful insights wherever possible. For their prompt and generous response to an inquiry, my sincere thanks also go to these distinguished associates of the Athens Historical Society in Athens, Georgia: Randy L. Reid, a scholar and educator at the Athens Academy; Gary Doster, an awarded local historian; and Steven A. Brown, archivist emeritus at the University of Georgia. In addition to his masterful biographies of two Harper's Ferry raiders, Steven Lubet, professor of law at Northwestern University, has also been personally helpful, especially when questions arose for me about Emperor's trial. Thanks also go to friend and filmmaker Jürgen Vsych for sharing generously from her extensive research. Of course, this book simply would not have become a reality without the genuine support, encouragement, and expert assistance of Clara Platter, my editor at New York University Press, as well as the capable support of Veronica Knutson, her editorial assistant, and Alexia Traganas, my production editor. Through NYU Press, too, my thanks go to the reviewers who were particularly helpful in making rigorous and insightful criticisms of some early chapter drafts. Last but not least, I am grateful to my wonderful wife, Michele Sweeting, and our beloved son, Louis Michael, who have supported this work from its inception with their love and patience throughout the whole process of research and writing.

Abbreviations

AFF   Benjamin Quarles, *Allies for Freedom: Blacks and John Brown* (1974)

DHSP Ferdinand J. Dreer John Brown Papers, Historical Society of Pennsylvania, Philadelphia

GLC   The Gilder Lehrman Collection at the New-York Historical Society, New York, N.Y.

HIN   Richard J. Hinton, *John Brown and His Men; with Some Account of the Roads They Traveled to Reach Harper's Ferry* (1894)

HMR   Tony Horwitz, *Midnight Rising: John Brown and the Raid That Sparked the Civil War* (2011)

JBW   Robert E. McGlone, *John Brown's War against Slavery* (2009)

LAL   Franklin B. Sanborn, *Life and Letters of John Brown* (1885)

LTFD *Life and Times of Frederick Douglass, Written by Himself* (1881)

NYDT *New York Daily Tribune* (1859)

NYH   *New York Herald* (1859)

OGV   John Brown-Oswald Garrison Villard Collection, Columbia University Rare Book and Manuscript Collection, New York, N.Y.

POF   David W. Blight, *Frederick Douglass: Prophet of Freedom* (2018)

RSY   Franklin B. Sanborn, *Recollections of Seventy Years*, vol. 1 (1909)

SCHF U.S. Congress, *Senate Select Commission on the Harper's Ferry Invasion* (1859)

SCHS South Carolina Historical Society, Charleston, S.C.

SWM   Ira Berlin, *Slaves without Masters: The Free Negro in the Antebellum South* (1974)

VFHF Osborne P. Anderson, *A Voice from Harper's Ferry* (1861)

VILL   Oswald G. Villard, *John Brown, 1800–1859* (1910, 1929)

Notes

PREFACE

1 "John Brown," *Rochester Democrat and Chronicle*, Jan. 27, 1874, 4.

2 Two other raiders, Aaron D. Stevens and Albert Hazlett, were also found guilty but were not executed until March 1860.

3 Frederick Douglass to James Redpath, June 20, 1860, in *Douglass' Monthly*, Sept. 1860, reprinted in *The Life and Writings of Frederick Douglass*, vol. 5, edited by Philip S. Foner (New York: International Publishers, 1975), 467–68.

4 Online correspondence with Kevin Wilmott, Jan. 1, 2019; also see "Incidentally," *New York Daily News*, July 8, 1996, 280. This report states that actors Denzel Washington and Harrison Ford were considered for the roles of Shields Green and John Brown, respectively. Anecdotally, the late Paul Newman also eyed the role of John Brown but chose not to go forward with the project because of ideological differences with the late Rupert Murdoch, who was by then a part owner of the Fox Entertainment Group, which was undertaking the project. When I inquired of Nell Newman whether she could confirm this account about her father, she kindly responded, writing that she had asked around and could not confirm it. "But I must say," she concluded, "it sure sounds like Pop!" Electronic mail from Nell Newman to author, Nov. 19, 2019.

5 See Craig Webb, "Akron Sculptor Learns John Brown Is Still a Larger-Than-Life Rebel," *Akron Beacon-Journal*, May 9, 2019, retrieved from beaconjournal.com; "John Brown Raiders Portrait Exhibition to Open in Harpers Ferry," National Park Service Harpers Ferry website, May 2, 2019, retrieved from nps.gov.

6 Amanda N'Duka, "'The Hunger Games' Actor Dayo Okeniyi to Star in Historical Drama 'Emperor,'" Deadline.com, Apr. 30, 2018; Mike Fleming Jr., "Briarcliff Lands U.S. Rights to Slave Rebellion Thriller 'Emperor' & Sets March 27 Release," Deadline.com, Jan. 15, 2020; "The Good Lord Bird," IMDb.com.

7 John Brown to Mary Brown, Nov. 8, 1846, in *VILL*, 35–36.

8 Frederick Douglass, speech at the First Baptist Church of Brooklyn, N.Y., May 5, 1886, in "John Brown," *Brooklyn Daily Eagle*, May 18, 1886, 1.

CHAPTER 1. EMPEROR MYSTERIOUS

1 See "Owen Brown's Story of His Journey from Hagerstown to Kennedy Farm, with Shields Green, a Colored Man," 2, transcription in Horatio N. Rust Collection, Henry Huntington Library, San Marino, Calif.

2 *SWM*, 181.

3 See Anne Brown Adams 1866 Recollections, transcription in the Clarence S. Gee Collection, Hudson Library and Historical Society, Hudson, Oh. (original in Chicago Historical Society), henceforth cited as Anne Brown Adams 1866 Recollections; Katherine Mayo's interviews and notes in OGV; also see an extended transcription in *VILL*, 416–20; interview material in *HIN*; and her letter describing John Brown's men to Garibaldi Ross, the son of the fraudulent "friend" of John Brown, Alexander M. Ross, Dec. 15, 1882, GLC3007.03, in GLC.

4 Katherine Mayo's transcription of Anne Brown Adams to Richard Hinton, Feb. 15, 1893 (based upon the Hinton Papers, Kansas Historical Society), in Shields Green folder, Box 8, OGV.

5 *AFF*, 85.

6 *SWM*, 269.

7 Sylvia Green, a free black woman, age twenty-two, died on July 17, 1854, from consumption; Emma J. Green, an enslaved woman, age thirty-eight, died Oct. 29, 1854, from consumption; and Elizabeth Greene, a free black woman, age thirty, died Dec. 16, 1854, from consumption. See Return of Deaths in Charleston, S.C., City of Charleston Health Department Records for Jan. 1853–Dec. 1857, in SCHS.

8 See "Rochester at Harper's Ferry," *NYDT*, Oct. 22, 1859, 7.

9 *LTFD*, 322.

10 *AFF*, 85 and 211, n. [57] and 58.

11 Meyer, *Five for Freedom*, 72 and note, "Shields Green," 236.

12 John R. McKivigan, *Forgotten Firebrand: James Redpath and the Making of Nineteenth-Century America* (Ithaca, N.Y.: Cornell University Press, 2008), 69.

13 "Biographies of John Brown's Men . . . Shields Green," *Pine and Palm*, July 6, 1861, 2.

14 See W. C. Nell to "Dear Mr. Editor," under "Biographies of John Brown's Men. Introductory Note," *Pine and Palm*, July 6, 1861, 2. After publishing Nell's letter, Redpath prefaced the piece, "Shields Green," with the statement: "At present the materials from which to furnish a sketch of this courageous Martyr for Freedom are meagre indeed." The spelling of "meagre" possibly suggests a British hand, either Redpath or Hinton.

15 "Biographies of John Brown's Men . . . Shields Green," *Pine and Palm*; Frederic May Holland, *Frederick Douglass: The Colored Orator* (New York: Funk and Wagnalls, 1891), 270.

16 "Biographies of John Brown's Men . . . Shields Green," *Pine and Palm*.

17 "Annual Dinner of the Pen and Pencil Club, Commemorative of the Anniversary of the Birth of Frederick Douglass," *Washington Bee*, Feb. 23, 1907, 4. I am indebted to Lisa Hayes, researcher for the South Carolina Historical Society, for locating this article.

18 *LTFD*, 322.

19 Nicholas Spicer [Alban S. Payne], "John Brown and His Coadjutors," *Spirit of the Times* (New York), Feb. 2, 1860, 615; "Execution of Green and Coupland [*sic*]," *Wilmington (N.C.) Journal* (from the *Baltimore Sun*), Dec. 22, 1859, 2.

20 *AFF*, 85.

21 Spicer [Payne], "John Brown and His Coadjutors."

22 *HIN*, 508.

23 J.T., "Old Brown and His Fellow Prisoners," *Spirit of the Times* (New York), Dec. 3, 1859, 21. Emphasis in italics is mine.

24 See "Our Special Despatch from Charlestown. The Trial of the Conspirators," *NYH*, Nov. 5, 1859, 1. This report states that "the count of treason was abandoned since it was not proven that Green was a free person."

25 As to Green's free status, a survey of the capitation taxes (levied on free blacks in Charleston) from the later 1840s to the early 1850s reveals that there were a number of free people, male and female, named Green, but there is no mention of Shields Green. Of course, it is possible that one of the Greens listed was a parent or relative and that he was employed by them, although this is speculation. It is also possible that he had evaded taxes in rebellion against his oppressors. Conversely, neither is there evidence that Green was born in slavery as is commonly believed. According to the Slave Schedule for 1850, a man named William Green enslaved thirty-one people in the St. James Santee Parish area of Charleston, including a male born between 1820 and 1830. However, there is no way to connect this anonymous man to Shields Green. It should be noted also that a survey of available capitation tax records from 1841 to 1860 likewise uncovered no mention of an Esau Brown. Reports of research consultant Lisa Hayes, South Carolina Historical Society, Charleston, S.C., to author, Dec. 6, 2018, and Feb. 2, 2019.

26 *SWM*, xiv.

27 Ibid., 216, 223, 225.

28 Bernard E. Powers, *Black Charlestonians: A Social History, 1822–1885* (Fayetteville: University of Arkansas Press, 1994), ch. 2.

29 *Reminiscences of Lucy N. Colman* (Buffalo: H. L. Green, 1891), 57–58. My emphasis in italics.

30 Ira Berlin, "Southern Free People of Color in the Age of William Johnson," *Southern Quarterly* 43, no. 2 (Winter 2006): 15.

31 H. M. Henry, "The Police Control of the Slave in South Carolina" (Ph.D. diss., Vanderbilt University, 1914), 183.

32 Leonard P. Curry, "Free Blacks in the Urban South: 1800–1850," *Southern Quarterly* 43, no. 2 (Winter 2006): 40, 50.

33 *LTFD*, 224–27.

34 Michael Schoeppner, "Peculiar Quarantines: The Seaman Acts and Regulatory Authority in the Antebellum South," *Law and History Review* 31, no. 3 (August 2013): 564, 575–76.

35 See the fascinating short video *Charleston Old City Jail*, featuring Harlan Greene, historian and archivist of the College of Charleston, C-SPAN, June 30, 2011, retrieved from c-span.org.

36 "Biographies of John Brown's Men . . . Shields Green," *Pine and Palm*.

37 J.T., "Old Brown and His Fellow Prisoners." My italics for emphasis.

38 Spicer [Payne], "John Brown and His Coadjutors."

39 See Katherine Mayo's handwritten notes from the manuscript of the memoir of Rev. George Leech, Baltimore Conference, Methodist Episcopal Church, in JB First Days in Charlestown Jail folder, Box 4, OGV; "The Executions at Charlestown . . . Executions of Green and Copeland," *Richmond (Va.) Daily Dispatch*, Dec. 19, 1859, 1.

40 See Anne Brown Adams to Alexander M. Ross, Oct. 21, 1892, GLC 3007 2/4, and May 12, 1895, GLC 3007 2/4, GLC.

41 See untitled piece in the *Cleveland Gazette*, Feb. 5, 1898, 2, where Anne Brown Adams (now living in Petrolia, Calif.) inquired of sources in Ohio's Western Reserve about the black raiders.

42 *RSY*, 179. Emphasis in the text is mine.

43 Katherine Mayo's transcription of Anne Brown Adams to Richard Hinton, Feb. 15, 1893 (based upon the Hinton Papers, Kansas Historical Society), in Shields Green folder, Box 8, OGV.

44 *LTFD*, 322.

45 A profile of Shields Green was published by the *Rochester Democrat* on Oct. 21, 1859, and a complete transcription of the *Democrat* piece was published as "Rochester at Harper's Ferry," *NYDT*, Oct. 22, 1859, 7. An abbreviated version of the same article appeared in the *NYH*, Oct. 29, 1859, 10.

46 "Additional Details from Our Own Reporter," *Baltimore Daily Exchange*, Oct. 20, 1859, 1; "The Executions at Charlestown . . . Executions of Green and Copeland," *Richmond (Va.) Daily Dispatch*, Dec. 19, 1859, 1.

47 *SWM*, 234–36.

48 *AFF*, 85. "His precise age we are unable to give, but in all probability he was not far from 25." "Biographies of John Brown's Men . . . Shields Green," *Pine and Palm*.

49 A correspondent from the *Baltimore Sun* claimed that Green was twenty-two years old. See "Execution of Green and Coupland [*sic*]." The *Rochester Democrat* set his age at twenty-five years. See *NYDT*, Oct. 22, 1859, 7 (relayed from the *Rochester Democrat*, Oct. 21, 1859).

50 See "Trial of the Insurgents," in Zittle, *Correct History of the John Brown Invasion*, 106. This work is a compilation of uncited press reports from the time of the raid.

51 John Brown Jr. to John H. Kagi, Aug. 11, 1859, in DHSP.

52 See *HIN*, 261.

53 The researcher, who is known only by an online identification, listed Green's birth year as 1825 and birthplace as Charleston, South Carolina, on the International Genealogical Index (IGI), a major source of information provided by the Church of Jesus Christ of Latter-Day Saints. Unfortunately, this researcher has proven harder to discover than Shields Green himself, although there is more reason to trust this source than to question it. In one attempt to locate the researcher, I was advised by the administrators of the IGI that if there was no working link for this person's online identification, the researcher may be dead. Retrieved from Family Search website, International Genealogical Index (IGI), Aug. 20, 2018.

54 See "The Attempt to Establish Freedom," *Anti-Slavery Bugle*, Oct. 29, 1859, 1. Other Iowa references for Green are found in "The Insurrection at Harper's Ferry," *Rutland (Vt.) Weekly Herald and Globe*, Oct. 21, 1859, 2; and *Perry County Democrat* (Bloomfield, Pa.), Oct. 20, 1859, 2.

55 "The Insurrection at Harper's Ferry; Authentic Details," *Washington (D.C.) Evening Star*, Oct. 19, 1859, 2.

56 "Virginia Insurrection," *Yorkville (S.C.) Enquirer*, Oct. 27, 1859, 2; and "The Insurrection at Harper's Ferry," *Wilmington (N.C.) Daily Herald*, Oct. 22, 1859, 2.

57 See two separate descriptions of Green under "Insurrection at Harper's Ferry," *Baltimore Sun*, Oct. 19, 1859, 1.

58 "The Late Rebellion; From Our Own Reporter," *Baltimore Daily Exchange*, Oct. 19, 1859, 1.

59 "Additional Details from Our Own Reporter," *Baltimore Daily Exchange*, Oct. 20, 1859, 1.

60 See *VILL*, 687.

61 See Don Papson and Tom Calarco, *Secret Lives of the Underground Railroad in New York City* (Jefferson, N.C.: McFarland, 2015), 111.

62 Gerald G. Eggert, "The Impact of the Fugitive Slave Law on Harrisburg: A Case Study," *Pennsylvania Magazine of History and Biography* 109, no. 4 (Oct. 1985): 538–39; R. J. M. Blackett, *Making Freedom: The Underground Railroad and the Politics of Slavery* (Chapel Hill: University of North Carolina Press, 2018), 32–33, 65; Papson and Calarco, *Secret Lives of the Underground Railroad*, 111.

63 "Additional Particulars," *NYH*, Oct. 19, 1859, 3. This report was filed by a Baltimore reporter on the afternoon of October 18. It does not appear to

have been widely republished but appeared under "The Harper's Ferry Riot! Additional Details of the Fight!," *Cleveland Weekly Plain Dealer*, Oct. 19, 1859, 2.

64 There already was a Fugitive Slave Law in the United States, which was passed by Congress and signed into law by President George Washington in February 1793. However, the 1850 Fugitive Slave Law both reinvigorated and increased the power that slaveholders had over human chattel and those who had sought to undermine slavery in the North.

65 Blackett, *Making Freedom*, 33–37; Eggert, "Impact of the Fugitive Slave Law," 546. For contemporary reports, see "Excitement in Harrisburg," *Wayne County Herald* (Honesdale, Pa.), Aug. 28, 1850, 3; and "Harrisburg Slave Excitement," *Baltimore Sun*, Aug. 27, 1850, 1.

66 See "Oberlin and a Noted Resident," *Rochester (N.Y.) Democrat and Chronicle*, Jan. 12, 1885, 4; and Wilbur G. Burroughs, "Oberlin's Part in the Slavery Conflict," *Ohio Archaeological and Historical Society* 20 (1911): 298.

67 See Katherine Mayo's note, "Oberlin College Records," in Shields Green folder, Box 8, OGV; and J. M. Fitch, "A Monument," *Weekly Anglo-African*, Jan. 14, 1860, 3.

68 Manisha Sinha, "Frederick Douglass and Fugitivity," *Black Perspectives*, Nov. 26, 2018, retrieved from aaihs.org. See her extensive discussion about the leadership of "self-emancipated slaves" in the abolitionist movement in *The Slave's Cause: A History of Abolition* (New Haven: Yale University Press, 2016), 421–60. Sinha is quite aware of Shields Green and identifies him in her masterful work as "a South Carolinian fugitive" (552).

CHAPTER 2. EMPEROR ENLISTED

1 Bernard E. Powers Jr., *Black Charlestonians: A Social History, 1822–1885* (Fayetteville: University of Arkansas Press, 1994), 38; also see *SWM*, 195–98.

2 Douglas R. Egerton, *He Shall Go Out Free: The Lives of Denmark Vesey* (Lanham, Md.: Rowman and Littlefield, 2004), 76.

3 *SWM*, 305.

4 Ibid., 258.

5 Electronic mail to author from Harlan M. Greene, director of archival and reference services at the College of Charleston, Aug. 2, 2019.

6 *LTFD*, 203.

7 "Race and Antebellum New York City: The New York African Free School Collection," New-York Historical Society website, retrieved from nyhistory. org; Leon F. Litwack, *North of Slavery: The Negro in the Free States, 1790–1860* (Chicago: University of Chicago Press, 1961), 111, 155, 159, 168.

8 See "The Rev. Dr. Pennington Forcibly Ejected from a Car," and "Dr. Pennington," *NYDT*, May 25, 1855, 7, and May 30, 1855, 4.

9 John Brown to John Brown Jr., Apr. 25, 1850, in John Brown Jr. Papers, Ohio Historical Society.

10 Obviously, the basis for this provisional sketch of Green's origins is based upon conclusions already drawn in the first chapter.

11 *POF*, 194–95.

12 *LTFD*, 269.

13 *POF*, 243.

14 Lecture on "John Brown," Charlestown, Mass., Dec. 9, 1873, in Frederic May Holland, *Frederick Douglass: The Colored Orator* (New York: Funk and Wagnalls, 1891); "Rochester at Harper's Ferry," *NYDT*, Oct. 22, 1859, 7.

15 Eleanor Bird, "Former Slaves and Free Blacks in Canada West: Using Early American Newspapers to Trace the Circulation of a Slave Narrative," *ReadEx Report* 10, no. 3, retrieved from readex.com; DeCaro, *"Fire from the Midst of You,"* 247.

16 See Adam Arenson, "After the Underground Railroad: Finding the African North Americans Who Returned from Canada," *BlackPast*, Jan. 12, 2011, retrieved from blackpast.org; Adam Arenson, "Crossing the Border after the Underground Railroad: The Emancipation Generation of African North Americans in the United States and Canada, 1860s–1930s," on the website History and Memory on American Borders, retrieved from adamarenson.com.

17 Larson, *Bound for the Promised Land*, 159–62. Thus, Brown wrote that Tubman had "hooked on" her "whole team." See letter excerpt, John Brown to John Brown Jr., April 8, 1858, in *LAL*, 452.

18 John Brown to John Brown Jr., April 14, 1858, John Brown Jr. Papers, Ohio Historical Society, Columbus.

19 Stanley J. Smith, "Chatham in Brown's Day," *London (Ontario) Free Press*, Oct. 10, 1959.

20 Stanley J. Smith, "Old John Brown in Ingersoll," *Ingersoll Tribune* (centennial ed., 1967), 22; Larson, *Bound for the Promised Land*, 160.

21 Smith, "Old John Brown in Ingersoll"; *Oxford Herald* (Ingersoll), April 15, 1858, transcribed under letter of Stanley J. Smith to Fred Landon, January 5, 1956, RP02–0183, in John Brown/Boyd B. Stutler Collection, West Virginia Archives and History, Charleston.

22 Smith, "Chatham in Brown's Day"; [Frances E. Rollin], *Life and Public Services of Martin R. Delany* (1883; reprint, New York: Arno, 1969), 85–86.

23 For a detailed discussion about Brown's activities in Canada, see Louis A. DeCaro Jr., "The Useful Frontier: John Brown's Detroit River Preface to the Harper's Ferry Raid," in *A Fluid Frontier: Slavery, Resistance, and the Underground Railroad in the Detroit River Borderland*, edited by Karolyn Smardz Frost and Veta Smith Tucker (Detroit: Wayne State University Press, 2016), 229–44.

24 "The Insurrection at Harper's Ferry. Interesting Details," *Washington (D.C.) Evening Star*, Oct. 20, 1859, 2. This report was picked up also by the *Alexandria (Va.) Gazette*, Oct. 21, 1859, 2.

25 Reynolds, *John Brown, Abolitionist*, 247–48; *POF*, 298–300.

26 *LTFD*, 322.

27 John Brown to John H. Kagi, Apr. 16, 1859, in DHSP.

28 *LTFD*, 322.

29 Letters of John Brown Jr. to John Henrie Kagi, Aug. 11 and 17, 1859, in DHSP. Junior's letter of August 17, written from Rochester, reads: "On my way up to our friend[']s [Douglass] house, I met his son Lewis who informs me that his father left here on Tuesday [Aug. 15] via N York & Philadelphia. . . . That other young friend [Shields Green] went on from here to visit you yesterday [Aug. 16]."

30 *LTFD*, 322.

31 *POF*, 291–92, 318.

32 *Reminiscences of Lucy N. Colman* (Buffalo: H. L. Green, 1891), 58.

33 *VFHF*, 23.

34 When F. B. Sanborn called this error to his attention in 1885, Douglass wrote back, acknowledging that Sanborn was correct about the Chambersburg meeting having taken place on August 19, 1859. His explanation, that he "took no note as to the exact time," is true on the face of it but is hardly satisfying considering that Douglass clearly glossed over a lot of details pertaining to the last few months prior to the raid. He likewise acknowledged that a group of black Philadelphians wrote to him after the Chambersburg meeting, urging him to support Brown's efforts. See *LAL*, 540–41.

35 See my discussions in *John Brown—The Cost of Freedom*, 64–69, and *Freedom's Dawn*, 26–30. Also see *POF*, 300–303.

36 *LTFD*, 322–23.

37 Hannah N. Geffert, "John Brown and His Black Allies: An Ignored Alliance," *Pennsylvania Magazine of History and Biography* 126, no. 4 (Oct. 2002): 599.

38 *LTFD*, 324–25.

39 "John Brown's Invasion; Cook's Confession," *NYDT*, Nov. 26, 1859, 7.

40 See Owen Brown's statement, dated May 5, 1885, in *LAL*, 541, and *RSY*, 183.

41 "Owen Brown's Story of His Journey from Hagerstown to Kennedy Farm, with Shields Green, a Colored Man," 1, transcription in Horatio N. Rust Collection, Henry Huntington Library, San Marino, Calif.

42 Virginia Ott Stake, *John Brown in Chambersburg* (Chambersburg, Pa.: Franklin County Heritage, 1977), 11–12; also see "Mary W. Welsh Ritner" [1818–1894], Find a Grave, retrieved from findagrave.com.

43 "Owen Brown's Story of His Journey," 1.

44 DeCaro, *"Fire from the Midst of You,"* 93–94; see "Governor Joseph Ritner," Pennsylvania Historical and Museum Commission, retrieved from phmc.state. pa.us.

45 See Franklin Keagy, "John Brown and His Men; Inmates of the Ritner Boarding House," *Public Opinion* (Chambersburg, Pa.), Feb. 13, 1891, SC02–0067A-E, and Franklin Keagy to Franklin B. Sanborn, Mar. 24, 1891, Transcript, MS13–0006 A-Q, both in John Brown/Boyd B. Stutler Collection, West Virginia Archives and History, Charleston.

46 Stake, *John Brown in Chambersburg*, 37.

47 Andrew N. Rankin, letter to editor, Oct. 21, 1882, under "Memories of the John Brown Raid," *New York Tribune*, Oct. 28, 1882, 7.

48 *LTFD*, 497.

49 Stake, *John Brown in Chambersburg*, 34, 37–39.

50 Lubet, *John Brown's Spy*, 84–85.

51 "Owen Brown's Story of His Journey," 2, 7.

52 Ibid., 8–9.

53 There are various references in John Brown's letters to Owen's arm, but most notably see John Brown to Jeremiah R. Brown, Nov. 28, 1859, in DeCaro, *John Brown Speaks*, 67; and Ralph Keeler, "Owen Brown's Escape from Harper's Ferry," *Atlantic Monthly*, March 1874, 344.

54 "Owen Brown's Story of His Journey," 2.

55 Ibid., 3–6.

56 Ibid., 10–14.

57 Ibid., 14–16.

58 Ibid., 16–21.

59 Lubet, *John Brown's Spy*, 85.

60 Neither John Junior nor Jason Brown was willing to go to Virginia with their father, although John acted as his father's agent prior to the raid. An Ohio friend named Jerome Noxon afterward defended John as a good man, but far less brave than his brother Owen. "It was said that he meant to go to Harper's Ferry. Knowing him, I believe that he *never* would have gone there." Jason, according to his father, was "bashful and retiring in his habits," and "too tender of people's feelings to get from them his just deserts." See Katherine Mayo's interview with Jerome B. Noxon, Wayne, Oh., Jan. 1909, in Mr. and Mrs. John Brown Jr. folder, Box 6, OGV; and John Brown to Rebecca Spring, Nov. 24, 1859, in *LAL*, 600.

61 Notably, John Junior rejected Protestant orthodoxy and did not hesitate to elevate spiritualism, almost to the point of misrepresenting his father as having begun to move in heterodox directions before he died, something that is quite untrue. As to Freemasonry, John joined the Lodge in later life despite the fact that his father had quit the Masons and adamantly opposed them

thereafter. Finally, he made a public show of support by sending a gift of homegrown grapes to the men accused of the Haymarket bombing in 1886. While Brown senior might very well have sympathized with the political grievances of the anarchists later in the nineteenth century, it is doubtful that he would have readily affirmed people accused of blowing up policemen and civilians during a protest. Even in the controversial Pottawatomie killings of 1856, Brown had targeted only those specifically and evidentially involved in a plot to violently attack his family and other free state settlers.

62 Transcription of Mary Brown to Isabelle Thompson Brown, Sept. 27, 1862, in Edwin N. Cotter Collection, University of Plattsburgh Library, Plattsburgh, N.Y. Also see DeCaro, *Freedom's Dawn*, 261–62.

63 Keeler, "Owen Brown's Escape from Harper's Ferry," 343, 344.

64 "Letter from Mr. Owen Brown," *Atlantic Monthly*, July 1874, 101. "All our men" rendered in italics for emphasis.

65 See Elaine L. Kinsella, Timothy D. Ritchie, and Eric R. Igou, "On the Bravery and Courage of Heroes: Considering Gender," *Heroism Science* 2, no. 1 (2017): 2–4.

66 Katherine Mayo's interview with Anne Brown Adams, Petrolia, Oct. 2–3, 1908, in Anne Brown Adams folder, Box 1, OGV.

CHAPTER 3. EMPEROR AMONG THE "INVISIBLES"

1 Alexander Boteler, "Recollections of the John Brown Raid by a Virginian Who Witnessed the Fight," *Century*, July 1883, 402.

2 Testimony of John C. Unseld, *SCHF*, 1–2.

3 Boteler, "Recollections of the John Brown Raid"; "The Extensive Restoration Before, During and After," John Brown Raid Headquarters website, retrieved from johnbrown.org; *SCHF*, 5.

4 Anne Brown Adams to Garibaldi Ross, Dec. 15, 1882, GLC.

5 Franklin B. Sanborn, *Memoirs of John Brown, Written for Rev. Samuel Orcutt's History of Torrington, Ct.* (Concord, Mass., 1878), 80, 82.

6 Watson Brown quoted in *LAL*, 549. Also see Katherine Mayo's transcription from a handwritten copy of Watson's original letters in Watson Brown folder, Box 6, OGV.

Besides Watson's letter, the plight of enslaved people in the vicinity of the Maryland farm is described by Osborne P. Anderson with some discrepancies. Watson wrote that there were five deaths, including the suicide, but he did not name the latter. Anderson says that there were "no less than four deaths among the slaves," including the suicide by "Jerry." Watson attributed the suicide to Jerry's wife having been sold farther south, but Anderson wrote that the man committed suicide rather than be sold south. In either case, Jerry's master had become insolvent. Anderson remembered a letter from Brown's son being written about these deaths, but mistakenly attributed it to Oliver instead of Watson, whose wife was back in North Elba. See *VFHF*, 20.

7   Mary D. [Brown] to [John Brown], June 29, 1859, in DHSP.

8   John Brown to Mary Brown, July 5, 1859, transcription in *VILL*, 404–5.

9   Anne Brown Adams 1866 Recollections, 2.

10 See Laughlin-Schultz, *Tie That Bound Us*, n. 15, 191–92.

11 Anne Brown Adams 1866 Recollections, 2.

12 Ibid.

13 Undated portion of letter from Anne Brown Adams to A. M. Ross [?], GLC 3007 2/4, GLC; *SCHF*, 3.

14 *HIN*, 248, 250.

15 *LAL*, 531.

16 *HIN*, 248.

17 "I would always ask him in, but he would never go in, and, of course, I would not go in his house." *SCHF*, 4.

18 *SCHF*, 4; Anne Brown Adams 1866 Recollections, 3–4.

19 See Anne Brown Adams's reminiscences in *HIN*, 265, and *RSY*, 172; George and Elizabeth Huffmaster, 1860 Census, Washington County, Sandy Hook District, Maryland, June 30, 1860, 353, NARA microfilm publication M653 (Washington, D.C.: National Archives and Records Administration, n.d.).

20 *HIN*, 265; Anne Brown Adams 1866 Recollections, 7; *VILL*, 418–19.

21 *RSY*, 172; Anne Brown Adams 1866 Recollections, 7–8.

22 See Katherine Mayo's handwritten note, "Arrival of Men," Kennedy Farm folder, Box 11, OGV.

23 According to H. W. Flournoy, editor of *The Calendar of Virginia State Papers*, one of the several letters found on the body of Dangerfield Newby from his enslaved wife was dated August 18, 1859, and first had been forwarded to raider Dwight Stevens (a.k.a. Whipple) from an Ohio associate on August 27, 1859. This associate, E. A. J. Lindsey, apparently had hosted Newby en route to join Brown in Maryland, but the letter was delivered literally on the same day of Newby's departure. Lindsey thus added a note of explanation, including a postscript: "Aug. 27. This letter is for Mr. G. [*sic*] Newby; he left our houes [*sic*] this morning." *The Calendar of Virginia State Papers from January 1, 1836–April 15, 1869*, vol. 11 (Richmond: Virginia State Library; printed in New York, 1893), 311. Assuming that Newby was still in Ohio on Saturday, August 27, he may have reached Chambersburg before the end of the month with only a short wait there before being smuggled into Maryland.

24 See Meyer, *Five for Freedom*, 13–26.

25 Mayo, Kennedy Farm Notes; "Life on Kennedy Farm," based upon Richard Hinton's interview of Anne Brown Adams, May 23, 1893, from the Kansas Historical Society, in Anne Brown Adams folder, Box 1, OGV.

26 *VILL*, 418–19; Kennedy Farm Notes based upon interview with Anne Brown, an incomplete typewritten mss., in Anne Brown Adams folder, Box 1, OGV; *VFHF*, 25.

27 See DeCaro, *"Fire from the Midst of You,"* 85–86.

28 "Life on Kennedy Farm"; *HIN*, 250; *RSY*, 179.

29 *Faded Flowers* (Washington, D.C.: Charles H. Anderson, n.d.), retrieved from loc.gov.

30 *VFHF*, 24; *VILL*, 417; "Life on Kennedy Farm."

31 *VFHF*, 25; *HIN*, 706.

32 See Meyer, *Five for Freedom*, 46–63.

33 Excerpt of letter from Barclay Coppic to Anne Brown Adams, Jan. 13, 1860, in Edwin & Barclay Coppic folder, Box 7, OGV.

34 "Arrival of Men," note in Kennedy Farm folder, Box 11, OGV; *VFHF*, 24.

35 *RSY*, 173.

36 Ibid., 179.

37 Anne Brown Adams 1866 Recollections, 4–5; *HIN*, 265.

38 Anne Brown Adams 1866 Recollections, 6–7.

39 Mayo, Kennedy Farm Notes; *RSY*, 174. Anne described the dog as "either a mixture of all breeds, or else of no breed at all—the ugliest brute I ever saw." A local resident wrote that a large dog was found tied to the front entrance of the Kennedy farm after the raid. He described it as a "huge, savage looking mastiff." See Zittle, *Correct History of the John Brown Invasion*, 74.

40 As a prisoner in Virginia, Brown wrote to one associate: "Strange *change in morals political*; as well as *Christian*; since 1776." See John Brown to Thomas B. Musgrave, Nov. 17, 1859, in DeCaro, *John Brown Speaks*, 28.

41 See Katherine Mayo's interview with Mary Thompson, Aug. 22–Sept. 1, 1908, in Henry & Ruth Thompson folder, Box 17, OGV; Brown quoted in *VILL*, 358; John Brown Jr. to Clifton Tayleure, June 13, 1879, in John Brown Collection, Robert Woodruff Library, Atlanta University.

42 Quoted from a piece of paper that Brown handed to one of his Virginia jail guards on the day of his execution, in which he stated his basic inclination— that he had hoped to eliminate slavery without extensive violence, but finally concluded that slavery would never end without a great deal of bloodshed. See "The So-Called Prophecy ('Autograph' for Hiram O'Bannon), December 2," in DeCaro, *John Brown Speaks*, 122–23.

43 See his various founding documents written between 1851 and 1859, in *HIN*, 585–697.

44 See Reynolds, *John Brown, Abolitionist*, 251–52.

45 Robert L. Tsai, "John Brown's Constitution," *Boston Law Review* (2010): 4.

46 See *Provisional Constitution and Ordinances for the People of the United States by John Brown*, preface by Boyd B. Stutler (Weston, Mass.: M&S Press, 1969).

47 The original copy of "A Declaration of Liberty" is held by the Historical Society of Pennsylvania. See "About This Document: A Declaration of Liberty by the Representatives of the Slave Population of the United States of America," Preserving American Freedom section, Historical Society of Pennsylvania website, retrieved from digitalhistory.hsp.org. Also see *HIN*, 637–43.

48 Ibid. The editor mistakenly assumes that the document was dictated by Brown to his son Owen, but although the document is in Owen's handwriting, the writing style is clearly that of John Brown, particularly in its use of semicolons, ampersands, and so forth. It is far more likely that Owen copied out the document based upon his father's first draft.

49 *HMR*, 122–23.

50 A half-page features Sanborn's sketches and notes and on the verso in Brown's handwriting, "F.B.S. design 1858," in the Sanborn folder, Houghton Library Collection, Harvard University. Thanks to Jürgen Vsych for bringing this to my attention.

51 See Rebecca Onion, "John Brown's Passionate 'Declaration of Liberty,' Written on a Lengthy Scroll," *The Vault* (blog), *Slate*, Dec. 2, 2013, retrieved from slate.com.

52 See "Sambo's Mistakes," in *HIN*, 588–92. Brown's actual title was "Sambo Mistakes," his focus being on behaviors, not on racial stereotypes.

53 Ibid., 585–88.

54 See Louis A. DeCaro Jr., "History, Black and Blurred: John Brown and Malcolm X according to James Smalls," Feb. 8, 2007, *John Brown the Abolitionist: A Biographer's Blog*, retrieved from abolitionist-john-brown. blogspot.com.

55 John Oliver Killens, *Black Man's Burden* (New York: Pocket Books, 1965, 1969), 28.

56 "A Declaration of Liberty," Pennsylvania Historical Society website. Italics added for emphasis.

57 *JBW*, 213–15. Robert E. McGlone must be singularly credited among Brown's biographers for his thoughtful consideration of "A Declaration of Liberty."

58 Henry Hudnall to Henry Wise, Nov. 17, 1859, in DHSP.

59 Hudnall's precise transcription of "A Declaration of Liberty" is also in DHSP.

60 See Rachel Moloshok, "Enduring the Past," Nov. 6, 2013, on the website of the Historical Society of Pennsylvania, retrieved from hsp.org. *HIN* includes "A Declaration of Liberty" in the appendices, published four years after the document was acquired by the Historical Society of Pennsylvania.

61 *VFHF*, 28.

62 Ibid., 26.

63 "John Brown's Invasion; Cook's Confession," *NYDT*, Nov. 26, 1859, 7.

64 See *Provisional Constitution and Ordinances for the People of the United States*, 15.

CHAPTER 4. THE RAID AND THE BLACK WITNESS

1 Tony Horwitz to author, Sept. 8, 2011.

2 *HMR*, 84, 205–6; and Horwitz to the author, Sept. 8, 2011. In fairness to Tony, he did not argue that Brown was "crazy," and he readily acknowledged in his book and in correspondence that making a diagnosis in historical retrospect was problematic. In our correspondence, Tony went so far as to agree with my argument that probably there is more evidence that Abraham Lincoln was mentally ill than there is for Brown's alleged mental illness. Still, he was insistent that Brown clearly was somewhere on the "broad spectrum" of manic depression—a position that I find, after more than twenty years of biographical research, without basis.

3 David S. Reynolds, "Reading the Sesquicentennial: New Directions in the Popular History of the Civil War," *Journal of the Civil War Era* 2, no. 3 (Sept. 2012): 423–24.

4 David S. Reynolds, "An Angry Prophet," *Wall Street Journal*, Oct. 22, 2011, C6.

5 Paul Finkelman, "John Brown: America's First Terrorist?," *Prologue* 43, no. 1 (Spring 2011): 27.

6 Paul M. Angle to Boyd B. Stutler, July 11, 1950, RP07–0017, in John Brown/Boyd B. Stutler Collection, West Virginia Archives and History, Charleston.

7 *HMR*, 221–23.

8 Reynolds, "Angry Prophet."

9 Horwitz's account of the raid develops accordingly based almost exclusively upon the experiences of local whites: watchmen Patrick Higgins and Bill Williams (129–30), Daniel Whelan (130), slaveholder Lewis Washington (133–37), William Throckmorton, night clerk (138), Andrew Phelps, train conductor (138), Armistead Ball, armory superintendent (141), Thomas Boerly, tavern keeper (143–44), John Starry, doctor (144), Terence Byrne, local resident (144–45), Jennie Chambers, schoolgirl (149), George Chambers, saloon keeper (149–50), and James Hoof, slave supervisor (150).

10 Tony Horwitz's approach to writing history is described as "participatory" in Sam Roberts, "Tony Horwitz Dies at 60; Prize-Winning Journalist and Best-Selling Author," *New York Times*, May 28, 2019, retrieved from nytimes.com.

11 See *HMR*, 153, where the black raider Dangerfield Newby, first identified as "one of the insurgents," is shot down by a sniper, and is only afterward introduced and his backstory provided.

12 *HMR*, 237, 199.

13 Paul M. Angle, "John Brown," *Chicago History* 5, no. 9 (Fall 1959): 257–58.

14 Reynolds, "Reading the Sesquicentennial," 424.

15 "He was easily bored with conventional explanations." See Roberts, "Tony Horwitz Dies at 60." For the record, I had mixed feelings about presenting

my criticisms of *Midnight Rising* following the sorrowful news of Tony Horwitz's death. However, he was still with us when I set out to write this manuscript, and a chapter on the Harper's Ferry raid was inevitable; certainly this meant engaging his work. It was my privilege to have met and conversed with Tony at Yale University in 2009, and from the first our differences regarding John Brown in no way diminished my cordial feelings toward him, or my respect for his professional accomplishments. He was a brilliant, thoughtful, and engaging fellow, and his skills as a scholar and writer were exceptional. Prior to the publication of *Midnight Rising*, he extended to me an opportunity to read and criticize a bound draft of the book. In response, I presented my sincere but frank criticisms, to which Tony responded kindly, countering some points but otherwise leaving me unsatisfied. When *Midnight Rising* was published, he sent me a copy of the book with a friendly inscription, adding "in memory of the 'Old Man.'" I believe that, on his own terms, Tony felt a sense of appreciation for John Brown, but for reasons that were both intuitive and ideological for him, I suppose, he was inclined to view Brown with a journalist's cynicism that I find unnecessary as a thoroughly steeped biographer of the man. In 2015 we had a brief correspondence over some secondary historical matter, after which I mentioned something that he had told me some years back about rearing boys, to which I also attached a picture of me and my son LouMike. Tony responded warmly, including an almost elegant photograph of his son Bizu, running through a grassy field. Although Tony and I were not frequent correspondents, I am glad to have known him and was sorrowed by the news of his death. Besides a profound personal loss to his family and friends, Tony's passing is also a great loss for historical writing in this generation. I would have loved another exchange on the "Old Man" with him.

16 Meyer, *Five for Freedom*, 51–59.

17 *VFHF*, 15.

18 DeCaro, *"Fire from the Midst of You,"* 258.

19 *VFHF*, 28.

20 For a discussion about Frederick Douglass's objections to Brown's plan, see DeCaro, *Freedom's Dawn*, 25–30.

21 The raiders who supported Brown's plan to seize Harper's Ferry were, according to Owen Brown, Kagi, Green, the later arriving "colored men" (Anderson, Leary, and Copeland), and Merriam. *LAL*, 541. Also see Sanborn, *Recollections of Seventy Years*, vol. 1, 182–83; and Anne Brown Adams 1866 Recollections, 13–14, transcription in Gee Collection, Hudson Library and Historical Society, Hudson, Oh. (original owned by Chicago Historical Society, Chicago).

22 *LAL*, 541–42.

23 See "The Plan, from Kans. Hist. Society, Hinton Papers, interview with Annie
    Brown Adams, Petrolia, Feb. 15, 1893," in Anne Brown Adams folder, Box 1,
    OGV.

24 Lubet, *John Brown's Spy*, 52–53, 277, n. 19.

25 *LAL*, 542; *RSY*, 184.

26 Owen Smith to "Dear Sir," Aug. 18, 1859, in DHSP.

27 Lubet, *John Brown's Spy*, 52, 277, n. 19.

28 Anne Brown Adams 1866 Recollections, 13–14. The following year, Tidd told
    abolitionist Thomas W. Higginson that Brown's only mistake was taking
    fewer than twenty-five men to Harper's Ferry. However, he does not seem to
    have questioned the plan itself in retrospect. See Thomas W. Higginson's
    "Conversation with [C. P. Tidd]," Feb. 10, 1860, transcription in Thomas
    Wentworth Higginson folder, Box 9, OGV.

29 *VFHF*, 26.

30 *Autobiography of Dr. William Henry Johnson* (Albany, N.Y.: Argus, 1900), 194–96.
    This book is not properly an autobiography or memoir as much as it is a
    compendium of documents, articles, speeches, and photographs, published in
    Johnson's honor after a long career as a leader in New York State. His
    reminiscences of the Brown-Douglass episode do not seem entirely without
    stylization and should not be used without consideration of this fact. However,
    there is no reason to doubt Johnson's testimony as an eyewitness to and young
    participant in the counsels of Brown, Douglass, and other black leaders in
    Philadelphia in 1859. The vignette offered not only coincides with Anderson's
    remembrance of Brown's Philadelphia meeting and sorrowful return just prior
    to the raid, but also resonates with other accounts in which Douglass
    withheld his assistance and even used his influence to discourage black
    support of Brown's raid. See my discussion in *Freedom's Dawn*, 26–30, and my
    earlier treatment in *John Brown—The Cost of Freedom*, 66–69. Johnson
    confuses the Shiloh Presbyterian Church in New York City for the Shiloh
    Baptist Church in Philadelphia, where J. J. Simons spoke prior to the Harper's
    Ferry raid in 1859 (195).

31 *VFHF*, 27.

32 John H. Kagi to John Brown Jr., Oct. 10, 1859, in *VILL*, 422–23.

33 Owen Brown told an interviewer: "The conflict at Harper's Ferry was precipi-
    tated by treachery before we were ready, and father was compelled to act at
    once and unprepared." Lewis B. Sperry, "At Las Cacitas: Recollections of a
    Visit to the Late Owen Brown, in California," *Chicago Inter-Ocean*, Feb. 1889,
    in Connelley Scrapbook, Vol. 3, Reel 5, John Brown/Boyd B. Stutler Papers,
    microfilm version, West Virginia Archives and History, Charleston.

34 *VILL*, 424. Villard dismissed Anderson as a reliable source, and in this case
    classified his remarks about the circumstances immediately prior to the raid as

among "frequent stories." By diminishing Anderson's trustworthiness, Villard set a trend that unfortunately continued well into the next century among Brown's biographers.

35 *VFHF*, 27. What Anderson says should not be confused with Horwitz's observation that "scores of rifles" were relocated within the armory grounds several weeks prior to the raid as a result of a flood threat. See *HMR*, 149. Moving arms to avoid water damage was probably an internal issue and certainly would not have created the wider consternation and concern that Anderson describes as the moving of "several thousand stand of arms . . . to some other point." Also see DeCaro, *Freedom's Dawn*, 374, n. 22, where the flood threat is mentioned.

36 William A. Phillips, "Three Interviews with Old John Brown," *Atlantic Monthly*, Dec. 1879, 743–44.

37 DeCaro, *Freedom's Dawn*, 56.

38 For instance, during Brown's trial, Armistead Ball, the master machinist, claimed that Brown had told him at the time of the raid that he was going to seize the weapons to arm "the blacks to defend themselves against their masters." "Trial of John Brown," *NYDT*, Oct. 29, 1859, 7. Another claim made after the fact came from Brown's Maryland neighbor, John C. Unseld, in testimony before the Senate investigation committee in January 1860. Unseld gave two reasons, allegedly from Brown's mouth, for his invasion of Virginia, the first being, "I knew there were a good many guns there that would be of service to me." The second reason was that once it had begun in Virginia, his movement would move quickly into the South. See *SCHF*, 7. Neither testimony should be taken at face value and both should be considered hostile witnesses and therefore open to interrogation.

39 [Edward H. House], "John Brown's Invasion . . . What Brown's Plan Really Was," *NYDT*, Nov. 9, 1859, 5; "The Virginia Insurrection. Old Brown's Doings," relayed from the *New York Times* in *NYDT*, Oct. 20, 1859, 6.

40 The most that actually can be asserted confidently regarding the Harper's Ferry weapons is that according to an armory official named W. S. Downer, two of Brown's men guarding the arsenal did open two boxes of guns to examine them during the raid. This they did of their own interest, not from Brown's command, and even Downer did not say that these guns were seized. DeCaro, *Freedom's Dawn*, 55–56. Tony Horwitz recognizes the incongruity between the claim that Brown wanted the armory weapons and the lack of evidence to support it, but because of his cynical presuppositions about John Brown, he treats the incongruity as indicating Brown's instability instead of questioning its Southern source. Nor does Horwitz seem to have known that Brown discussed the matter with journalists and does not even provide a citation for his claim that Brown "had chosen to target the town because of its vast supply of arms." *HMR*, 236.

41 When questioned by the senatorial investigation committee in 1860, Andrew Hunter, who prosecuted Brown and his men in court, testified that he had taken part in an initial interview with Brown after his defeat. When the question of arms had come up, Hunter recalled: "He said he was prepared to arm about 1,500, but not perfectly. Further inquiry was made on this point—I sometimes presenting the questions, but chiefly the governor—and he then replied he had 200 Sharp's rifles and about 200 revolver pistols, and had expected 1,500 spears, but the contractor had failed, and he had received only about 950." To be clear, Brown said *nothing* to his questioners about the arms in the arsenal, which is quite consistent with the fact that he made neither preparation nor effort to remove the Harper's Ferry guns. See Hunter's testimony, *SCHF*, 61–62.

42 *VFHF*, 27.

43 The publication of John Cook's statement in the *Tribune* was no small thing, since the text was clandestinely provided by Edward House, who was Horace Greeley's undercover agent in Charlestown. The "Confession" afterward was published for sale to raise money for a Virginian wounded during the raid, so its release in the *Tribune* probably rattled authorities in Charlestown. See "John Brown's Invasion; Cook's Confession. Correspondence of the N.Y. Tribune," *NYDT*, Nov. 26, 1859, 7.

44 *VFHF*, 28–29. The difference between Anderson's rendering and Cook's version is almost negligible except for punctuation, case, and a variant of "press" and "impress."

45 Ibid., 29–30.

46 [George A. Townsend], "GATH. American Art and Artists . . . Reminiscences of Old John Brown, of Harper's Ferry," *Cincinnati Enquirer*, May 2, 1883, 1.

47 *VFHF*, 31, 34.

48 Ibid., 34, 60.

49 Ibid., 59.

50 Wise's speech of Dec. 5, 1859 is found in *Doc. No. I. Governor's Message and Reports of the Public Officers of the State, of the Boards of Directors, and of the Visitors, Superintendents, and Other Agents of Public Institutions or Interests of Virginia* (Richmond: William F. Ritchie, 1859), in West Virginia Archives and History, Charleston, retrieved from wvculture.org.

51 "It was owing alone to the loyalty and well-affected disposition of the slaves that he did not succeed in inciting a servile war. . . . It is very certain from the proofs before the committee, that not one of the captured slaves, although arms were placed in their hands, attempted to use them; but on the contrary, as soon as their safety would admit, in the absence of their captors their arms were thrown away and they hastened back to their homes." *SCHF*, 7.

52 *JBW*, 269–70, 296–97.

53 Lincoln's Cooper Union Address, Feb. 27, 1860, in Abraham Lincoln Online, edited by Rhoda Sneller, retrieved from abrahamlincolnonline.com.

54 *VFHF*, 37, 38, 41, 59.

55 Wise, speech, Dec. 5, 1859, in *Doc. No. I. Governor's Message and Reports*. While more inclined to insinuate, the official federal report expressed in the majority opinion of Senator James Mason of Virginia likewise concluded that Harper's Ferry was selected by Brown not only for its strategic value, but also for its "large deposit of arms in the arsenal of the United States there situated." See *SCHF*, 17.

56 *HMR*, 236.

57 Douglas R. Egerton, *He Shall Go Out Free: The Lives of Denmark Vesey* (Lanham, Md.: Rowman and Littlefield, 2004), 140. Also see DeCaro, *Freedom's Dawn*, 24–25.

58 Meyer, *Five for Freedom*, 159–60; Hannah Geffert, "They Heard His Call: The Local Black Community's Involvement in the Raid on Harper's Ferry," in *Terrible Swift Sword*, edited by Peggy A. Russo and Paul Finkelman (Athens: University of Ohio Press, 2005), 32. Like most of us, Geffert follows the conventional notion that Shepherd was a manumitted slave. However, Meyer has ruled out any notion of Shepherd having been in slavery, and shows that he was from a long-standing free black family.

59 See Mary Johnson, "An 'Ever Present Bone of Contention': The Heyward Shepherd Memorial," *West Virginia History* 56 (1997): 1–26.

60 See DeCaro, *Freedom's Dawn*, 18, 366, n. 20.

61 *VFHF*, 35, 41. Also see DeCaro, *Freedom's Dawn*, 15–18, 364, nn. 5–6, and 365, nn. 12 and 19.

62 *VILL*, 435–36.

63 According to the slaveholder Lewis Washington, when he was brought in by the raiders to the armory and led into the engine house, he met John Brown for the first time. "You will find a fire in here, sir; it is rather cool this morning," Brown told him. See Washington's testimony, *SCHF*, 34.

64 See Brown's interview with the undercover journalist Edward House, in "John Brown's Invasion . . . What Brown's Plan Really Was," *NYDT*, Nov. 9, 1859, 5.

65 *VFHF*, 36.

66 DeCaro, *Freedom's Dawn*, 34.

67 *VFHF*, 37.

68 Ibid., 38. See my extended description of Brown's tactical errors in *Freedom's Dawn*, chapter 3.

69 *VFHF*, 38.

70 See *HMR*, 152–53; and Stephen B. Oates, *To Purge This Land with Blood: A Biography of John Brown* (New York: Harper Torchbooks, 1970), 294. Villard

privileges the Virginians' accounts too, but at least he acknowledged that the Jefferson Guard had a "sharp exchange of volleys" with Brown's men. *VILL*, 438.

71   *VFHF*, 39–40.

72   *JBW*, 284.

73   *VILL*, 438.

74   Meyer, *Five for Freedom*, xi, 17–24.

75   Leech, *Raid of John Brown*, 8.

76   *VILL*, 439.

77   *VFHF*, 40; Meyer, *Five for Freedom*, 90.

78   *VFHF*, 40.

79   Ibid., 42.

80   Villard says that William Thompson was first sent out with a prisoner under a flag of truce and was captured, and afterward both Watson Brown and Aaron Stevens were subsequently sent out with a flag of truce and were fired upon. *VILL*, 439. In contrast, Anderson says that Watson Brown and Aaron Stevens were sent out with a flag of truce successively, one after the other, and that Jeremiah Anderson, another raider, was also wounded. He says that Thompson was captured as he entered town, returning from the Kennedy farm. He also says that Jeremiah Anderson was wounded at this time. See *VFHF*, 43.

81   *VILL*, 440; *VFHF*, 44.

82   *VFHF*, 36; *VILL*, 445.

83   *VILL*, 445.

84   Meyer, *Five for Freedom*, 94.

85   See "The Late Rebellion," *Baltimore Daily Exchange*, Oct. 19, 1859, 1. Based on the evidence of the informant's description, the victim certainly was one of the raiders, not a local black man, and undoubtedly was Lewis Leary by description and age. The report is consistent with the record of what happened with the men who fled from the rifle factory, including John Copeland being captured without being wounded. The only other "mulatto" raider was thirty-four-year-old Dangerfield Newby, who had already been shot and killed. See Thomas Featherstonaugh, "The Final Burial of the Followers of John Brown," *New England Magazine*, April 1901, 133. Leary is elsewhere described as a "yellow fellow." See testimony of John Starry, *SCHF*, 27.

86   Hinton wrote that James Holt, a Harper's Ferry resident, "was seen to club the body of Leary, after the capture of the raiders." *HIN*, 317. Also see Richard J. Hinton, "John Brown's Comrades," *NYDT*, Sept. 18, 1899, 7.

87   *VFHF*, 4.

88   Anderson also argues that the raid proved that the conduct of the slaves was a "strong guarantee of the weakness" of Southern slavery, and that "the colored

people, as a body, were well represented by numbers, both in the fight, and in the number who suffered martyrdom afterward." *VFHF*, 60.

89 Ibid., 41.

90 *SCHF*, 5–6.

91 *VFHF*, 42.

92 See Robert Baylor to Henry Wise, Oct. 22, 1859, 5, in DHSP.

93 For example, see the appendix in *HMR*.

94 Consider this reporter's statement, based upon a lecture given by an expert in 2019: "The raid was designed to start a slave rebellion like the 1831 Nat Turner Rebellion in Southhampton County and supply slaves with rifles to kill their white oppressors." Of course, this is entirely incorrect. First, the Turner revolt was an insurrection carried out with the explicit intention of killing slaveholders, including children. Brown defied any notion of servile war or insurrection, and as we have observed, his tactics during the raid were so aversive of insurrectionary violence that he apparently undermined his own efforts. As we have also observed, there is no evidence that Brown intended to arm the slaves with guns from the arsenal, and Brown denied it as well. The point here is that the claims of slaveholders are still so ingrained in the culture of the United States that they are constantly rehearsed as historical facts. See Evan Goodenow, "Lecture Details Winchester Man's Role in Harpers Ferry Raid," *Winchester (Va.) Star*, Aug. 5, 2019, retrieved from winchesterstar.com.

95 *VFHF*, 43.

96 *VILL*, 445.

97 *VFHF*, 45, 47.

98 *VILL*, 446.

99 Villard not only dismissed Anderson's account as containing "many erroneous statements" (685), but previously had followed a similar tack in demeaning W. E. B. Du Bois's *John Brown* (1909), which also suffered from errors in detail despite its profound and insightful interpretation of the abolitionist. See Louis A. DeCaro Jr., "Black People's Ally, White People's Bogeyman," in *The Afterlife of John Brown*, edited by Andrew Taylor and Eldrid Herrington (New York: Palgrave Macmillan, 2005), 11–26.

100 See Libby et al., *John Brown Mysteries*, 31.

101 Eight of the wounded Martinsburg fighters, including a county sheriff, are listed in "Execution of Brown To-Day," *NYH*, Dec. 2, 1859, 1. Also see "Domestic Intelligence. The Arrival of Troops and First Fighting," *Harper's Weekly*, Oct. 29, 1859, 694–95; and "John Brown's Raid," *Washington Post*, July 1, 1883, 3.

102 *VFHF*, 46, 47. Italics in the original.

103 After interviewing Brown, Edward House of the *New York Daily Tribune* wrote: "The reason of the change was, he avers, that as the night of the rising

was very severely cold, he suddenly concluded to have the prisoners taken to the Armory, where they would not be exposed to the weather, anticipating no trouble in moving off with them, in case he should not be able to effect the exchanges with negroes before the general alarm should spread." "John Brown's Invasion . . . What Brown's Plan Really Was," *NYDT*, Nov. 9, 1859, 5. An interview with the *New York Times* included this exchange: "I asked if he did not expect to encounter the Federal troops. 'Not if I had followed up my plans. I intended to remain here but a few hours, but a lenient feeling toward the citizens led me into a parley with them as to compromise, and by prevarication on their part I was delayed until attacked, and then in self-defense was forced to entrench myself.'" See literal transcription of *Times* interview in "The Virginia Insurrection. Old Brown's Doings," *NYDT*, Oct. 20, 1859, 6. Brown made the same point in letters. To a Quaker sympathizer, Brown wrote: "It is solely my own fault, in a military point of view, that we met with our disaster—I mean that I mingled with our prisoners and so far sympathized with them and their families, that I neglected my duty *in other* respects." Brown to "E.B.," Nov. 9, 1859; to an old associate he wrote: "I have been *a good deal* disappointed as it regards *myself* in not keeping up *to my own plans* . . . but I was induced to act very *contrary* to my *better judgment*." Brown to Herman Vaill, Nov. 15, 1859; to a very critical kinsman, Brown answered: "I will only add, that it was in yielding to my feelings of humanity (if I ever exercised such a feeling), in leaving my proper place and mingling with my prisoners to quiet their fears, that occasioned our being caught." Brown to Heman Humphrey, Nov. 25, 1859. See DeCaro, *John Brown Speaks*.
104 *VFHF*, 62, 40.

CHAPTER 5. ALIAS EMPEROR

1 *HMR*, 143–44, 163–64.

2 In his account, Anderson does not name Boerly or the raider who shot him, but describes the scene: "Edwin Coppic, one of the sentinels at the Armory gate, was fired at by one of the citizens, but the ball did not reach him, when one of the insurgents close by put up his rifle, and made the enemy bite the dust." See *VFHF*, 37.

3 Former Virginia congressman Alexander Boteler wrote that Newby killed both Boerly and Turner. See "Recollections of the John Brown Raid," *Century*, July 1883, 406. Richard Hinton likely repeats Boteler in attributing both shootings to Newby, although his text has a number of careless mistakes. See *HIN*, 511. Simpson Donavin, who was a reporter for the *Baltimore Daily Exchange* at the time of the raid, later attributed Turner's death to Newby. See S. K. Donavin, "John Brown at Harper's Ferry and Charlestown," *Ohio Archaeological and Historical Publications* 30 (1921): 312. Avey, another eyewitness, attributes the

killing of Turner to the "sentinel at the arsenal gate," which likely was Newby. See Avey, *Capture and Execution of John Brown*, 127.

4 Leech, *Raid of John Brown*, 8–9. Leech also claimed that Shields Green had shot and killed Fontaine Beckham, but this is quite unlikely, as one of the hostages confidently identified raider Edwin Coppic as the one who had shot the mayor. See *VILL*, 441.

5 J.T., "Old Brown and His Fellow Prisoners," *Spirit of the Times* (New York), Dec. 3, 1859, 21.

6 The Mason report thus reads: "It would seem that, for his safety, [Turner] had taken a gun offered to him by someone in the village, and was proceeding along the street, unattended, with it in his hand, when he also was killed by a rifle ball." *SCHF*, 6. This is reiterated in Zittle, *Correct History of the John Brown Invasion*, 34. Another Harper's Ferry narrator, "Josephus Jr." (Joseph Barry), acknowledged that Turner was taking aim with his musket at the time he was shot, although he was killed by accident, the shot having been intended for another target. This seems more a bias on the part of "Josephus Jr." to diminish the episode. Yet even he admits that the bullet struck Turner's shoulder first. Rather than acknowledge that the projectile probably glanced off Turner's shoulder bone and struck him in the neck, the writer much preferred to portray the shot entirely as a fluke. See *Annals of Harper's Ferry*, 37.

7 See 1860 U.S. Federal Census Slave Schedules.

8 Donavin, "John Brown at Harper's Ferry and Charlestown," 311–12.

9 Libby et al., *John Brown Mysteries*, 18; also see transcript of lecture by researcher Jean Libby, delivered at the John Brown Farm, Lake Placid, N.Y., Oct. 21, 2000, 7 and n. 11.

10 See under "Mrs. Brown's Interview with Her Husband . . . Brown's Interview with His Fellow-Prisoners," *NYDT*, Dec. 3, 1859, 7; and "The Execution," *NYH*, Dec. 3, 1859, 1.

11 Compare *VFHF*, 40, and Leech, *Raid of John Brown*, 8. While there are some discrepancies between these two accounts, both writers agree that Newby was struck twice.

12 Compare Boteler, "Recollections of the John Brown Raid," and Leech, *Raid of John Brown*, 7–8. Leech may have been an eyewitness, but his account was written a good many years after the Boteler piece was written, and he may have imperfectly plagiarized from it in order to fill out his own story, at least regarding Newby's death. Leech writes that he observed as Newby lay on the ground, dying in great pain, surrounded by outraged Virginians. This is quite unlikely. Boteler wrote that by the time he saw the angry Virginians encircling Newby, the raider was already dead.

13 *VFHF*, 90.

14 See *JBW*, 292, 295; and *VFHF*, 46.

15 *VFHF*, 46.

16 *JBW*, 422, n. 73.

17 See Robert Baylor to Henry Wise, Oct. 22, 1859, 5–7, in DHSP. Brown's response is also found in *VILL*, 447, and *JBW*, 291.

18 John E. P. Daingerfield, "John Brown at Harper's Ferry," *Century*, June 1885, 267. After his defeat, Brown told his interrogators: "I exercised my best judgment, not believing the people would wantonly sacrifice their own fellow citizens, when we offered to let them go on condition of being allowed to change our position about a quarter of a mile. The prisoners agreed by vote among themselves to pass across the bridge with us. We wanted them only as a sort of guarantee of our own safety; that we should not be fired into." "The Harper's Ferry Outbreak. Verbatim Report of the Questioning of Old Brown by Senator Mason, Congressman Vallandigham, and Others," *NYH*, Oct. 21, 1859, 1

19 *VILL*, 452; *JBW*, 298–99. Neither Villard nor McGlone recognize the assault of the railroad men on the engine house as the reason for the ladder being found near the engine house. Villard simply states that "a heavy ladder lay near by" (452), and McGlone writes that a heavy ladder lay outside the doors of the engine house "by chance" (299).

20 Baylor to Wise, Oct. 22, 1859, 9.

21 *JBW*, 299. McGlone makes much of the fact that Lee did not mention that the marines fired a volley before entering. To be sure, the marines fired a volley before they entered; but he errs in concluding that there was an immediate and rapid exchange between the marines and the raiders.

22 "Harper's Ferry Outbreak. Verbatim Report," 1.

23 Bernard C. Nalty, "At All Times Ready: The Marines at Harper's Ferry, 1859" (Marine Corps Historical Reference No. 10, 1962), 7.

24 "Harper's Ferry Outbreak. Verbatim Report."

25 "The Attack on the Armory—Old Brown" (relayed from the *Baltimore Daily Exchange*), *NYDT*, Oct. 20, 1859, 6.

26 See *JBW*, 302–3; also see DeCaro, *Freedom's Dawn*, 39–40. One official narrative of the U.S. Marines states that Israel Green entered the engine house first, but the evidence marshaled by McGlone is more persuasive. See Nalty, "At All Times Ready."

27 See DeCaro, *Freedom's Dawn*, 40, 371, n. 35.

28 Ned House, the undercover journalist for the *Tribune*, described "the horrible long red splash" of blood on the wall of the engine house, which had "poured from [Brown's] face as Lieut. Green struck him with his saber, while he lay prostrate before him." "John Brown's Invasion . . . The Engine Room at Harper's Ferry," *NYDT*, Nov. 11, 1859, 5. In another report, House wrote: "It is true that [Israel Green] was among the first to confront the invaders; but it is

also true that he completely lost control of himself when in their presence, and slashed about at random with wildest fierceness, and did not cease his blows until long after his opponents were subdued." House then included a transcription of Israel Green's cross-examination during the trial of one of the raiders:

MR. SENNOTT: 'You say that when Brown was down you struck him in the face with your saber?'

LIEUT. GREEN: 'Yes, Sir.'

MR. SENNOTT: 'This was after he was down?'

LIEUT. GREEN: 'Yes, Sir; he was down.'

MR. SENNOTT: 'How many times, Lieut. Green, did you strike Brown in the face with your saber after he was down?'

LIEUT. GREEN: 'Why, Sir, he was defending himself with his gun.'

See "John Brown's Invasion . . . Lieut. Green," *NYDT*, Nov. 18, 1859, 5.

29 DeCaro, *Freedom's Dawn*, 38–39, 49; "Harper's Ferry Outbreak. Verbatim Report."

30 See testimony of Thomas Allstadt in DeWitt, *Life, Trial and Execution of Captain John Brown*, 57; John Daingerfield and Armstead Ball did not think that Brown fired his weapon. See *JBW*, 300, 425, n. 120.

31 See testimony of John Daingerfield in "Trial of John Brown. The Fourth Day's Proceedings," *NYDT*, Oct. 31, 1859, 5.

32 "An Officer here stated that the orders to the marines were not to shoot anybody; but when they were fired upon by Brown's men and one of them killed, they were obliged to return the compliment." "Harper's Ferry Outbreak. Verbatim Report"; *JBW*, 299.

33 See DeCaro, *Freedom's Dawn*, 39–40, 371, n. 31.

34 *VFHF*, 44.

35 "But when the attack came on, he had thrown off his hat and all his equipments, and was endeavoring to represent himself as one of the slaves." Washington's testimony, *SCHF*, 37. Also see DeCaro, *Freedom's Dawn*, 371, n. 32.

36 *VILL*, 687. See David Levering Lewis, *W. E. B. Du Bois: Biography of a Race, 1868–1919* (New York: Henry Holt, 1993), 477–78, where Lewis describes Villard as a spokesman "for what might have been called the Fourteenth and Fifteenth Amendment reformers, the privileged white people who championed the constitutional rights of black people but were distinctly unsympathetic to aspirations of 'social equality.'" Also see 85 and 399–400.

37 *VFHF*, 40, 45.

38 Washington's testimony, *SCHF*, 37.

39 Josephus Jr. [Joseph Barry], *Annals of Harper's Ferry*, 53.

40 Statement of Lewis Washington (mistakenly rendered as John A. Washington), "The Insurrection in Virginia . . . Special Report to the New York Herald," *NYH*, Oct. 24, 1859, 1; Testimony of Lewis Washington, in *SCHF*, 37; Lubet,

John Brown's Spy, 160; report of the *Baltimore Sun*, Oct. 18, relayed in "Insurrection in Virginia," *Weekly Raleigh Register*, Oct. 26, 1859, 1.

41 "The Insurrection in Virginia . . . Special Report to the New York Herald," *NYH*, Oct. 24, 1859, 1.

42 "All the insurgents would have been killed on the spot, had the Virginians been able to distinguish them with certainty from their prisoners." Avey, *Capture and Execution of John Brown*, 131.

43 Clifton W. Tayleure to John Brown Jr., June 15, 1879, in John Brown Jr. Letters, Charles E. Frohman Collection, Rutherford B. Hayes Presidential Library, Fremont, Oh.

44 For a description of the conditions immediately after Brown's defeat and his concerns over the threat of being lynched, see DeCaro, *Freedom's Dawn*, 45–47.

45 "The Charlestown jail was a place where slaves were lodged on their way to the far South." Spring, *Book of Remembrance*, 153. Spring, who corresponded with Brown and some of the raiders in prison, probably learned this from Aaron Stevens, with whom she had an extended correspondence. Spring says that while "the two young men who there awaited death"—Aaron Stevens and Albert Hazlett—were still incarcerated, they heard the anguished cries of a slave mother who was sold away from her children by a jealous mistress.

46 Ibid., 67–69.

47 John Brown to Herman Vaill, Nov. 15, 1859, in DeCaro, *John Brown Speaks*, 22.

48 *Virginia Free Press*, Nov. 10, 1859, 4.

49 Katherine Mayo's interview with a woman identified only by the last name of Duke-McFaden, Mar. 21, 1908, in Harper's Ferry Raid folder, Box 9, OGV.

50 McGinty, *John Brown's Trial*, 97.

51 See journalist's transcription in DeWitt, *Life, Trial and Execution of Captain John Brown*, 55; "Our Charlestown Correspondence. Appearance of the Prisoners in Court—Brown's Speech and Defiant Attitude," *NYH*, Oct. 28, 1859, 2; McGinty, *John Brown's Trial*, 85–88.

52 DeWitt, *Life, Trial and Execution of Captain John Brown*, 55–56.

53 Ibid., 56–57.

54 McGinty, *John Brown's Trial*, 87.

55 DeWitt, *Life, Trial and Execution of Captain John Brown*, 50.

56 Steven Lubet observes that Richard Parker resided in nearby Winchester, Virginia, and owned ten people as slaves. See *John Brown's Spy*, 128.

57 McGinty, *John Brown's Trial*, 81–82. Also see Daniel C. Draper, "Legal Phases of the Trial of John Brown," *West Virginia History*, Jan. 1940, 99–102. Draper lays blame on Brown's lawyers for not appealing to the federal courts but finally admits that the "prevailing Southern view of states rights" dealt "this blow to Federal power" (102).

58 McGinty, *John Brown's Trial*, 286.

59 "The Harper's Ferry Conspirators," *Daily National Intelligencer* (Washington, D.C.), Nov. 5, 1859, 3; DeCaro, *Freedom's Dawn*, 99–100.

60 See Lubet, *"Colored Hero" of Harper's Ferry*, 10–13; Lubet, *John Brown's Spy*, 159–62; and McGinty, *John Brown's Trial*, 236–37.

61 See "John Brown's Invasion . . . A Revival of Wrath. Correspondence of the N.Y. Tribune," *NYDT*, Nov. 7, 1859, 6.

62 Lubet, *"Colored Hero" of Harper's Ferry*, 12.

63 Lubet writes: "Most effective was his motion to dismiss the treason charge 'on the strength of the Dred Scott decision, which deprives negroes of citizenship, and consequently of their treasonable capabilities.' In *Dred Scott*, decided only two years earlier, the United States Supreme Court had infamously observed that a black man had 'no rights which the white man was bound to respect.'" Lubet, *"Colored Hero" of Harper's Ferry*, 11–12. Also see McGinty, *John Brown's Trial*, 236.

64 "John Brown's Invasion. Correspondence of the N.Y. Tribune," *NYDT*, Nov. 7, 1859, 6; "John Brown's Invasion. Correspondence of the N.Y. Tribune . . . Affairs in Court," *NYDT*, Nov. 8, 1859, 6.

65 "The Harper's Ferry Affair . . . More Humors of the Local Press," *NYDT*, Nov. 9, 1859, 5; Nicholas Spicer [Alban S. Payne], "John Brown and His Coadjutors," *Spirit of the Times* (New York), Feb. 2, 1860, 615.

66 Lubet, *"Colored Hero" of Harper's Ferry*, 16. Lubet quotes from "Our Charlestown Correspondence . . . Green's Trial," *NYH*, Nov. 10, 1859, 5, col. 5.

67 McGinty, *John Brown's Trial*, 98–99; "John Brown's Invasion. Correspondence of the N.Y. Tribune . . . Affairs in Court," *NYDT*, Nov. 8, 1859, 6; "John Brown's Invasion . . . Personal Portraits," *NYDT*, Nov. 17, 1859, 5.

68 Handwritten transcriptions of Andrew Hunter to Henry Wise, Oct. 22, 1859, and Nov. 2, 1859, both in Andrew Hunter folder, Box 10, OGV. Also see McGinty, *John Brown's Trial*, 98–99.

69 Andrew Hunter, "John Brown's Raid; Recollections of Prosecuting Attorney Andrew Hunter," *New Orleans Times Democrat*, Sept. 5, 1887, 6–7.

70 McGinty, *John Brown's Trial*, 236.

71 "Personal Portraits," *NYDT*, Nov. 14, 1859, 6.

72 Letter of George Sennott under "Aaron D. Stevens. To the Editor of the N.Y. Tribune," *NYDT*, Nov. 28, 1859, 6.

73 "The Harper's Ferry Outbreak . . . Our Special Despatch from Charlestown. The Trial of the Conspirators," *NYH*, Nov. 5, 1859, 1; electronic communication from Steven Lubet, Aug. 24, 2019.

74 "John Brown's Invasion . . . Affairs in Court. Correspondence of the N.Y. Tribune," *NYDT*, Nov. 8, 1859, 6.

75 For example, see DeCaro, *Freedom's Dawn*, 307–8.

76 "Visit to Old Brown . . . Green's Trial" and "The Harper's Ferry Outbreak; Our Charlestown Correspondence [Nov. 7]," *NYH*, Nov. 10, 1859, 5.

77 "The Harper's Ferry Outbreak. Sentence of Cook and Other Insurrectionists," *NYH*, Nov. 12, 1859, 1; "John Brown's Invasion . . . Sentences of Coppic, Cook, Green, and Copeland," *NYDT*, Nov. 14, 1859, 7.

78 "Sentence of the Harper's Ferry Insurgents," *Alexandria Gazette and Virginia Advertiser*, Nov. 15, 1859, 2.

79 "The Virginia Panic" (relayed from the *Baltimore American*), *NYDT*, Nov. 22, 1859, 6; handwritten transcription of memoir of Rev. George Leech, Baltimore Conference, Methodist Episcopal Church, in JB First Days in Charlestown Jail folder, Box 4, OGV.

80 "The Execution of John Brown," *New-York Illustrated News*, Dec. 10, 1859, 53.

81 Lubet, *John Brown's Spy*, 150.

82 "The Execution of John Brown"; "The Trials at Charlestown. Correspondence of the N.Y. Tribune; Brown and His Place of Confinement," *NYDT*, Nov. 12, 1859, 6; "Copeland's Confession," *NYDT*, Nov. 4, 1859, 6. A shorter version of Brown's words to Copeland and Green is found in "Sympathy for John Brown in the North. Brown's Interview with His Fellow-Prisoners," *NYH*, Dec. 3, 1859, 1.

83 See "Request to Gov. Wise for the Bodies of the Colored Men," *NYDT*, Dec. 17, 1859, 5; and "Request to Gov. Wise for the Bodies of the Colored Men," *NYH*, Dec. 17, 1859, 5.

84 "The Executions at Charlestown . . . The Prisoners Yesterday," *NYH*, Dec. 17, 1859, 1; "The Charlestown Executions," *NYH*, Dec. 17, 1859, 5; Spring, *Book of Remembrance*, 149; "Letter from Cook and Coppic on Their Attempted Escape," *NYH*, Dec. 19, 1859, 2. According to Frank Leslie, there was a heavy snow that night that covered the jailhouse. See advertisement for *Frank Leslie's Illustrated Newspaper* in *NYH*, Dec. 19, 1859, 1.

85 Douglas Fermer, *James Gordon Bennett and the New York Herald* (New York: St. Martin's Press/Royal Historical Society, 1986), 149.

86 Ibid., 6; James L. Crouthamel, *Bennett's New York Herald and the Rise of the Popular Press* (Syracuse, N.Y.: Syracuse University Press, 1989), 70–71. Also see Louis M. Starr, "James Gordon Bennett: Beneficent Rascal," *American Heritage* 6, no. 2 (Feb. 1955), retrieved from americanheritage.com.

87 "Execution of the Harper's Ferry Traitors To-Day," *NYH*, Dec. 16, 1859, 4.

88 "The Burial of John Brown," *NYDT*, Dec. 12, 1859, 4.

89 "The Bodies of Green and Copeland," *NYDT*, Dec. 16, 1859, 6.

90 DeCaro, *Freedom's Dawn*, 120.

91 My description of the hangings is based upon the following reports: "The Executions at Charlestown," *Richmond (Va.) Daily Dispatch*, Dec. 19, 1859, 1; "The Executions at Charlestown, Virginia," *National Era* (Washington D.C.), Dec. 22, 1859, 202; "The Charlestown Executions," *NYH*, Dec. 17, 1859, 5; Meyer, *Five for Freedom*, 118.

CHAPTER 6. EMPEROR SEEN

1 See "John Brown's Invasion. Correspondence of the N.Y. Tribune," *NYDT*, Nov. 8, 1859, 6; and DeCaro, *Freedom's Dawn*, 123–24, 127–28.

2 House identifies a "traveling daguerreotype operator" but also speaks of two men. It may be that the other man was Dinkle, whom House took to be from out of town as well. See "John Brown's Invasion. Correspondence of the N.Y. Tribune," *NYDT*, Nov. 7, 1859, 6; Lewis Graham Dinkle was born in 1829 and appears in the 1860 census as an "artist." See Richard L. Armstrong, "7th Virginia Cavalry," 1992, CivilWarScholars.com.

3 See "Soldiers from Richmond Grays at execution of abolitionist John Brown in Charles Town, West Virginia" (Washington, D.C.: Library of Congress), illus. in E468.7 .M64 1911 [P&P], image available online at loc.gov. One of these images was used on the cover of Francis Trevelyan Miller, *The Opening Battles: The Photographic History of the Civil War* (1957) and David Donald, *Why the North Won the Civil War* (1966), and at other times has been mistaken for a Civil War photograph.

4 Arthur F. Loux, *John Wilkes Booth: Day by Day* (Jefferson, N.C.: McFarland, 2014), 35.

5 DeCaro, *Freedom's Dawn*, 184–85.

6 According to Brackett, Brown made no objection to the procedure. "He was merely indifferent, uninterested; but ceded at once when he understood it was the desire of Phillips, Howe, and Stearns that a bust should be made." See memoir of Edwin Brackett, in JB First Days in Charlestown Jail folder, Box 4, OGV.

7 "John Brown's Invasion. Correspondence of the N.Y. Tribune," *NYDT*, Nov. 8, 1859, 6; DeCaro, *Freedom's Dawn*, 127–28.

8 Lydia M. Child, "Brackett's Bust of John Brown," *NYDT*, Feb. 11, 1860, 9.

9 See letter of George H. Hoyt to E[dward] A. Brackett, Dec. 21, 1859, in "Brackett's Bust of John Brown," *Liberator*, Jan. 1, 1860, 3.

10 *Boston Commonwealth*, July 17, 1863, quoted in Earl Conrad, *Harriet Tubman* (New York: Paul S. Ericsson, 1943, 1969), 143; also see a story about the recent recovery and restoration of Brackett's bust, Geoff Edgers, "Finding John Brown: Solving the Mystery of a Lost Masterpiece in the Tufts Art Collection," Nov. 2, 2016, *Tufts Now*, retrieved from now.tufts.edu.

11 "John Brown's Invasion. Correspondence of the N.Y. Tribune," *NYDT*, Nov. 8, 1859.

12 See Jean Libby, *John Brown Photo Chronology: Catalog of the Exhibition at Harpers Ferry 2009* (Palo Alto, Calif.: Allies for Freedom, 2009).

13 Sarah Barber, "Fine Art: The Creative Image," in *History beyond the Text: A Student's Guide to Approaching Alternative Sources*, edited by Sarah Barber and Corinna M. Peniston-Bird (New York: Routledge, 2009), 27.

14 DeCaro, *Freedom's Dawn*, 145–47.

15 Ibid., 142–48; also see Boyd B. Stutler to Elliot Evans, Nov. 7, 1951, RP04–0135, John Brown/Boyd B. Stutler Collection, West Virginia Archives and History, Charleston.

16 "Bogus Illustrations," *Frank Leslie's Illustrated Newspaper*, Nov. 12, 1859, 367–68 [1–2].

17 See *New-York Illustrated News*, Dec. 17, 1859, 66; *NYH*, Dec. 19, 1859, 1; and "Enterprise and Truth versus Laziness and Lying; The New-York Illustrated News versus Frank Leslie's Newspaper," *NYH*, Dec. 19, 1859, 5.

18 See "A Golden Horseshoe; West Virginia Encyclopedia," *West Virginia Hillbilly*, Dec. 31, 1968. Also see John A. Cuthbert, "David Hunter Strother," *e-WV: The West Virginia Encyclopedia*, retrieved from wvencyclopedia.org.

19 See "The Late Invasion at Harper's Ferry," *Harper's Weekly*, Nov. 5, 1859, 712–14.

20 David H. Strother's 1868 speech, A&M 2894, Box 8, FF16, West Virginia and Regional History Collection, West Virginia University Libraries.

21 "John Brown's Invasion," *NYDT*, Nov. 15, 1859, 6.

22 Salmon Brown recalled a visit by abolitionist Franklin Sanborn, who told him, "I think your father looks like an Eagle." His brother Watson replied, "Yes, or some other carnivorous bird." See Katherine Mayo's interview with Salmon Brown, Oct. 11–13, 1908, in Salmon Brown folder, Box 6, OGV.

23 Barber, "Fine Art," 18.

24 Derek Sayer, "The Photograph: The Still Image," in Barber and Peniston-Bird, *History beyond the Text*, 53, 54.

25 Henry S. Olcott, "How We Hung John Brown," in *Lotus Leaves: Original Stories, Essays, and Poems*, edited by John Brougham and John Elderkin (Boston: William F. Gill, 1875), 234.

26 Sayer, "The Photograph," 53.

27 I assume here that Barber would permit this description to apply as much to sketches as to painting portraiture. See Barber, "Fine Art," 18.

28 Ibid., 19.

29 Barber and Peniston-Bird, *History beyond the Text*, 8.

30 "It is increasingly evident that German immigrant opposition to slavery was so pervasive that it may have been a crucial, albeit ignored factor in the victory of the Union forces." Kenneth Barkin, "Ordinary Germans, Slavery, and the U.S. Civil War," *Journal of African American History* 93, no. 1 (Winter 2008): 70.

31 See Lincoln's Cooper Union Address, Feb. 27, 1860 in Abraham Lincoln Online, retrieved from abrahamlincolnonline.com; *NYDT*, Oct. 19, 1859, 4.

32 Lubet, *"Colored Hero" of Harper's Ferry*, 187.

33 "The Insurrection at Harper's Ferry," *Baltimore Sun*, Oct. 19, 1859, 1; [Simpson Donavin], "Additional Details from Our Own Reporter," *Baltimore Daily Exchange*, Oct. 20, 1859, 1.

34 *Rochester Democrat*, Oct. 21, 1859, reprinted in "A Rochester Man in the Harper's Ferry Insurrection," *NYH*, Oct. 29, 1859, 10.

35 See testimony of Washington, in *SCHF*, 37.

36 "The Late Invasion at Harper's Ferry," *Harper's Weekly*, Nov. 5, 1859, 714.

37 See *Harper's Weekly*, Nov. 19, 1859, 1.

38 *VFHF*, 45.

39 See Timothy Marr, "The American Zouave: Mania and Mystique," Sept. 15, 2016, Military Images, retrieved from militaryimages.atavist.com.

40 *Reminiscences of Lucy N. Colman* (Buffalo: H. L. Green, 1891), 57–58.

41 *SCHF*, 37; see also Clifton Tayleure to John Brown Jr., June 15, 1879, in John Brown Jr. Letters, Charles E. Frohman Collection, Rutherford B. Hayes Presidential Library, Fremont, Oh.

42 See *VILL*, 685.

43 [Simpson Donavin], "The Harper's Ferry Insurrection; Additional Details," *Baltimore Daily Exchange*, Oct. 21, 1859, 1.

44 Nicholas Spicer [Alban S. Payne], "John Brown and His Coadjutors," *Spirit of the Times* (New York), Feb. 2, 1860; J.T., "Old Brown and His Fellow Prisoners," *Spirit of the Times* (New York), Dec. 3, 1859; DeCaro, *Freedom's Dawn*, 67.

45 Lubet, *"Colored Hero" of Harper's Ferry*, 187; also see "Our Charlestown Correspondence . . . Green's Trial," *NYH*, Nov. 10, 1859, 5, col. 5.

46 "Our Charlestown Correspondence," *NYH*, Oct. 28, 1859, 2.

47 *Reminiscences of Lucy N. Colman*, 58.

EPILOGUE

1 Meyer, *Five for Freedom*, 129.

2 John Copeland to Henry Wise, Dec. 4, 1859, and telegram from John Copeland to Henry Wise, Dec. 12, 1859, in Wise Family Papers, Library of Congress Collection, Washington, D.C.

3 See copies of telegrams between Copeland and Wise in John Copeland folder, Box 7, OGV; Lubet, *"Colored Hero" of Harper's Ferry*, 203; James Monroe, *Oberlin Thursday Lectures, Addresses and Essays* (Oberlin: Edward J. Goodrich, 1897), 170.

4 Lubet, *"Colored Hero" of Harper's Ferry*, 203–7; Meyer, *Five for Freedom*, 129–32. James Monroe recounted this episode in *Oberlin Thursday Lectures*, 158–84.

5 J. M. Fitch, "A Monument," *Weekly Anglo-African*, Jan. 14, 1860, 3.

6 Monroe, *Oberlin Thursday Lectures*, 175.

7 Fitch, "A Monument"; Monroe, *Oberlin Thursday Lectures*, 175. See Ron Gorman, "The Election of 1857 and Oberlin's Dissent," *Oberlin Heritage Center Blog*, Nov. 19, 2016, retrieved from oberlinheritagecenter.org. Although Monroe's retrospect is not dated as to its original presentation, he says that

none of the material in his book was delivered earlier than the 1880s, which certainly suggests a post-Reconstruction context.

8 "City Affairs; Crumbs," *Charleston Daily News*, June 7, 1870, 3.

9 See 1869 and 1875 city directories for Charleston, South Carolina, in SCHS.

10 W. E. B. Du Bois, *Black Reconstruction in America, 1860–1880* (New York: Atheneum, 1983), 378.

11 Reynolds, *John Brown, Abolitionist*, 472, 479.

12 See "Important from Washington . . . Views of Mr. Lincoln and the Statesmen of the Country," *NYH*, Dec. 10, 1861, 3. See also Reynolds, *John Brown, Abolitionist*, 471.

13 *LTFD*, 364.

14 See "A Black Hero," *Douglass' Monthly*, Aug. 1861; "Fighting Rebels with Only One Hand," *Douglass' Monthly*, Sept. 1861; "Men of Color, To Arms!" *Douglass' Monthly*, March 1863; and *POF*, 345, 393–95.

15 Blight, *Race and Reunion*, 316–17, 397.

16 Du Bois, *Black Reconstruction in America*, 714.

17 "News and Sentiment; From Colored Exchanges," *Huntsville Gazette*, Apr. 1, 1882, 2.

18 Electronic mail from Steven Brown, Aug. 26, 2019; electronic mail from Randy L. Reid, Aug. 26, 2019; Robert Cumming Wilson, *Drugs and Pharmacy in the Life of Georgia, 1733–1959* (1959; reprint, Athens: University of Georgia Press, 2010), 182.

19 Electronic mail from Steven Brown, Aug. 26, 2019; electronic mail from Randy L. Reid, Aug. 26, 2019.

20 Annabel Jane Wharton, *Selling Jerusalem: Relics, Replicas, Theme Parks* (Chicago: University of Chicago Press, 2006), 9.

21 Transcription of "History of the Medical Profession," in William A. Carlton, *History of Athens and Clarke County*, USGenWeb Archives (2005), retrieved from files.usgwarchives.net.

22 See C. Vann Woodward, *Reunion and Reaction: The Compromise of 1877 and the End of Reconstruction* (New York: Oxford University Press, 1966), 8. Also see Michael W. Fitzgerald, *Reconstruction in Alabama: From Civil War to Redemption in the Cotton South* (Baton Rouge: Louisiana State University Press, 2017), 8.

23 Chick Hodgson, "Life at the Lyndon House," *Athens Historian* 1 (1996), Athens Historical Society (Athens, Ga.), retrieved from athenshistorical.org.

24 Lecture on "John Brown," Charlestown, Mass., Dec. 9, 1873, quoted in Frederic May Holland, *Frederick Douglass: The Colored Orator* (New York: Funk and Wagnalls, 1891), 271.

25 "John Brown," *Shepherdstown (West Va.) Register*, Mar. 7, 1874, 1 (relayed from the *Boston Globe*). I assume that the occasion reported by the *Globe* is the same

speech that Holland cites in the previous note, although he sets it as Dec. 9 and the *Globe* sets it as Dec. 15.

26 Frederick Douglass, *John Brown: An Address by Frederick Douglass at the Fourteenth Anniversary of Storer College, May 30, 1881* (Dover, N.H.: Morning Star, 1881), 27.

27 "The Revenges of Time," *New England Farmer*, June 4, 1881, 2. According to an eyewitness, when Hunter met the abolitionist orator, he told him: "Douglass, had we got you, you would have been hung with John Brown. I came here to oppose you but—" at which point he grasped Douglass's hand, shook it warmly and said, "Let us go on." Douglass returned the sentiment, saying to Hunter, "In union together." See extract from letter of J. R. Clifford, Martinsburg, West Va., in Frederick Douglass file, Box 7, OGV.

28 *LTFD*, 325–26.

29 *Douglass' Monthly*, Nov. 1859, in *The Life and Writings of Frederick Douglass*, vol. 2, *Pre–Civil War Decade*, edited by Philip S. Foner (New York: International Publishers, 1950, 1975), 464.

30 *VILL*, 687.

31 *VFHF*, 45.

32 *HIN*, 507–8, 151.

33 W. E. B. Du Bois, *John Brown*, centennial ed. (New York: International Publishers, 1962), 347.

34 *VILL*, 687.

35 *AFF*, 97.

36 Anne Brown Adams to Alexander M. Ross [?], GLC 3007 2/4, GLC.

37 Katherine Mayo's transcription of Anne Brown Adams to Richard Hinton, Feb. 15, 1893 (based upon the Hinton Papers, Kansas Historical Society), in Shields Green folder, Box 8, OGV; and interview with Anne Brown Adams, Oct. 2–3, 1908, Anne Brown Adams folder, Box 1, OGV.

38 *POF*, 313–14.

39 See Anne Brown Adams 1866 Recollections; and Katherine Mayo's interviews and notes in Anne Brown Adams folder, Box 1, OGV. Also see an extended transcription in *VILL*, 416–20; interview material in *HIN*; and her letter describing John Brown's men to Garibaldi Ross, Dec. 15, 1882, GLC3007.03, in GLC.

40 See DeCaro, *John Brown—The Cost of Freedom*, 66.

41 Franklin Sanborn's claim that a group of blacks from Philadelphia wrote to Douglass urging him to support Brown and pledging their support is no rumor. A transcription of the letter to Douglass is provided in *RSY*, 153–54. There is no reason to doubt the authenticity of the transcription. Likewise, it is no rumor that Brown and Douglass met with the black leaders of Detroit and Chatham, Ontario, in March 1859. There is also sufficient evidence that

they clashed during this meeting. Notably, Benjamin Quarles, an authority on Brown's involvement with black leaders, believed that this episode was true. See *AFF*, 60–61. Likewise, Brown aficionado Boyd Stutler never questioned whether the Douglass-Brown conflict took place in Detroit. See Stutler's research notes, "John Brown in Detroit," RP02–0193, Boyd Stutler Collection. Also see Richard J. Hinton, "John Brown and His Men," *Leslies Popular Monthly*, June 1889; Rossiter Johnson, "Richard Realf," *Lippincott's Magazine*, March 1879, 293–300; and Ulysses W. Boykin, *A Hand Book on the Detroit Negro; A Preliminary Edition* (Detroit: Minority Study Associates, 1943), 12.

42   "He misjudged the negroes as well as the soldiers of the standing army." Katherine Mayo's undated notes from an interview with Anne Brown Adams, in Anne Brown Adams folder, Box 1, OGV. It should be added that Anne's assessment of the raid and its aftermath is of the least value compared to her memories of childhood and the Kennedy farm in 1859. Anne's retrospectives on Brown's strategy and the outcome of the raid are not trustworthy. Indeed, her reminiscences in later life are tainted by her ambitions and prejudices, including her condescending attitude toward blacks. Her notions about the outcome of the raid seem to reflect the common assumptions of the later nineteenth century rather than historical facts.

43   Anne Brown Adams to Alexander M. Ross [?], GLC 3007 2/4, GLC.

Selected Bibliography

Anderson, Osborne P. *A Voice from Harper's Ferry*. Boston, 1861.

Avey, Elijah. *The Capture and Execution of John Brown: A Tale of Martyrdom.* Chicago: Brethren Publishing House, 1906.

Barry, Joseph [Josephus Jr.]. *The Annals of Harper's Ferry with Sketches of Its Founder and Many Prominent Characters Connected with Its History.* Martinsburg, West Va., 1872.

Berlin, Ira. *Slaves without Masters: The Free Negro in the Antebellum South.* New York: Pantheon, 1974.

Blight, David W. *Frederick Douglass: Prophet of Freedom.* New York: Simon and Schuster, 2018.

———. *Race and Reunion: The Civil War in American Memory.* Cambridge, Mass.: Harvard Belknap Press, 2001.

DeCaro, Louis A., Jr. *"Fire from the Midst of You": A Religious Life of John Brown.* New York: New York University Press, 2002.

———. *Freedom's Dawn: The Last Days of John Brown in Virginia.* Lanham, Md.: Rowman and Littlefield, 2015.

———. *John Brown—The Cost of Freedom.* New York: International Publishers, 2007.

———. *John Brown Speaks: Letters and Statements from Charlestown.* Lanham, Md.: Rowman and Littlefield, 2015.

DeWitt, Robert, ed. *The Life, Trial and Execution of Captain John Brown.* New York: Robert M. DeWitt, 1859. Reprint, New York: DaCapo, 1969.

Douglass, Frederick. *Life and Times of Frederick Douglass, Written by Himself.* Hartford, Conn.: Park Publishing, 1881. Reprint, Secaucus, N.J.: Citadel, 1983.

Hinton, Richard J. *John Brown and His Men; with Some Account of the Roads They Traveled to Reach Harper's Ferry.* New York: Funk and Wagnalls, 1894.

Horwitz, Tony. *Midnight Rising: John Brown and the Raid That Sparked the Civil War.* New York: Henry Holt, 2011.

Larson, Kate Clifford. *Bound for the Promised Land: Harriet Tubman, Portrait of an American Hero.* New York: One World/Ballantine, 2004.

Laughlin-Schultz, Bonnie. *The Tie That Bound Us: The Women of John Brown's Family and the Legacy of Radical Abolitionism.* Ithaca, N.Y.: Cornell University Press, 2013.

Leech, Samuel V. *The Raid of John Brown at Harpers Ferry as I Saw It*. [Washington, D.C.?]: Published by the author, 1909.

Libby, Jean, et al. *John Brown Mysteries*. Missoula, Mon.: Pictorial Histories, 1999.

Lubet, Steven. *The "Colored Hero" of Harper's Ferry: John Anthony Copeland and the War against Slavery*. New York: Cambridge University Press, 2015.

———. *John Brown's Spy: The Adventurous Life and Tragic Confession of John E. Cook*. New Haven, Conn.: Yale University Press, 2012.

McGinty, Brian. *John Brown's Trial*. Cambridge, Mass.: Harvard University Press, 2009.

McGlone, Robert E. *John Brown's War against Slavery*. New York: Cambridge University Press, 2009.

Meyer, Eugene L. *Five for Freedom: The African American Soldiers in John Brown's Army*. Chicago: Lawrence Hill Books, 2018.

Quarles, Benjamin. *Allies for Freedom: Blacks and John Brown*. New York: Oxford University Press, 1974. Reprint, New York: DaCapo, 2001.

Reynolds, David S. *John Brown, Abolitionist*. New York: Knopf, 2005.

Sanborn, Franklin B. *Life and Letters of John Brown*. Boston, 1885. Reprint, New York: Negro Universities Press, 1969.

———. *Recollections of Seventy Years*. Vol. 1. Boston: Richard C. Badger, 1909.

Spring, Rebecca Buffum. *A Book of Remembrance* (MSS). Department of Special Collection, Stanford University Library.

U.S. Congress, Senate Select Commission on the Harper's Ferry Invasion. Washington, D.C.: 36th Congress, First Session, June 12, 1859.

Villard, Oswald G. *John Brown, 1800–1859*. Garden City, N.Y.: Doubleday and Doran, 1910, 1929.

Zittle, John, ed. *A Correct History of the John Brown Invasion at Harper's Ferry, West Va., Oct. 17, 1859*. Hagerstown, Md.: Mail Publishing, 1905.

Index

About the Author

LOUIS A. DECARO, JR. is Associate Professor at Alliance Theological Seminary, where he teaches courses on church history and theology. A lifetime student of John Brown, he has published *John Brown the Abolitionist: A Biographer's Blog* since 2005. He is a graduate of Geneva College and Westminster Theological Seminary and earned his doctorate at New York University. He lives in Morningside Heights, Manhattan, with his wife, Michele Sweeting, and their son, Louis Michael.